D1514914

MICHAEL J. PELCZAR, JR.

PROFESSOR OF MICROBIOLOGY
AND VICE PRESIDENT FOR GRADUATE STUDIES
AND RESEARCH
UNIVERSITY OF MARYLAND

E. C. S. CHAN

ASSOCIATE PROFESSOR OF MICROBIOLOGY
McGILL UNIVERSITY

THIRD EDITION

LABORATORY EXERCISES IN

MICROBIOLOGY

McGRAW-HILL BOOK COMPANY

NEW YORK / ST. LOUIS / SAN FRANCISCO / DÜSSELDORF
JOHANNESBURG / KUALA LUMPUR / LONDON / MEXICO
MONTREAL / NEW DELHI / PANAMA / RIO de JANEIRO
SINGAPORE / SYDNEY / TORONTO

LABORATORY EXERCISES IN MICROBIOLOGY

07-049227-1

5 6 7 8 9 0 B A B A 7 9 8 7 6 5 4

This book was set in Spartan Book by Black Dot, Inc.,
and printed and bound by George Banta Company, Inc.
The designer was Edward A. Butler;
the drawings were done by John Cordes, J. & R. Technical Services, Inc.
The editors were James R. Young and Diane Drobnis.
Matt Martino supervised production.

CONTENTS

PART 5   PURE-CULTURE TECHNIQUES

PART 6   BIOCHEMICAL ACTIVITIES OF BACTERIA

PART 7   CHARACTERIZATION OF UNKNOWN CULTURES

PART 8   HIGHER PROTISTS: MOLDS, YEASTS, PROTOZOA, AND ALGAE

PART 9   VIRUSES

PART 10   CONTROL OF MICROBIAL POPULATIONS: PHYSICAL AGENTS

The experiments in this manual are designed for an introductory course in microbiology for college or university students, regardless of their background or field of specialization. Satisfactory completion of the exercises should acquaint the student with the basic techniques of microbiology and the fundamental characteristics of microorganisms.

It is not an exaggeration to state that microbial cells are prototypes, as well as models, of biological structure and processes such as cellular anatomy, biological energetics, biosynthesis, molecular genetics, and cellular physiology. Studies on microorganisms can also make their contribution to the broad areas of ecology and evolution. Microbes not only provide the tools for an understanding of living processes at a molecular level but also the specific systems used in solving the reactions, enzymatic, genetic, or synthetic that form the basis of life as a whole. Indeed we find in microbes the simplest ideal systems for the study of life in all its manifestations. We can see then that microbiology, as an independent discipline, has much to offer in unifying and integrating biological science as advances in modern biology crumble the barriers between its divisive (and traditional) branches. It is inconceivable today to learn genetics, biochemistry, or even evolution without first getting a clear understanding of the life of microorganisms. As a discipline microbiology has helped in no small measure to change the nature of biology from a largely descriptive science to a quantitative, precise science sharing many of the characteristics of physics and chemistry.

One must also not forget the extensive applications of microbial knowledge in man's environment. These applications range from improvements in fermentation, agriculture, and medicine to modern extensive industries based upon the activities of selected microorganisms. Acids and alcohols, vitamins and enzymes, flavoring substances and antibiotics, hormone derivatives, and a host of other products are now produced by microbes.

From what has been said about microbiology, the student may gather that he can do his "thing" in microbiology, whatever his interests are in the broad spectrum of biological activities. It is hoped that this manual will serve as the first turn of the key to the kingdom of microorganisms.

The exercises are intended to be brief and to include only the steps required to accomplish the particular experiment. Details such as composition and preparation of staining solutions, media, and other reagents are given in the Appendixes. Appendix material has been expanded in this edition to include information to the instructor for each exercise where deemed necessary, e.g., helpful demonstrations, visual aids, and mechanisms of reactions of certain tests. However, the laboratory instructor will generally supplement the brief introductory remarks to each exercise with further explanation of the principles or techniques that he thinks will be helpful to the student. It is essential that the student understand the what, the how, and the why of each exercise before performing it.

The student is encouraged to supplement interpretation of results, explanations of the various biological phenomena, and so on, by reading the corresponding chapters of the text "Microbiology," by Pelczar and Reid, cited near the beginning of each exercise. A list of references on selected laboratory subjects is also included in Appendix E.

The number and choice of experiments in this edition of the manual can be programmed by the instructor to accommodate laboratory classes which meet either two days per week for one semester or once a week for the academic year. In the latter case, the availability and use of refrigerated incubators (inoculated cultures are refrigerated until 24 to 48 hr before the next class, when the incubators will be brought up to incubation temperature) make this schedule quite convenient.

We thank Miss Petra Tobber for modelling for the many illustrations.

Michael J. Pelczar, Jr.
E. C. S. Chan

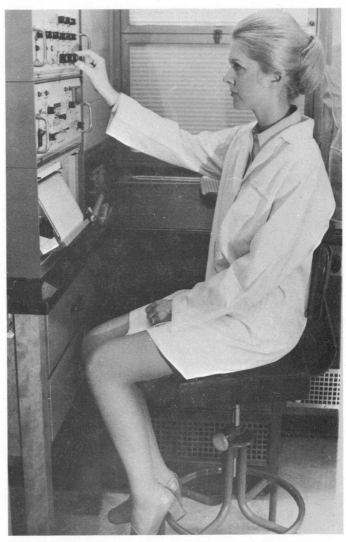

A MICROBIOLOGIST is working with a gas chromatography apparatus.

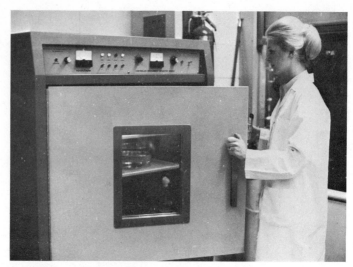

A refrigerated incubator (ambient plus and low temperature) for use in microbiology laboratories (see Preface).

Instruments for measuring radioactivity, such as this liquid scintillation counter, are also used in microbiology.

LABORATORY EXERCISES IN

MICROBIOLOGY

Among living organisms, there are two fundamental and different cell organizational patterns: the eucaryotic and the procaryotic (protocaryotic) types. They may be compared as follows.

	PROCARYOTIC CELLS	EUCARYOTIC CELLS
Groups where found as unit of structure	Bacteria, blue-green algae	Most algae, fungi, protozoa, higher plants and animals
Nucleus:		
Nuclear membrane	Absent	Present
Mitotic division	Absent	Present
Chromosome number	1	More than 1
Movement:		
Cytoplasmic streaming	None	May occur
Locomotor organelles	Simple	Complex
Ameboid movement	None	May occur
Functional structure:		
Chloroplasts	None	May be present
Mitochondria	None	Present

On the basis of this division and the mode of nutrition (photosynthesis, absorption, or ingestion), the world of living organisms can be classified into five kingdoms: Monera, Protista, Fungi, Plantae, and Animalia. Of interest to microbiologists are the first three kingdoms (usually lumped together into the kingdom Protista of Haeckel):

Kingdom Monera, the procaryotic cells
Kingdom Protista, the unicellular eucaryotic organisms
Kingdom Fungi, the multinucleate eucaryotic higher fungi

Viruses, a very important group of microorganisms studied by microbiologists, are not included in the scheme of living things above because they are not regarded as cellular entities.

We can see then that the microbes encountered by microbiologists include all the microscopic forms of life. They can be autotrophic and heterotrophic; chlorophyll-free and chlorophyll-containing; aerobic and anaerobic; acellular, unicellular, and multicellular; depending for their nitrogen on fixed compounds or on gaseous nitrogen; saprophytic and parasitic; capable of living within the cells of higher forms of life or of living outside of cells; and ranging from viruses and bacteria to algae, fungi, protozoa, and even certain worms. This kaleidoscopic array of microbial forms is the concern of the student of microbiology.

GENERAL
LABORATORY
DIRECTIONS

1. You must familiarize yourself *in advance* with the exercise(s) to be performed.
2. Preliminary instructions and demonstrations will be given at the beginning of each exercise by the laboratory instructor. You should be prepared to ask any questions concerning the procedure to be followed and should thoroughly understand the purpose of the exercise. Do not attempt to start work before receiving instructions.
3. Accurate and detailed results are to be recorded at the completion of each exercise. Use the tables and other spaces provided for recording results and answering questions. Drawings of microscopic findings should be enclosed within the circular outlines. In making your drawing of a specimen, do not attempt to draw everything in the microscopic field. Simply select a few representative specimens, i.e., cells, their arrangements, or structures.
4. The writing of a laboratory exercise is to be completed within 1 week from the time the exercise was performed unless directed otherwise by the instructor.
5. A permanent slide collection is helpful. A representative stained slide (or slides) from each exercise that calls for stained preparations should be properly labeled and placed in a slide box after appropriate examinations have been made. This collection will prove useful in reviewing your work.

LABORATORY RULES

The following rules must be observed for the safety and convenience of everyone working in the laboratory:

1. Wearing apparel not worn should be left outside the laboratory on the clothes racks provided.
2. Pencils, labels, or any other materials should never be placed in your mouth.
3. Transfer needles and loops are sterilized by heating the entire length of the wire to redness *before* and *after*

using. Spattering is avoided by first holding the needle above the flame.

4. If a culture is spilled, cover the area with disinfectant (5% Lysol solution) and notify the instructor.

5. Cultures are never to be taken from the laboratory.

6. Inoculated media placed in the incubator must be *properly labeled,* i.e., with your name, date, and the nature of the specimen, and put on the assigned shelf.

7. Gas burners must be turned down or off when not in use during the laboratory period. Be sure gas burners are turned off at the end of the laboratory period.

8. Eyepiece, lenses, and objectives, as well as the microscope stage, should be clean before and after use. Lenses of the microscope must be wiped off with lens paper only.

9. All reagents and equipment must be returned to their proper place at the end of each laboratory period.

10. All used tubes, petri dishes, pipettes, etc., must be placed in designated receptacles at the end of the laboratory period.

11. All scraps of paper, cotton, etc., must be placed in wastebaskets and not left on desk tops or on the floor.

12. The laboratory desk top should be cleaned with a disinfectant (5% Lysol) at the beginning and end of each laboratory period.

13. Personal accidents, such as cuts and burns, must be reported immediately to the instructor.

14. Every student should wash his hands — if necessary, with a disinfectant — before leaving the laboratory.

EQUIPMENT AND SUPPLIES NEEDED BY EACH STUDENT
SUPPLIES CUSTOMARILY FURNISHED BY THE STUDENT

Drawing pencil (4H)
Wax glass-marking pencil (red)
Celluloid metric rule (6-in.)
Microscope slides (3 by 1 in.), one box
Microscope slide box (50 capacity)
Microscope slide labels
  (box or booklet)
Culture microscope slide
  (one depression)
Lens and bibulous paper (booklet)
Cover slips ($^7/_8$-in. square), $^1/_2$ oz.
Safety matches
Cheesecloth, 1 yd

PERMANENT EQUIPMENT GENERALLY FURNISHED

Microscope
Microscope lamp
Loop transfer needle
Straight transfer needle

Forceps
Staining tray or trough
Bunsen burner
Staining block complete with stains

SOME
EQUIPMENT
OF THE
MICROBIOLOGY
LABORATORY

petri dishes (sterile, plastic,
disposable ones come in a
plastic bag);

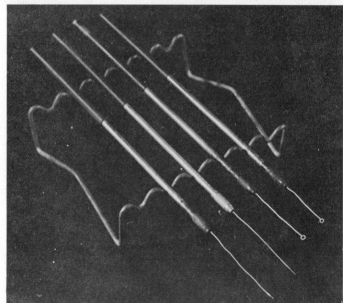

inoculating needles
(straight transfer needles
and loop transfer needles);

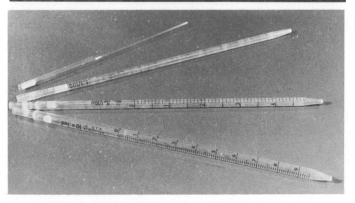

Pasteur pipette (top) and
serological pipettes;

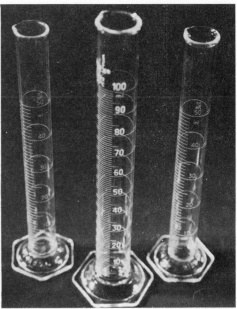

Erlenmeyer flasks (may be used with screw-caps or with cotton-plugs);

graduated cylinders;

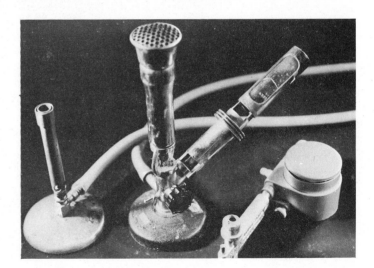

several types of bunsen burners;

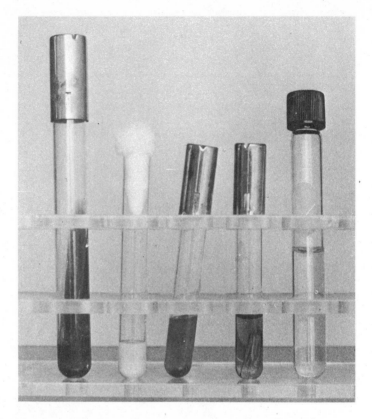

Tubed media: left to right; agar slope with metal (stainless steel) cap; litmus milk and cotton plug; gelatin stab with metal cap; broth with inverted inner fermentation vial and metal cap; broth with screw cap.

SOME BASIC LABORATORY TECHNIQUES ILLUSTRATED
PREPARATION OF STAINED SMEAR

Specimen is removed with transfer loop.

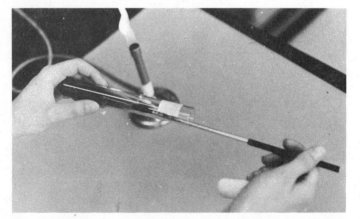

Material on transfer loop is spread (smeared) over an area approximately the size of a dime on a clean slide. Smear is allowed to dry.

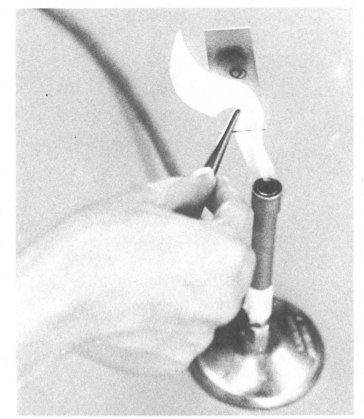

The smear is fixed by passing the slide (smear side up) over the flame of a laboratory burner. Excessive heat is to be avoided.

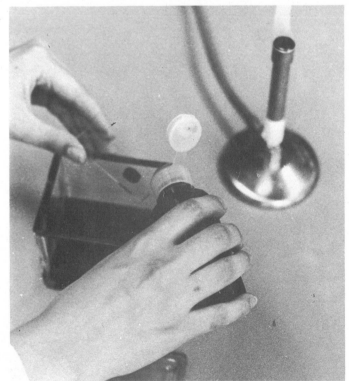

Staining solution(s) should be applied and washed off. The smear is then dried and observed with the microscope.

The smear can also be stained by immersing the slide in staining solution contained in a Coplin jar.

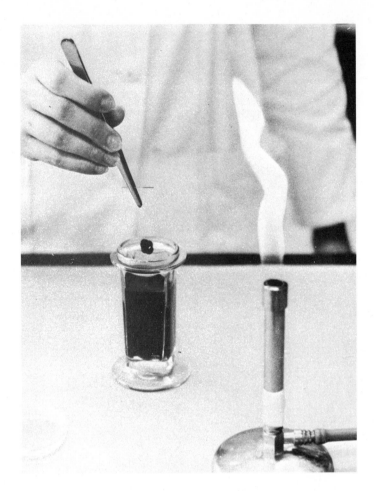

INOCULATION OR TRANSFER OF A CULTURE

The transfer needle is sterilized by holding it in the flame of the burner.

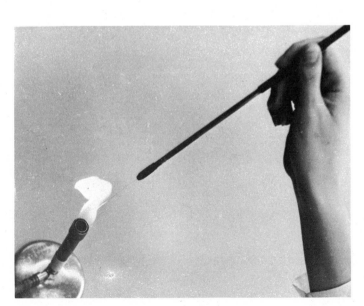

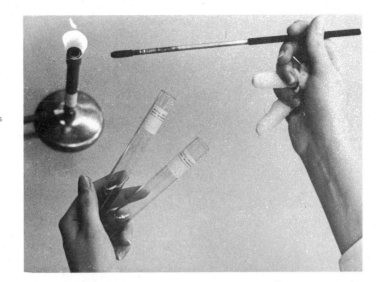

Cotton plugs from the tubes
are removed by grasping
them between the fingers
of the hand holding the
transfer needle.

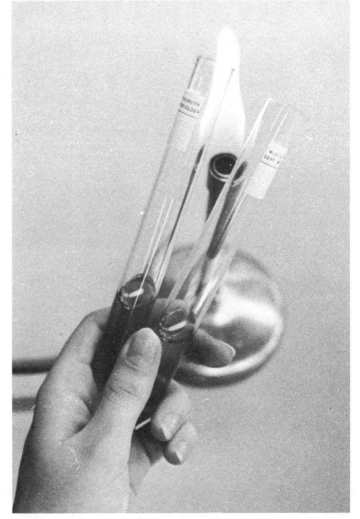

The mouths of the tubes are
passed through the flame
of the burner to eliminate
any potential contamination.

The transfer needle is inserted into the tube containing the culture (inoculum) and then introduced into the tube of medium to be inoculated. Following this, the mouths of the tubes are again flamed, the cotton stoppers replaced, and the transfer needle sterilized by holding it in the flame.

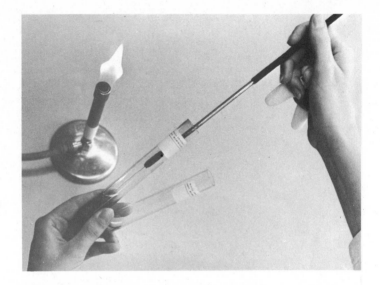

POURING AGAR MEDIUM INTO A PETRI DISH

One edge of the lid of the petri dish is raised sufficiently high to permit placement of the mouth of the tube (or bottle or flask) containing medium. Approximately 15 to 20 ml of the agar medium is added per plate.

STREAKING AN AGAR MEDIUM PLATE

The lid of the petri dish is removed and the needle is moved back and forth over the surface of the agar in a manner to effect good distribution of organisms.

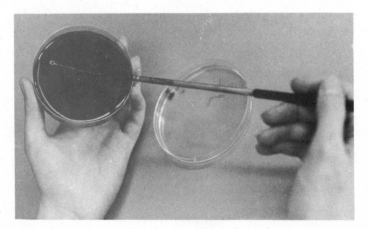

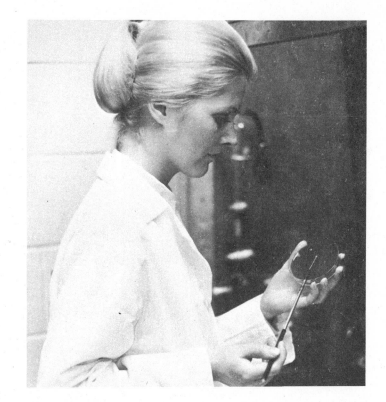

Routine technique of streaking a plate.

USE OF THE PIPETTE

Liquid material is drawn into the pipette by gentle suction. Control of the liquid in the pipette is accomplished by holding the pipette as shown; gentle release of pressure exerted by the forefinger will allow liquid to run out.

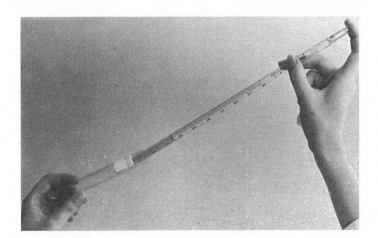

Laboratory Exercises in Microbiology

HOW MICROORGANISMS ARE STUDIED

Before beginning work on specific experiments, it is instructive for a student to grasp an overall idea of how microorganisms are studied. The accompanying schematic diagram summarizes various ways of studying microorganisms. It also gives a general impression of the broad scope of microbiology. With this in mind, the individual experiments that follow become more meaningful when placed in the context of the diagram.

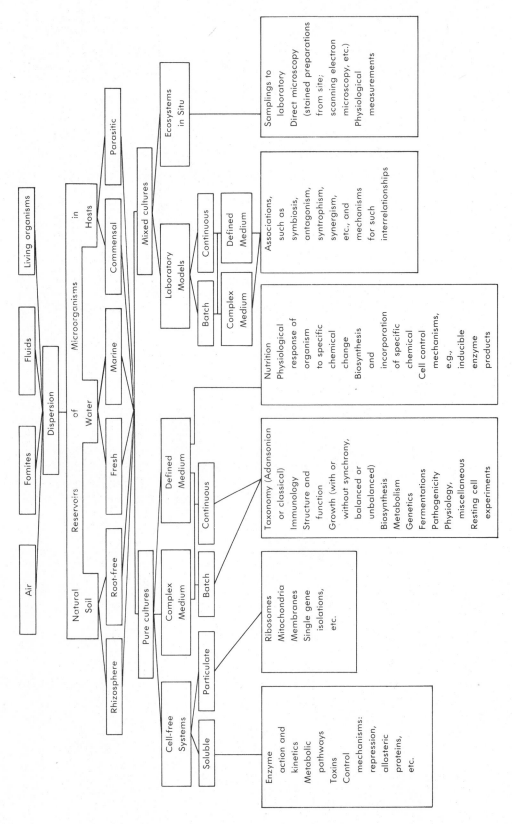

PART ONE
THE UBIQUITY
OF MICROORGANISMS

Microorganisms are abundant and ubiquitous in our environment. The exposure of a petri dish containing sterile nutrient agar to room air will demonstrate this. After the petri dish has been incubated, colonies of microorganisms become visible, indicating that the plate had been inoculated from the microorganisms being circulated by air currents. The origin of these microbes includes such sources as soil, dust, and the upper respiratory tract of human beings. Pond water or a sample of hay infusion provides a menagerie of microbes — bacteria, yeasts, molds, protozoa, and algae. Some concept of the diversity of morphological types among microorganisms can be gained by careful microscopic examination of such specimens. Considerable variation among these organisms can be found in their shape, cellular structures, type of motility, and size.

EXERCISE ONE
MICROORGANISMS
IN THE ENVIRONMENT

The laboratory, like all other environments, is populated with many microorganisms suspended in air or settling with dust on various surfaces. This is of particular significance to the laboratory worker. He must practice techniques that will prevent these organisms from contaminating materials he works with, such as media, sterile solutions, and sterile equipment.

MATERIALS

1. 1 100-ml bottle or 5 15- to 20-ml tubes nutrient agar*
2. 5 sterile petri dishes
3. 1 sterile cotton swab

PROCEDURE

1. Melt nutrient agar and cool to approximately 45°C.
2. Pour 15 to 20 ml nutrient agar into each of five sterile petri dishes.
3. Upon solidification of the medium, inoculate the petri dishes (plates) in the following manner:
   a. Remove the cover from first plate and allow it to be exposed for 30 min.
   b. Using a cotton swab, wipe an area on your laboratory desk and then streak the entire surface of second agar plate with this cotton swab. *Do not cut into the agar.*
   c. Remove the cover from third plate, and with your head held directly over the plate, run your fingers vigorously through your hair.
   d. Touch the agar surface of the fourth plate in several places with your fingers.
   e. Remove the cover from fifth plate and cough or sneeze directly onto the agar surface.
4. Incubate plates at 35°C until the next laboratory period.

*The term "tube of agar," as used throughout the exercises in this manual, refers to a tube containing a sufficient amount of an agar medium (approximately 15 ml) to pour into one petri dish (or "plate"). It is generally more convenient to dispense the agar medium in bottles (about 100 ml per bottle) and to have students pour plates from this source. However, the reference to number of tubes required provides a means for calculating the amount of plating agar and petri dishes required by the class.

RESULTS

1. Examine the plates and count the number of colonies on each.
2. Describe in general terms the appearance of these colonies, i.e., size, color, shape, and texture.
3. Draw representative colonies from each plate to illustrate different colonial types.

SPECIMEN	NUMBER OF COLONIES ON PLATE	SKETCH OF REPRESENTATIVE COLONY	WORD DESCRIPTION OF PREDOMINANT COLONY
a			
b			
c			
d			
e			

QUESTIONS

1. What is the source of the microorganisms found in the laboratory air and on laboratory surfaces?

_____

_____

_____

_____

_____

_____

_____

2. What is a bacterial colony?

_____

_____

_____

_____

_____

_____

_____

3. Does a bacterial colony continue to increase in diameter upon prolonged incubation? Explain.

_____

_____

_____

_____

_____

_____

_____

4. Of what practical significance are airborne microorganisms to the laboratory worker?

_____

_____

_____

_____

_____

5. What precautions should be taken to control laboratory contaminants?

_____

_____

_____

_____

_____

PART TWO
MICROSCOPY AND MICROBIAL MORPHOLOGY

The microscope is one of the most important tools of the micro-biologist. An understanding of this instrument and knowledge of its proper use must be achieved early in your experience in microbiology. This is the reason for the length of the introduction to the exercises on the use of the microscope.

ANATOMY OF THE MICROSCOPE

The illustration depicts the main parts of the microscope. The *eyepiece*, or *ocular*, is slipped into the upper end of the *draw tube*. The number on it indicates its magnification. This number multiplied by the magnification of the objective gives the total magnification of the object under examination. There are two kinds of oculars, the *regular*, or *Huygenian*, ocular for use with *achromatic* objectives and the *compensating ocular* for use with *apochromatic* objectives. (The terms *achromatic* and *apochromatic* are defined below.)

The fixed draw tube (*mechanical tube length*) of the monocular microscope as shown in the illustration is 160 mm. In a binocular microscope, the draw tube is replaced by a *binocular tube*, the ocular sleeves of which can be displaced in relation to each other

The microscope.

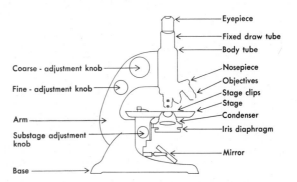

by a sliding action to adjust for the interpupillary distance of the examiner. The fields of view seen by both eyes should coincide exactly. The value indicated on the central wheel must then be set on each of the eyepiece sleeves to restore the correct mechanical tube length, which has been changed by the interpupillary distance setting. This also ensures that the objectives are *parfocal* (see below). However, if your vision is not the same in both eyes, you may adjust the eyepiece sleeve on the poor side until both eyes see the same sharp image.

The *nosepiece* is for quick exchange of *objectives*, the lens systems nearest the specimen. Certain designations on each objective should be noted. For example, consider

100/1.30
160/ —

These numbers mean the following:

100 = objective magnification is 100×.
1.30 = *numerical aperture* (see below).
160 = computed for mechanical tube length of 160 mm.
— = insensitive to *larger* than ±0.01 mm deviations of cover-slip thickness when cover slip is 0.17 mm thick. (If the number here is 0.17, this means that the objective is to be used with a cover slip of 0.17 ± 0.01 mm thickness; 0 means corrected for zero cover-slip thickness or for uncovered specimens.)

Other designations on an objective indicate what kind of an objective it is, e.g., whether it is an oil-immersion objective, a phase-contrast objective, or a flat-field objective.

Microscopes in most microbiological laboratories are equipped with three objectives: the low-power objective (16 mm), the high-dry objective (4 mm), and the oil-immersion objective (1.8 mm). The 16, 4, and 1.8 mm designate the *focal length* of each objective. It follows that the shorter the focal length of the objective, the shorter the *working distance* of the lens, i.e., the distance between the specimen and the objective.

Formerly, changing objectives was rather inconvenient because the draw tube had to be raised before turning the nosepiece and every objective had to be focused separately. Nowadays the objectives are parfocal, which means that objectives can simply be swung into place and only slight focusing with the fine adjustment will bring the specimen into sharp focus.

There are two kinds of lenses in objectives, *achromats* ("without color") and *apochromats* ("with separated colors"). A theoretically perfect achromat (nonexistent) would bring all wavelengths of light to a common focus so that all images would be of the same size. But because of light dispersion and refraction by a glass lens (blue components bend more than the red components of light), this is not possible in practice. Instead an attempt is made to bring together those colors, red and green, to which the eye is particularly sensitive. The residual blue color fringe of the image is not readily detected by the eye and vanishes completely against a blue background. For this reason manufacturers usually provide a disk of blue (or green) glass to be placed in front of microscope lamps. Achromatic lenses are relatively cheap and are adequate for most purposes.

Apochromatic lenses are made on an entirely different principle and must be used with special eyepieces. The colors are intentionally widely separated, or overcorrected, and then brought back to a nearly common focus by a compensating eyepiece. An apochromatic objective used with a regular eyepiece gives a much poorer image than the much cheaper achromatic objective. Its use is justified only in color photography and in the most critical kind of research.

The *stage* with its *spring* or *stage clips* is for holding the slide containing the specimen. To facilitate examination, the clips are usually replaced with a *mechanical stage,* which allows smoother and better-controlled movements of the slide.

In the substage position are the *condenser* and the *iris diaphragm.* The two main types of condensers in use today are the *Abbe* and the *achromat.* The first type is used with achromatic objectives and the second with both apochromatic and achromatic objectives. Every substage condenser is furnished with an iris diaphragm, the only function of which is to control the numerical aperture (see below) of the condenser. (The iris diaphragm should never be used to decrease light intensity because this results in loss of fine detail or even introduction of detail that is not there.)

The ordinary Abbe condenser, with a maximum numerical aperture of about 0.9, is perfectly adequate for most work. The resolution of an oil-immersion objective of numerical aperture 1.2, working at numerical aperture 0.9 with an Abbe condenser, is good enough for most routine work. It should be remembered that the Abbe condenser, unlike the achromatic one, has spherical and chromatic aberration.

The numerical aperture 1.4 achromatic condenser is required when color correction is sought with apochromatic objectives or when oil-immersion lenses are to be used at numerical apertures greater than 1. In this case, the condenser, as well as the objective, must be oiled to the slide.

Many condensers are equipped with a swinging or sliding lens immediately under the condenser. This is necessary because the image of most light sources produced by high-power condensers is too small for low-power objectives. Unfortunately, this lens not only expands the beam of light but also throws it out of focus, so that the corrections and resolution of the low-power objectives are seriously affected. The only functional use of these lenses is to permit a field to be searched with low power to locate an object for examination under high power. Other condensers are equipped with a swing-out front lens; as soon as a low-power objective requires more light to illuminate the field than the condenser provides, the iris diaphragm is opened fully and the front lens is swung out.

The correct position of the condenser is always at its upper stop. It is lowered *slightly* only for the Kohler method of illumination (discussed below).

The light source is an integral part of the microscope system. It can be built in or separate. The separate illuminator, of course, requires a mirror to direct light into the condenser.

The minimum requirements for a separate microscope illuminator for use with a microscope with a substage condenser are as follows.

1. A high-intensity lamp with a compact filament. An ideal light source would be a point. A compact filament is the most practical source.
2. A lens (*field condenser*) at least 3 in. in diameter, mounted in a focusing device, which will produce a sharp image of the filament at a distance of from 6 to 12 in. This lens is required to gather the rays leaving the filament and condense them into a beam of useful size and direction. In practice this lens is the light source by which the substage condenser forms an image on the slide.
3. An iris diaphragm, or *field iris*, in front of the lens used to limit the size of the light image. It should not be used to decrease light intensity; the same rule is applied to the condenser iris diaphragm. (There are two ways to decrease the intensity of illumination: lowering the voltage applied to the lamp has the disadvantage of making the light redder as the intensity is decreased; the better method is to place neutral-density filters in the filter holder.)
4. Filter holder in front of the iris.
5. A housing that can be tilted.

Many modern microscopes have the illuminant, field condenser, and field iris built into the *base* of the instrument. This has the great advantage of convenience but also has the disadvantage of lack of flexibility.

COMMON OPTICAL AND MECHANICAL PROPERTIES RELATED TO MICROSCOPES
MAGNIFICATION

The objective magnifies the specimen and produces a *real image* (illuminated by the lamp and the condenser). The ocular magnifies the real image, yielding a *virtual image,* which is seen by the eye. In general practice, the useful limit of magnification is at the most 1,000 times the numerical aperture of the objective. However, in microscopy, magnification is secondary to resolution.

RESOLUTION (RESOLVING
POWER)

The resolving power of a lens is its ability to show two closely adjacent points as distinct and separate. For example, we are interested in knowing whether a microscope can show two adjacent bacterial flagella as two separate elements instead of as one. Thus the largest image a microscope reproduces is not actually the most useful.

This characteristic of a microscope is a function of the wavelength of light used and the numerical aperture (a characteristic of a lens system explained below). The limit of resolution, or maximum resolving power, can be determined as follows.

If NA_{obj} and NA_{cond} are the numerical apertures of the objective and the condenser and λ is the wavelength of the light used for observation in micrometers, then the smallest resolvable separation d between two points, in micrometers, is

$$d = \frac{\lambda}{NA_{obj} + NA_{cond}}$$

To illustrate this further, assume the use of a green filter resulting in light of $\lambda = 0.55$ μm. The oil-immersion objective used has an NA of 1.25 and the condenser has an NA of 0.9. Substituting these values into the equation, we have

$$d = \frac{0.55}{1.25 + 0.9} = 0.255 \ \mu m$$

NUMERICAL APERTURE

The accompanying diagram shows an objective front lens and specimen.

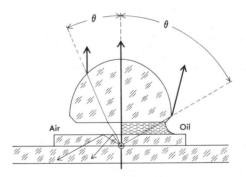

The angle θ subtended by the optical axis and the outermost rays still covered by the objective is a measure of the aperture of the objective; it is the aperture angle. The magnitude of this angle is expressed as a sine value. The sine value of the half aperture angle multiplied by the refractive index n of the medium filling the space between the front lens and the cover slip gives the numerical aperture: $NA = n \sin \theta$

With dry objectives the value of n is 1 since 1 is the refractive index of air. When immersion oil is employed as the medium, n is 1.56, and if θ is 58°, then

$$NA = n \sin \theta = 1.56 \times \sin 58° = 1.56 \times 0.85 = 1.33$$

From this example it becomes obvious that an oil-immersion objective accomplishes a big gain in numerical aperture.

ILLUMINATION

Proper illumination is essential for the efficient utilization of the magnification and resolution of a microscope.

In microscopes with mirrors, the light from the illuminating source is reflected into the condenser by the mirror. The flat surface is used with microscopes equipped with a condenser. (The concave side is used with microscopes without condensers, since it concentrates the light rays.)

There are two kinds of illumination, *critical illumination* and *Kohler illumination*. In critical illumination the image superimposed on the object is that of the light source itself, i.e., an image of the glowing filaments of the electric bulb. Unfortunately, the brightly glowing coiled filaments are a distraction.

Kohler illumination uses a disk of light limited by the field iris as the illuminant. The size of such a disk can be varied by closing and opening the field iris. It is possible by this means to fill the field of view of any objective since different objectives have different size fields of view. This type of illumination allows precise control of the light path and is widely used today.

SETTING UP A MICROSCOPE FOR MICROBIOLOGICAL EXAMINATION

There are essentially three things that should be done by a microbiologist in setting up a microscope before examination.

1. Set up Kohler illumination with the lamp properly centered and the field iris in focus.
2. Every time the objective is changed, rematch the condenser to it with the substage iris.
3. Whenever the slide is changed, refocus the substage condenser.

SETTING UP KOHLER ILLUMINATION

1. Align the microscope illuminator or lamp with the plane mirror of the microscope so that an image of the spiral lamp filaments is focused on the substage iris with the aid of the field condenser. This is done by first focusing the filament of the lamp on a piece of paper laid on the microscope mirror and then, having moved the piece of paper up until it rests against the underside of the substage condenser, adjust the focus with the field condenser until the filaments are again sharp. (A small mirror held in the hand will allow one to see clearly what is going on underneath the stage.) The lamp should be tilted and moved backward and forward and the mirror again tilted until the image of the filament, when twice focused, is centered both on the mirror and on the substage.
2. Rack the condenser up to the top. Remove the eyepiece from the tube. Keep adjusting the mirror until the back

lens of the objective is filled with light. It is advisable to dim the light by a neutral-density filter. Insert the eyepiece and focus the specimen with a 10× objective.

3. Close the iris diaphragm of the illuminator (field stop) almost completely and move its blurred image on the specimen into the center of the field of view by rotating and tilting the mirror. (For microscopes with a built-in illuminator, step 1 and part of step 2 are omitted. Under step 3, centering is not accomplished with the aid of a mirror but by the centering screws of the condenser.)

4. Focus the edge of this diaphragm image by slightly lowering the condenser. Both the specimen and the field stop are now sharply defined. Open the field stop until the entire field of view is just clear.

5. Slightly readjust the lamp socket or the lamp condenser, until the field of view is evenly illuminated.

6. At first open the condenser iris completely and then close it only far enough to eliminate glare in the most important image elements and to render them with satisfactory contrast. (Do not use the iris diaphragm to reduce light intensity.)

7. With low-power objectives the front lens of the condenser (when present) may have to be swung out to illuminate the field fully. The condenser iris is opened fully, and contrast is controlled with the lamp diaphragm.

The diagram summarizes the steps to be taken in setting up Kohler illumination.

The four stages in setting up Kohler illumination. The stages are numbered, but the main things to remember are that an image of the lamp filament is first formed on the substage iris with the aid of the field condenser; then an image of the field iris is formed in the plane of the object with the substage condenser. (*From Peter Gray, "The Use of the Microscope." Copyright 1967. McGraw-Hill Book Company. Used by permission.*)

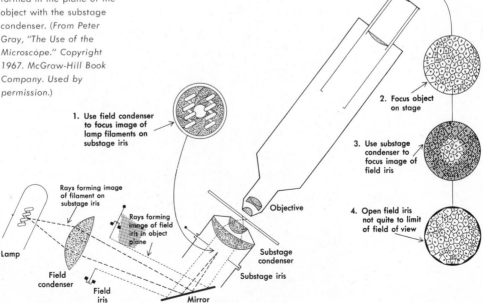

1. Use field condenser to focus image of lamp filaments on substage iris

2. Focus object on stage

3. Use substage condenser to focus image of field iris

4. Open field iris not quite to limit of field of view

Rays forming image of filament on substage iris

Rays forming image of field iris in object plane

Objective

Lamp

Field condenser

Field iris

Mirror

Substage condenser

Substage iris

Laboratory Exercises in Microbiology

MATCHING THE
CONDENSER TO THE
OBJECTIVE

Remove the eyepiece and look down the barrel from at least 10 in. away and then open or close the substage iris until it cuts off about the outer tenth of the back lens of the objective. With oil-immersion objectives the substage iris is opened to its full extent. No further adjustment is necessary, since the maximum aperture of the substage is normally matched to the oil-immersion objective.

REFOCUSING THE
SUBSTAGE CONDENSER

When another slide is put in place, swing back to the 10X objective and refocus the substage condenser to produce a sharp image of the field iris. This is necessary because slides vary in thickness.

PRECAUTIONS TO
BE OBSERVED IN
USING THE
MICROSCOPE

Microbiologists also use the electron microscope to study the fine structures of microorganisms.

1. Do *not* touch the lenses. If they become dirty, clean them by wiping gently with lens paper.

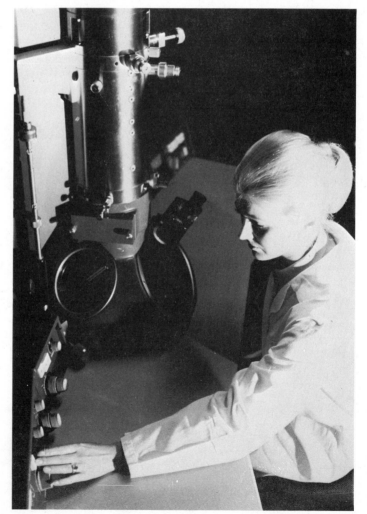

2. With lens paper, wipe the oil off the oil-immersion objective after use to prevent the oil from drying or dust from collecting.

3. Do not tilt the microscope when working with the oil-immersion objective. Otherwise the oil may flow into hard-to-clean places and dry there.

4. Keep the instrument free of dust by keeping it covered when not in use.

5. Carry the instrument by the arm and with both hands.

6. Preliminary focusing to bring the object into view should always be done by *raising* the objective. Never allow the objective lens to touch the cover slip or the slide. (All knobs should turn freely and easily; never force any movable part of the instrument.)

7. Keep both eyes open when looking through the eyepiece of the monocular microscope. Closing one eye for a long period of time is tiring. Work with perfectly relaxed eyes. This can be done if you imagine that you are viewing the image as if it were at infinity. That is, look "through the microscope" but not "into the microscope." After some practice this should come easily.

EXERCISE TWO
THE USE
OF THE MICROSCOPE

REFERENCE: Text,* chap. 4.

The microscope is one of the most important instruments employed by the microbiologist. Although there are several types of microscopy, only the bright-field technique will be used in the exercises that follow. You must become thoroughly acquainted with the proper use of this instrument at the outset of the course.

MATERIALS

1. Microscope and microscope lamp
2. Microscope slide and cover slip
3. Immersion oil
4. Yeast cake
5. Test tube

PROCEDURE

1. Place the microscope on your desk with the arm of the microscope nearest you. With the aid of the previous illustration, locate the various parts of the instrument. Be sure that you understand the function of each working part. You should also become familiar with the terms frequently used in microscopy, some of which are described on the preceding pages. Consult with the laboratory instructor if you have any questions.
2. Connect the microscope lamp and position it in front of the mirror of the microscope. NOTE: Models of some microscopes have a built-in light source in the base of the instrument.
3. Prepare a suspension of yeast cells by transferring a very small piece of the yeast cake (about the size of a pinhead) into a test tube containing approximately 1 ml water. Place a loopful of the yeast suspension on a glass slide and cover it with a cover slip. Place this preparation on the stage of the microscope.

*References made to the "text" throughout this manual mean Michael J. Pelczar, Jr., and Roger D. Reid, "Microbiology," 3d ed., McGraw-Hill Book Company, New York, 1972.

4. Set up the microscope for microbiological examination as described in the preceding pages.
5. Note the size and shape of the yeast cells with the low-power (10X) objective.
6. Swing the high-dry objective into position over the slide. With parfocal objectives, only slight adjustment of the fine-adjustment knob will bring the yeast cells into sharp focus. Again note the size and shape of the yeast cells.
7. Swing the high-dry objective partially out of the way and place a drop of immersion oil on the center of the cover slip.
8. Swing the oil-immersion objective into position above the slide. Now look through the eyepiece and adjust the fine-adjustment knob. Examine; note the relative sizes of the yeast cells under each objective.
9. If time permits, repeat the above procedure, substituting a strand of hair or a piece of filter paper for the yeast.

RESULTS

Draw a few cells from a typical microscopic field of the yeast preparation as seen under each magnification.

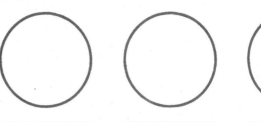

magnification: _____   _____   _____

objective: _____   _____   _____

QUESTIONS

1. The magnification obtained by the microscope is a product of the magnification of the ocular times that of the objective. The magnification of each objective is as follows: low-power (16 mm) = 10; high-dry (4 mm) = 44; oil-immersion (1.8 mm) = 95. What magnification was obtained in each of the examinations that you performed?

_____

_____

_____

_____

_____

_____

2. Why should preliminary focusing always be done upward?

_____

_____

_____

_____

_____

_____

3. What is the function of oil as used with the oil-immersion objective?

_____

_____

_____

_____

_____

_____

4. What is the limiting factor in obtaining useful magnifications through optical microscopes?

_____

_____

_____

_____

_____

_____

5. Describe one situation where the use of phase or dark-field microscopy would be distinctly preferable to bright-field microscopy.

_____

_____

_____

_____

_____

_____

6. Identify the following terms as they apply to microscopy: "resolution," "numerical aperture," "working distance."

_____

_____

_____

_____

_____

_____

_____

_____

EXERCISE THREE
MICROSCOPIC EXAMINATION
OF MICROORGANISMS

REFERENCE: Text, chap. 1

Microbes are widely distributed in natural environments. This can be demonstrated by microscopic examination of hay infusion (water in which hay has been allowed to soak for several days). Hay infusion should be prepared using pond or stream water since either is likely to contribute microorganisms to those already present on the hay. Nutrients that leach out from the hay support growth of some of the microbes. It is possible to observe bacteria, fungi (yeasts and molds), protozoa, and algae in such specimens.

MATERIALS

1. Cultures of a bacterium (*Bacillus cereus*), a yeast (*Saccharomyces cerevisiae*), a mold (*Aspergillus niger*), an alga (*Chlorella* sp.), and a protozoan (*Paramecium* sp.)
2. Beaker containing hay infusion
3. Glass slides and cover slips
4. Dropping pipette

PROCEDURE

1. Prepare a wet mount of each of the pure cultures provided by placing a small drop of water on a clean slide, adding some of the culture, and mixing by means of the transfer needle. Place a cover slip over this suspension. Examine these under low-power and high-dry magnification. Note their size, their shape, and any characteristics of motion.
2. By use of the dropping pipette, carefully obtain some liquid from the *surface* of the hay infusion and prepare a wet mount.
3. Examine this preparation under low-power and high-dry magnification. Pay particular attention to comparative sizes of microorganisms as well as to the shapes, structures, and movements of individual organisms. Compare the various types of organisms seen in the hay infusion with those observed in pure culture (step 1 above).

4. Repeat steps 2 and 3, using a drop of liquid taken from the *bottom* of the hay-infusion sample.

RESULTS

1. Sketch a few typical cells of each pure culture as seen under high-dry magnification. Make your sketches so that they reflect comparative sizes.

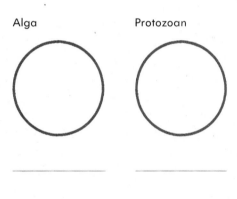

Bacterium   Yeast   Mold

species name: _____ _____ _____

magnification: _____ _____ _____

Alga   Protozoan

species name: _____ _____

magnification: _____ _____

2. Make drawings of a typical microscopic field (high-dry magnification) as observed from the *surface* and *bottom* specimens of hay infusion.

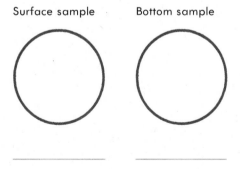

Surface sample   Bottom sample

magnification: _____ _____

QUESTIONS

1. What major kinds of microorganisms could you identify in the hay infusion? (Refer to Chap. 1 of text for general characteristics of microorganisms.)

2. Was there any difference in the numbers or types of organisms found in the surface and bottom specimens of hay infusion? How might one account for this?

3. Did you observe differences in motility among the various organisms? Explain.

EXERCISE FOUR
MEASUREMENT
OF MICROORGANISMS

REFERENCE: Text, chap. 5.

The dimensions of microorganisms are usually expressed in micrometers (μm), a unit of measurement which is 1/1,000 of a millimeter or 1/25,400 of an inch. Microorganisms of various types range in size from a fraction of a micrometer to high multiples of a micrometer. Their size can be measured by equipping the microscope with an *ocular micrometer,* which is then calibrated against a *stage micrometer.**

MATERIALS

1. Ocular micrometer
2. Stage micrometer
3. Prepared slides of a bacterium, yeast, mold, alga, and protozoan

PROCEDURE

CALIBRATION OF OCULAR MICROMETER

1. Center the stage micrometer on the stage of the microscope beneath the low-power objective.
2. Remove the eyepiece from your microscope and place the ocular micrometer on the metal shelf within it as shown in the sketch.

A. Ocular removed from microscope. The ocular may have a focusing eye lens. B. Eyepiece unscrewed from ocular to allow insertion of ocular micrometer.

*Note that the unit of length is pronounced micro·me′ter and the measuring device is pronounced mi·crom′e·ter

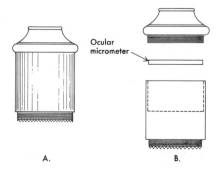

Ocular micrometer

A.

B.

3. Replace the eyepiece, focus the eye lens, and rotate the ocular micrometer so as to superimpose its lines upon those of the stage micrometer. The field should appear as shown. The graduations of the ocular micrometer superimpose and are parallel with those of the stage micrometer.

Ocular-micrometer
divisions.

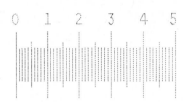

Stage micrometer
divisions (10 μm apart).

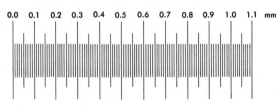

4. Align these two sets of graduations so that you can determine the number of ocular-micrometer spaces that fall within a given stage-micrometer space. From this information, you can calculate the distance between the ocular-micrometer spaces.

5. In a similar manner, repeat the procedure with the high-power and oil-immersion objectives.

MEASUREMENT OF
MICROORGANISMS

6. Replace the stage micrometer with one of the prepared slides of microorganisms and determine the dimensions of several individual cells. Repeat this for each of the different prepared specimens.

RESULTS

1. Record the following information pertaining to the standardization of your microscope.

Microscope number: _____	LENGTH OF ONE OCULAR DIVISION, MICROMETERS (μm)		
	LOW-POWER	HIGH-DRY ,	OIL-IMMERSION
Tube length: _____			

2. Record the measurements made of microorganisms in the following table.

SPECIES*	LENGTH		WIDTH	
	SEVERAL INDIVIDUAL CELLS	AVERAGE	SEVERAL INDIVIDUAL CELLS	AVERAGE
Bacterium				
Yeast				
Mold				
Alga				
Protozoan				

*Supply specific name.

QUESTIONS

1. How many micrometers are there in 1 inch? 1 centimeter? 1 millimeter? What is a nanometer?

_____

_____

_____

_____

_____

2. How much variation did you observe among the cells in the same species?

_____

_____

_____

_____

_____

_____

3. Would you expect unstained (living) cells to be different in size than the same cells examined in a stained preparation? Why?

_____

_____

_____

_____

_____

_____

4. Name a typical "average-size" bacterium, and give its dimensions. Name a bacterial species which is considerably larger and one that is considerably smaller than the average and give their dimensions. Do the same for algae and protozoa.

_____

_____

_____

_____

_____

_____

PART THREE
BACTERIAL
MORPHOLOGY AND
STAINING METHODS

One of the major characteristics of bacteria is morphology—size, shape, arrangement, and structure. These characteristics can be determined by examination of appropriately prepared specimens. When bright-field microscopy is used for the examination, it is desirable that the cells be stained to make them more readily visible. Unstained cells are practically transparent and are best observed by techniques that permit critical control of illumination, as in phase or dark-field microscopy.

Staining of a bacterial film (or smear) may be performed simply to reveal the shape, size, and arrangement of the cells. The cells are stained by the application of a single staining solution. However, it is possible to acquire additional information about the morphology of bacteria through the use of differential staining techniques. Differential staining procedures usually involve treatment of the smear with a series of reagents. The appearance of the cells following this treatment may permit one to distinguish between two different bacteria on the basis of the color they retain; e.g., one type might appear blue, another red. One may also distinguish between structural entities within the cell proper or exterior to the cell wall.

Careful examination of appropriately stained bacteria provides invaluable information for the morphological characterization and identification of the specimen.

Unstained bacterial cells are nearly transparent when observed by light microscopy and hence are difficult to see. Staining, by producing artificially colored microorganisms, renders them easier to visualize microscopically.

Apart from differentiating and rendering visible the cell in whole or in part, staining also aids in the identification of microorganisms. For example, the reaction of positiveness or negativeness in the gram stain is useful as a means of primary grouping.

Stains are made from dyes, which are classified as natural or synthetic. Natural dyes are mainly for histological purposes. Most bacterial stains are made from synthetic dyes, which are aniline (or more correctly coal-tar) dyes. They are all derivatives of benzene.

There are three groups of stains: acid, basic, or neutral. The most commonly used stains are salts. A salt is composed of a positively charged ion and a negatively charged ion. For example, methylene blue is actually the salt methylene blue chloride:

methylene blue$^+$ + chloride$^-$

When color of the stain is in the positively charged ion, it is a basic dye. Acid stains have the reverse situation, and the color is in the negative ion, an example being eosin, which is really sodium$^+$ eosinate$^-$. An acid dye is so called because, like an acid, the chromophore combines with a base (like NaOH) to form the dye salt, e.g., sodium eosinate. Thus a basic dye has a chromophore that behaves like a base; it combines with an acid (like HCl) to form the dye salt, e.g., methylene blue chloride.

Neutral stains are formed by mixing together aqueous solutions of certain acid and basic dyes. The coloring matter in neutral stains is contained in both negatively and positively charged components.

Why staining reactions occur is not fully understood. They are apparently a combination of physical and chemical reactions. Since bacterial cells are rich in nucleic acid, which has a negative charge, it follows that basic stains (chromophore is positively charged) will be attracted to them and stain them.

REFERENCES: Text, chap. 4; MMM,* chap. 2; MCM,* chap. 75.

Stained preparations are made by the simple process of spreading a drop of an aqueous suspension of cells on a glass slide, allowing it to dry, and applying gentle heat to "fix" the cells; this is followed by application of the staining solutions.

MATERIALS

1. Petri-dish mixed culture
2. Pure cultures of *Bacillus subtilis, Staphylococcus aureus,* and *Spirillum itersonii*
3. Staining solutions: Loeffler's methylene blue, Ziehl's carbolfuchsin, and Hucker's crystal violet

PROCEDURE

1. Wash and dry several microscope slides.
2. Place a small, clean drop of water on the slide by use of the transfer loop.
3. Flame the transfer needle, raise the top of the petri dish, and remove a portion of a colony on the tip of the transfer needle.
4. With a circular motion, emulsify this growth in the drop of water on the slide. Spread the drop out to approximate the size of a dime. Flame the needle again as soon as the smear is made.
5. Allow the smear to air-dry; then fix the smear by passing the slide through the flame (right side up) two or three times.
6. Select one of the following stains and cover the smear for the designated time: crystal violet, 2 to 60 sec; methylene blue, 1 to 2 min; carbolfuchsin, 15 to 30 sec.
7. After the smear has been exposed to the stain for the required time, remove excess stain by washing with a gentle stream of water; then blot dry with absorbent paper.

*Reference to MMM throughout this manual means the Committee on Bacteriological Technic, Society of American Bacteriologists, "Manual of Microbiological Methods," McGraw-Hill Book Company, New York, 1957. MCM means the American Society for Microbiology, "Manual of Clinical Microbiology," ASM, Bethesda, Md., 1970.

8. Examine the stained preparation under the microscope, using the oil-immersion objective.
9. Repeat this procedure, using other colonies from the plate and different stains so that all three stains are used.
10. Prepare and examine simple stain preparations of each of the pure cultures of bacteria.

RESULTS

NOTE: The accompanying illustrations provide guidance for the preparation of sketches from your microscopic preparations. Examples A and B show the microscopic field of a pure culture and an appropriate drawing from it. Note that a small area of the miscroscopic field provides adequate information on the shape and arrangement of this specimen. Examples C and D show a microscopic field from a mixed-culture specimen. *The drawing* shown in D is made of cells from different locations in the microscopic field to reveal the diverse morphological forms.

You should use the scheme illustrated as a guide for preparation of drawings from microscopic preparations.

A. Microscopic field of stained smear from a pure culture. B. Sketch from an area of the microscopic field illustrating shape and arrangement of cells. C. Microscopic field of stained smear from a mixed culture. D. Sketch of several cells selected from microscopic field to illustrate diverse morphology of cells.

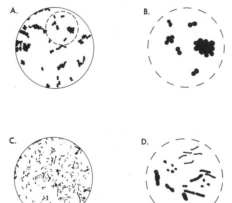

1. Make a drawing, and give a word description of the organisms found in each stained preparation made from a colony. Describe the type of colony from which each smear was made.

	STAIN USED		
	METHYLENE BLUE	CARBOLFUCHSIN	CRYSTAL VIOLET
Drawing of a few cells in a typical microscopic field			
Magnification			

	STAIN USED		
	METHYLENE BLUE	CARBOLFUCHSIN	CRYSTAL VIOLET
Word description of morphology			
Description of colony from which stain was made			

2. Draw a few representative cells of each of the three species which were provided in pure culture.

SPECIES	SKETCH OF CELLS	WORD DESCRIPTION OF MORPHOLOGY
Bacillus subtilis		
Staphylococcus aureus		
Spirillum itersonii		

QUESTIONS

1. What is meant by the term "fixing the smear," and what occurs during the process?

    _____

    _____

    _____

    _____

    _____

    _____

2. Why stain bacteria?

    _____

    _____

    _____

    _____

    _____

    _____

3. Were all your simple stain preparations equally good for purposes of noting the morphology of cells? If not, what characteristics made some better than others?

    _____

    _____

    _____

    _____

    _____

    _____

B. THE NEGATIVE STAIN

Unstained bacteria can be made clearly visible when they are prepared as a film in nigrosin. The nigrosin provides a dark gray background; the cells are clear and unstained. Since this method of preparing a smear for microscopic examination does not subject the cells to strong chemical agents or physical treatment, there is little chance of distortion of their morphology.

MATERIALS

1. Dorner's nigrosin solution
2. Trypticase-soy-agar cultures of *Spirillum itersonii*, *Staphylococcus aureus*, and *Bacillus subtilis*

PROCEDURE

One slide, which is held at an angle, is drawn just enough to the right to form contact with the droplet across its entire edge and the surface of the bottom slide. This same slide is then pushed across the surface of the bottom slide, drawing out the material in the droplet and forming a wide film.

1. Place a small drop of nigrosin near one end of a glass slide. Using the transfer needle, remove some organisms from one of the slant cultures and mix them in the drop. *Do not spread the drop out during this mixing.*
2. Using the edge of another clean slide, spread the drop out into a film following the technique illustrated.
3. Allow the film to *air-dry* and examine, using the oil-immersion objective of the microscope. The thickness of the film is not uniform, and hence the background in some

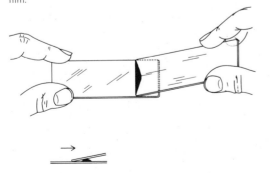

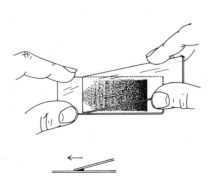

areas will be darker than in others. Search several locations to select the best field for characterizing the morphology of the bacteria.

4. Repeat the process for the other two cultures.

RESULTS

Select a suitable microscopic field from each of the preparations and make drawings of a few organisms. Note particularly the shape of individual cells, arrangements of cells, and the relative size of cells from the three species.

	BACTERIAL SPECIES		
	Bacillus subtilis	*Staphylococcus aureus*	*Spirillum itersonii*
Drawing of a few cells from a typical microscopic field	◯	◯	◯
Magnification			
Word description of morphology			

QUESTIONS

1. Why is this technique called a "negative" stain?

_____

_____

_____

_____

_____

_____

2. a. How does the negative-staining technique differ from the dark-field technique?

_____

2. b. Compare the general appearance of bacterial cells observed in a negative-stain preparation with the same bacteria as seen in a dark-field preparation.

3. Compare the size, shape, and arrangement of cells of each of the three species as determined by this technique with those observed in the preceding section.

C. THE GRAM STAIN

One of the most important and widely used procedures for characterizing bacteria is the gram stain. In general terms, bacteria are divided into two groups, based on whether they retain or lose the primary stain (crystal violet). Those organisms which retain the crystal violet (appear dark blue or violet) are designated *gram-positive*; those which lose the crystal violet and are subsequently stained by the safranin (appear red) are designated *gram-negative*.

MATERIALS

1. Nutrient-agar slant cultures of *Bacillus cereus, Escherichia coli, Staphylococcus aureus,* and *Neisseria perflava*
2. Staining solutions: Hucker's crystal violet, Gram's iodine solution, 95% ethyl alcohol, safranin
3. Sterile applicator stick

PROCEDURE

1. Prepare smears of *B. cereus* and *E. coli* side by side on the same slide. Fix the smears.
2. On a second slide, prepare and fix smears of *S. aureus* and *N. perflava*.
3. Stain smears with crystal violet solution for 1 min; then wash with water for a few seconds. Drain off excess water.
4. Apply Gram's iodine solution for 1 min; wash with water and drain.
5. Decolorize with 95% alcohol until free color has been washed off (approximately 30 sec). Wash slide with water, and drain.
6. Counterstain smears for 30 sec with safranin; wash, and blot dry.
7. Make microscopic examinations of each stained preparation.
8. Using a sterile applicator stick, take some scrapings from

the base of your teeth and gums. Prepare a smear from this and stain it by the gram method. Examine several areas of this film using the oil-immersion objective.

RESULTS

1. Identify the gram reaction of each of the four species used in this experiment.
2. Make a drawing from each preparation that will illustrate typical morphology of these organisms.
3. List the various morphological types of organisms, and their gram reaction, as seen in the smear from the gum scrapings.

_____

_____

_____

_____

	BACTERIAL SPECIES			
	Bacillus cereus	Escherichia coli	Staphylococcus aureus	Neisseria perflava
Drawing of a few cells from a typical microscopic field				
Magnification				
Word descrip-tion of morphology				
Color of stained bacteria				
Gram reaction				

QUESTIONS

1. Were all cells in each of the preparations from the pure cultures uniformly stained? If not, how could variations in staining be accounted for?

_____

_____

_____

_____

_____

_____

2. Explain what happens during each step of this staining procedure to a gram-negative cell and a gram-positive cell.

_____

_____

_____

_____

_____

_____

_____

_____

3. List several physiological characteristics which can be associated with gram-positive bacteria. Gram-negative bacteria.

_____

_____

_____

_____

_____

_____

4. Name 10 gram-positive species of bacteria and 10 gram-negative species of bacteria.

_____

_____

_____

_____

_____

_____

_____

_____

D. THE ACID-FAST STAIN

Some species of bacteria, particularly those in the genus *Mycobacterium,* do not stain readily by simple staining procedures. Staining of these organisms is facilitated by application of heat. Once stained, they retain the dye, even when treated with a decolorizing agent such as acid alcohol. They are designated as *acid-fast.* The acid-fast procedure employs initial treatment with carbolfuchsin followed by acid alcohol and methylene blue. Acid-fast organisms are not decolorized and hence appear *red;* non-acid-fast organisms are decolorized and counterstained by the methylene blue; hence they appear *blue.*

MATERIALS

1. Nutrient-agar slant cultures of *Mycobacterium smegmatis* and *Staphylococcus aureus*
2. Staining solutions: Ziehl's carbolfuchsin, acid alcohol, Loeffler's methylene blue
3. Egg albumin or serum
4. Strip of blotting paper approximately ¾ by 1½ in.
5. Prepared acid-fast stains of tuberculous sputum

PROCEDURE

NOTE: Smears of the bacteria should be prepared in a small drop of serum or egg albumin. The protein enhances the adherence of the bacteria to the glass surface and also provides material for light background staining.

1. Prepare and fix smears of *M. smegmatis* and *S. aureus* side by side on a glass slide. On a second slide, prepare a single smear containing a mixture of the two species.
2. Cover the smear with a strip of the blotting paper; the paper should not extend beyond the edges of the slide.

3. Saturate the paper with Ziehl's carbolfuchsin.

4. Heat the slide to steaming with a small flame or hot plate. *Do not allow the slide to dry.* If necessary, add more stain. Allow the staining to continue for 3 to 5 min, and remove blotting paper.

5. Wash the slide with tap water and then decolorize the smear for 10 to 30 sec with acid alcohol. Exercise care so that the smear is not overdecolorized. Wash the slide with tap water.

6. Apply methylene blue for 30 to 45 sec, wash, blot dry, and examine smears microscopically. Acid-fast organisms stain red; non-acid-fast organisms stain blue. The protein film (serum or albumin) will appear faintly blue.

7. Make a microscopic examination of the acid-fast stain of tuberculous sputum provided.

RESULTS

1. Record the color of organisms in each preparation, and indicate their acid-fast reaction.
2. Draw a representative portion of a typical microscopic field from each stained preparation.

	BACTERIAL SPECIES		
	Mycobacterium smegmatis	Staphylococcus aureus	Mixture
Drawing of a few typical cells in a microscopic field			
Magnification			
Word description of morphology			
Color of stained bacteria			
Acid-fast reaction			

QUESTIONS

1. What accounts for the acid-fast property of *Mycobacterium* species?

_____

_____

_____

_____

_____

2. Compare the morphological characteristics of *Mycobacterium smegmatis* and *M. tuberculosis*.

_____

_____

_____

_____

_____

_____

3. Explain why the acid-fast stain is a very useful diagnostic technique.

_____

_____

_____

_____

_____

_____

4. Is there any correlation between the gram and acid-fast reactions of bacteria? Explain.

_____

_____

_____

_____

_____

_____

EXERCISE SIX
STAINING FOR
CELL STRUCTURES
A. THE SPORE STAIN

Certain bacteria, e.g., species of *Bacillus* and *Clostridium*, develop a spore (or endospore) that possesses a remarkable resistance to physical and chemical agents. The spore develops in a characteristic position within the cell; and as development proceeds, the vegetative cell eventually gives way to the formation of a free spore. The nature of the spore necessitates a vigorous treatment for staining. Once stained, these spores are comparatively difficult to decolorize. The size of the endospore and its position in the cell are distinctive characteristics of sporeforming species.

REFERENCES: Text, chap. 5; MMM, chap. 2; MCM, chap. 75.

MATERIALS

1. Nutrient-agar slant cultures of *Bacillus coagulans* and *Bacillus subtilis*; fluid thioglycolate (with added calcium carbonate) cultures of *Clostridium butyricum* and *C. tetanomorphum*
2. Staining solutions: 5% aq. malachite green, 0.5% aq. safranin
3. Blotting-paper strips
4. Gram-stain reagents

PROCEDURE

1. Prepare and fix a smear of each culture; two smears can be made side by side on a single slide.
2. Cover the smears with a blotting-paper strip and then saturate the strip with the malachite green staining solution.
3. Heat the slide gently until it steams; allow solution to remain 2 to 3 min. (More solution may be added to prevent drying.)
4. Wash slide with tap water and then apply safranin solution for 30 sec.
5. Wash smear with tap water, drain, blot dry, and examine using the oil-immersion objective. The spores stain green, and the vegetative cells stain red.
6. Prepare and examine a gram stain of each species.

RESULTS

From a typical microscopic field of each specimen, draw several of the bacteria. Note the position and size of the spore within individual cells as well as the size and shape of free spores.

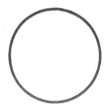

*Bacillus
coagulans*

*Bacillus
subtilis*

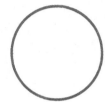

*Clostridium
butyricum*

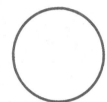

*Clostridium
tetanomorphum*

QUESTIONS

1. Why is a spore more difficult to stain than the vegetative cell?

_____

_____

_____

_____

_____

2. Is it possible to see spores in a preparation stained by the gram method? Explain.

_____

_____

_____

_____

_____

3. Is the location (position) of a spore in a bacterial cell the same for all sporeforming bacteria? List several specific examples to substantiate your answer.

_____

_____

_____

_____

_____

_____

4. What generalization can be made about morphology, gram reaction, and spore formation?

_____

_____

_____

_____

_____

_____

B. THE CAPSULE STAIN

The cell wall of many species of bacteria is surrounded by a mucilaginous substance referred to as a *capsule* or slime layer. Its size varies with the species and among strains of species. The composition of the medium may also influence the size of the capsule.

Among disease-producing bacteria the presence of a heavy capsule is generally an indication of a highly virulent form of the organism. The diagnosis of pneumonia and other diseases is assisted by using a capsule stain.

MATERIALS

1. Skim-milk culture and trypticase-soy-broth culture of *Flavobacterium capsulatum*, *Alcaligenes viscolactis*, and *Proteus vulgaris*
2. Staining solutions: Tyler's crystal violet and 20% aq. $CuSO_4 \cdot 5H_2O$
3. Gram-stain reagents

PROCEDURE

1. Prepare smears from each of the two *F. capsulatum* cultures side by side on a single slide. Allow the smears to air-dry. *Do not heat*. Do the same with the other two species.
2. Stain for 4 to 7 min with crystal violet.
3. Wash smear with $CuSO_4 \cdot 5H_2O$ solution.
4. Blot dry and examine microscopically, using the oil-immersion objective. Capsules appear faint blue, and the cells proper are dark blue.
5. Prepare and examine gram stains of each species from the trypticase-soy-broth cultures.

RESULTS

Make a drawing of a few cells from a typical microscopic field from the capsule stain of smears of each species prepared from the skim-milk culture and the trypticase-soy-broth culture. Record the gram reaction of each species.

	DRAWING OF A FEW CELLS FROM TYPICAL MICROSCOPIC FIELDS		
	Flavobacterium capsulatum	*Alcaligenes viscolactis*	*Proteus vulgaris*
Skim-milk culture			
Trypticase-soy-broth culture			
Magnification			
Word description of morphology and gram reaction			
Color: Capsule			
Cell proper			

QUESTIONS

1. What kind of chemical substance(s) constitute the capsules of bacteria?

_____

_____

_____

_____

_____

_____

_____

2. What are some of the physiological roles ascribed to capsular substances?

_____

_____

_____

_____

_____

_____

_____

3. What relationship exists between capsules of pneumococci and serological types of pneumococci?

_____

_____

_____

_____

_____

_____

_____

4. Compare capsules to the sheaths found on some of the higher bacteria.

_____

_____

_____

_____

_____

_____

5. Assume that you have a nutrient-agar slant culture of some bacterial species. A capsule stain is prepared from this culture, and upon microscopic examination the organism is seen to have a very small capsule. How might capsule formation by this organism be enhanced?

_____

_____

_____

_____

_____

_____

C. THE FLAGELLA
STAIN AND DETECTION
OF MOTILITY

Motile bacteria, particularly those regarded as true bacteria, possess one or more very fine threadlike appendages called *flagella*. These are regarded as organs of locomotion. They can be demonstrated by special staining procedures. Motile bacteria can also be detected by examination of the organisms in a wet preparation, where they are able to move about freely. Bacterial motility can also be determined indirectly by inoculating a special agar medium; motile bacteria spread throughout this as evidenced by their growth.

MATERIALS

1. Gray's flagella mordant and Ziehl's carbolfuchsin
2. Specially cleaned slides; 3 distilled 1 ml-water blanks
3. Depression slide and cover slips
4. 3 tubes of motility-test agar
5. 18- to 22-hr nutrient-agar slant cultures of *Pseudomonas fluorescens* and *Proteus vulgaris*; 18- to 24-hr spirillum-agar slant culture of *Spirillum serpens*
6. Small tube of petroleum jelly

PROCEDURE
FLAGELLA STAIN

1. Scrupulously cleaned slides are required and should be prepared as follows. Select new slides and carefully clean them in dichromate solution; remove, wash with water, rinse in 95% alcohol, and wipe dry with clean cheesecloth; pass the slides through the flame of the bunsen burner several times.
2. Prepare a light suspension of each culture in distilled water and incubate 10 to 15 min to develop and extend the flagella fully.
3. Transfer one loopful of the suspension of cells to one end of a clean slide. Tilt the slide, allowing the drop to run down. Air-dry this film. Do *not* heat-fix.

4. Flood the slide with flagella mordant and allow to stand for approximately 10 min.
5. Rinse the stain off gently with water.
6. Flood with Ziehl's carbolfuchsin for 5 min. Rinse off gently with water.
7. Air-dry (do not blot) and examine, using the oil-immersion objective.

HANGING-DROP PREPARATION

1. Ring the outer edge of the concave well of a depression slide with petroleum jelly. (Use it sparingly.)
2. Place a small drop of the bacterial suspension on a cover slip and then place the cover slip over the concave area as shown.

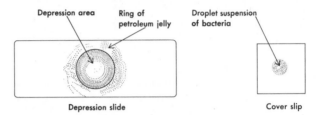

Depression area   Ring of petroleum jelly   Droplet suspension of bacteria

Depression slide   Cover slip

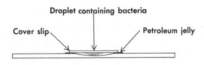

Droplet containing bacteria

Cover slip   Petroleum jelly

3. Observe the specimen, using the *high-dry* objective. Exercise discretion in focusing and adjusting light. Proper illumination is critical since this is an unstained preparation. (Concentrate on the edge of the droplet, where the organisms appear to be more active because of a greater oxygen supply.)

ALTERNATIVE WET PREPARATION

In place of the hanging-drop procedure described above, the following technique can be used:

1. Smear a drop of immersion oil over a glass slide to cover an area approximately the size of a cover slip.
2. Place a small drop of the bacterial culture on a cover slip and then invert and place this cover slip onto the slide with the immersion-oil film. Gently press the cover slip to the slide.
3. Observe the preparation using the oil-immersion objective and reduced illumination. Small droplets of the bacterial suspension will be observed to be trapped throughout the oil film. Motility of the organisms can be observed within these droplets.

INOCULATION OF MOTILITY-TEST AGAR

1. Make a stab inoculation from the agar slants of each culture into individual tubes of motility agar.
2. Incubate these tubes at 35°C for 24 to 48 hr.

RESULTS

1. Make drawings of each flagella-stain preparation. Note the number of flagella and the position of their attachment to the cell.
2. Describe the type of movement observed in the hanging-drop preparations.
3. Illustrate by a sketch the pattern of growth that developed in the motility-agar stab cultures.

	BACTERIAL SPECIES		
	Pseudomonas fluorescens	Proteus vulgaris	Spirillum serpens
Flagella stain: drawing of a few typical cells			
Magnification			
Word description of morphology			
Hanging-drop preparation: description of motion of cells			
Motility-test agar: drawing of growth in stab culture			

QUESTIONS

1. Compare the results relating to motility and presence of flagella as determined by the three techniques.

_____

_____

_____

_____

_____

_____

2. Why must meticulous care be exercised in preparing flagella stains?

_____

_____

_____

_____

_____

_____

3. Compare the type of flagellation between species in the orders Eubacteriales and Pseudomonadales.

_____

_____

_____

_____

_____

_____

4. What is Brownian motion? Do bacteria exhibit this type of motion? Explain your answer.

_____

_____

_____

_____

_____

_____

5. Summarize the morphological characteristics of all the species of bacteria that you have used thus far in the laboratory. Use the table on the next page for this purpose.

Bacterial Morphology and
Staining Methods:
Summary of Morphological
Characteristics of Bacteria
Studied

NAME OF ORGANISM	SHAPE AND ARRANGEMENT	GRAM REACTION	ACID-FAST REACTION	PRESENCE OR ABSENCE		
				SPORES	CAPSULES	FLAGELLA

D. THE CELL-WALL STAIN

The true bacteria have rigid cell walls. The cell wall of a bacterium is easily seen in the electron microscope. In the light microscope, it is difficult to distinguish it from the other components of the cell, but by using mordants the wall can be stained and observed.

MATERIALS

1. 24-hr nutrient-agar slant cultures of *Escherichia coli* and *Bacillus cereus*
2. Microscope slide
3. M/100 cetylpyridinium chloride; saturated aqueous congo red; methylene blue

PROCEDURE

1. Make smears of the cultures provided and fix with heat.
2. Add 3 drops of cetylpyridinium chloride solution to each smear.
3. Add 1 drop congo red to each smear. Mix the drops with a loop-transfer needle (do not scratch the smears).
4. Rotate the drops with a tilting motion by holding the slide in your hand.
5. Rinse off with water.
6. Counterstain for 10 sec with methylene blue.
7. Rinse and blot dry. Examine with the oil-immersion objective.

RESULTS

Make drawings of each cell-wall preparation. (Note the color of the cell wall and the cytoplasm.)

	BACTERIAL SPECIES	
	Escherichia coli	Bacillus cereus
Cell wall as observed by staining	◯	◯
Magnification		

QUESTIONS

1. Is there a difference between the cell wall of gram-positive and gram-negative bacteria? Explain briefly.

2. Name some chemical substances found in the cell walls of bacteria.

EXERCISE SEVEN
MORPHOLOGICAL
UNKNOWN

Morphological characteristics, including staining reactions, represent one of the major properties of bacteria. In identifying an organism, it is customary to determine the characteristics of morphology and staining such as those which have been described in the preceding exercises. In this exercise, you will be given pure cultures of bacteria identified by code rather than by name. You will determine the morphological properties of each of these unknown cultures.

MATERIALS

1. Staining solutions used in previous exercises
2. Agar slant cultures of two or more unknown bacteria identified by code only

PROCEDURE

1. Perform the following techniques on each unknown culture: gram stain, acid-fast stain, spore stain, capsule stain, and hanging-drop preparation. Use the procedures described in preceding exercises.
2. Make microscopic examinations of each preparation.

RESULTS

Tabulate results obtained for each unknown in the table provided.

	CODE NUMBERS OF UNKNOWNS		
Drawing of a few typical cells from gram-stain preparation	◯	◯	◯
Magnification			
Gram reaction			
Acid-fast reaction			
Spores, + or −; if present make drawing			
Capsules, + or −; if present, make drawing			
Motility, + or −			

QUESTIONS

1. Compare the characteristics of each of your unknown cultures with each of the pure cultures that you have used in Exercises 5 and 6. Which of these have morphological characteristics similar to your unknowns?

_____

_____

_____

_____

_____

_____

2. Give an example of how information on the morphology and staining reactions of a culture assists one in (a) identifying and (b) classifying the organism.

_____

_____

_____

_____

_____

_____

3. What broad generalizations can be made in terms of shape of cells and other morphological characteristics; e.g., are cocci generally sporeformers, acid-fast, or motile; do bacilli exhibit cellular arrangements such as occur in the cocci?

_____

_____

_____

_____

_____

Bacteria exhibit great diversity in their nutritional requirements; e.g., some are capable of growing in a medium consisting of inorganic compounds only, while others require several amino acids, vitamins and additional complex organic substances. The specific nutritional requirements have been determined for a great many species. However, the media usually used in the laboratory consist of a mixture of digests or extracts from plant or animal tissues. The most common of these are meat extract, yeast extract, peptone, and agar. These ingredients, except for the agar, are used to prepare broths or liquid media. The addition of agar results in a solid medium. Nutrient broth (peptone and meat extract) and nutrient agar (peptone, meat extract, and agar) may be considered basic liquid and solid media, respectively. They may be modified in a variety of ways by the addition of specific chemicals or complex supplements to produce a medium with some desired characteristic. For example, nutrient agar is enriched by the addition of sterile blood; as such, it will support the growth of nutritionally fastidious bacteria. Either nutrient broth or nutrient agar may be supplemented with some substrate for use as a biochemical test medium.

There are innumerable media available for use in microbiology, each formulation presumably offering some advantage for the isolation, maintenance, characterization, or growth of certain groups of organisms.

EXERCISE EIGHT
PREPARATION
OF NUTRIENT BROTH,
GLUCOSE BROTH,
YEAST-EXTRACT BROTH, AND
NUTRIENT AGAR

REFERENCES: Text, chap. 6; MMM, chap. 3; "American Type Culture Collection, Catalogue of Strains," pp. 160–186; MCM, chap. 74.

Media employed for the cultivation of bacteria, as well as for the cultivation of other microorganisms, may be liquid, solid, or semisolid. The ingredients range from pure chemical compounds to complex materials, such as extracts or digests of plant and animal tissues. The most common ingredients of bacteriological media used in routine laboratory work are beef extract and peptone for liquid media and beef extract, peptone, and agar for solid media. These basic ingredients may be supplemented with a variety of materials to provide a medium suitable for the cultivation or demonstration of a reaction for specific types or groups of bacteria.

MATERIALS

1. Beef extract
2. Peptone
3. Agar
4. Yeast extract
5. Glucose
6. 1 1,500- to 2,000-ml Erlenmeyer flask or other vessel suitable for dissolving media ingredients
7. 4 500-ml Erlenmeyer flasks
8. 100 18- by 150-mm test tubes
9. Balance
10. 1 500-ml graduate
11. Nonabsorbent cotton
12. pH meter
13. 1 N HCl
14. 1 N NaOH

PROCEDURE

1. Put a measured amount of water (approximately 500 ml) into a large (1,500- to 2,000-ml) flask. Weigh out 5 g

peptone and 3 g beef extract and place in the flask. Agitate and heat until solution is effected. Adjust the total volume to 1,000 ml by addition of water.

2. Divide the beef-extract-peptone solution prepared above into four equal parts (250 ml), placing each aliquot in a 500-ml Erlenmeyer flask, and treat as follows:

   a. Make no further additions. This is *nutrient broth*.

   b. Add 3.75 g agar. Agitate, and allow to soak for about 5 min; then heat to boiling with frequent agitation to dissolve the agar. This is *nutrient agar*.

   c. Add 1.25 g glucose and agitate to effect solution. This is *glucose broth*.

   d. Add 1.25 g yeast extract. Heat, and agitate to effect solution. This is nutrient broth *enriched* with yeast extract.

3. Adjust the reaction of the four media to pH 7.0 using a pH meter.

4. Dispense each of the media into test tubes, 10 ml per tube for the broth media and 20 ml per tube for the nutrient agar.

5. Stopper the tubes with cotton, after which sterilize in an autoclave at 15 lb pressure (121°C) for 20 min. NOTE: The laboratory instructor will demonstrate the operation of the autoclave.

6. After sterilization store at room temperature for use in Exercise 10.

RESULTS

Describe the physical characteristics of beef extract, yeast extract, and agar. Do the same for each of the four media prepared.

_____

_____

_____

_____

_____

_____

_____

_____

_____

_____

_____

QUESTIONS

1. What is a peptone? How is a peptone made? Name several commercially available peptones. What nutrients are supplied by a peptone?

_____

_____

_____

_____

_____

_____

_____

_____

_____

2. How are yeast extract and beef extract prepared? What specific nutrients does each of these media ingredients provide?

_____

_____

_____

_____

_____

_____

3. What are the advantages of using commercially prepared powdered or dehydrated media?

_____

_____

_____

_____

_____

_____

_____

4. What is the source of agar? What is its chemical nature? What is the principal function of agar as a culture-medium ingredient? At what temperature does nutrient agar liquefy? Solidify?

_____

_____

_____

_____

_____

_____

5. What is the pH range for the optimum growth of most bacteria?

_____

_____

_____

6. Name four pH indicators used in microbiology and give the pH range over which they are useful.

_____

_____

_____

7. What is meant by the term "buffer"? Name several buffers employed in microbiological media.

_____

_____

_____

A medium that consists of known chemical compounds is designated as a *chemically defined* or *synthetic* medium. Nutrient agar, nutrient broth, and other such media, which contain peptone and/or extracts of meat or other tissues, are not chemically defined. These extracts or digests consist of a complex variety of substances, including amino acids, vitamins, carbohydrates, and inorganic salts. Chemically defined media for the growth of some bacteria, e.g., *Escherichia coli*, are relatively simple in composition. The essential ingredients are glucose, an inorganic nitrogen source, and a few other inorganic salts. The composition of a chemically defined medium for lactobacilli is much more elaborate; many amino acids, vitamins, inorganic salts, and other compounds must be provided. In this exercise, a relatively simple chemically defined medium will be prepared.

REFERENCES: Text, chap. 6;
MMM, chap. 3.

MATERIALS

1. 0.5 g glucose
2. 0.5 g sodium chloride
3. 0.02 g magnesium sulfate
4. 0.1 g ammonium dihydrogen phosphate
5. 0.1 g dipotassium phosphate
6. 1 500-ml Erlenmeyer flask
7. 10 test tubes
8. Nonabsorbent cotton
9. 1 *N* HCl
10. 1 *N* NaOH

PROCEDURE

1. Add 100 ml distilled water to a clean 500-ml Erlenmeyer flask.
2. Weigh out the amounts of chemicals 1 through 5 listed above and place them in the flask. Mix to dissolve all chemicals.

3. Determine the pH of a portion with a pH meter. Adjust to pH 7.0 to 7.2 if necessary with acid or base.

4. Dispense the medium into test tubes, approximately 10 ml per tube.

5. Cotton-stopper the tubes and sterilize the medium by autoclaving (15 min at 121°C). Store the medium for use in Exercise 10.

RESULTS

1. Compare the appearance of the medium prepared in this exercise with that of the broths prepared in Exercise 8.

   _____

   _____

   _____

   _____

   _____

   _____

2. If the pH of the medium in the portion tested required adjustment, show the calculations made to determine the amount of NaOH or HCl needed for the rest of the medium.

   _____

   _____

   _____

   _____

   _____

   _____

   _____

   _____

   _____

QUESTIONS

1. From a nutritional standpoint, what does each ingredient of the medium prepared in this exercise provide?

   _____

   _____

   _____

   _____

   _____

2. What are the desirable features of using chemically defined media?

_____

_____

_____

_____

_____

_____

3. How might you enrich the chemically defined medium prepared in this exercise and still have it be a synthetic medium?

_____

_____

_____

_____

_____

_____

4. Is peptone broth a chemically defined medium? Explain.

_____

_____

_____

_____

_____

_____

EXERCISE TEN
EVALUATION OF MEDIA FOR
ABILITY TO SUPPORT
GROWTH OF BACTERIA

Bacteria manifest a wide range of requirements for nutrients. At the one extreme are the autotrophs, which require only a limited number of inorganic substances. At the other extreme are the fastidious heterotrophs, which must be supplied a variety of complex organic substances. Media of various formulations have been developed for the satisfactory cultivation of each nutritional group of microorganisms. In this experiment you will determine the nutritional adequacy of several media for several species of bacteria.

REFERENCE: Text, chap. 6.

MATERIALS

1. Media prepared in Exercises 8 and 9
2. Trypticase-soy-broth cultures of *Escherichia coli*, *Pseudomonas aeruginosa*, *Staphylococcus aureus*, *Neisseria catarrhalis*, and *Streptococcus lactis*

PROCEDURE

1. Transfer one loopful of each culture into one tube of the following media: nutrient broth, glucose broth, yeast-extract broth (Exercise 8), and the glucose-salts medium (Exercise 9).
2. Make a stab inoculation of each culture into the nutrient-agar "deep" tubes (Exercise 8).
3. Incubate all inoculated tubes at 35°C for 48 hr.
4. Make gram-stain preparations of *S. lactis* and *P. aeruginosa*. Examine these microscopically.

RESULTS

1. Observe each of the tubes of liquid media for amount of growth (turbidity). Use the following scheme for recording amount of growth: $+++$ = very turbid; $++$ = moderately turbid; $+$ = faintly turbid; 0 = no turbidity. Record results in the table provided.

BACTERIAL SPECIES	AMOUNT OF GROWTH IN MEDIA				
	NUTRIENT BROTH	GLUCOSE BROTH	YEAST-EXTRACT BROTH	NUTRIENT AGAR	GLUCOSE-SALTS
Escherichia coli					
Pseudomonas aeruginosa					
Staphylococcus aureus					
Neisseria catarrhalis					
Streptococcus lactis					

2. Observe the agar deep-stab cultures, and make a sketch of the amount of growth along the line of inoculation.

Growth of Bacterial
Species in Stab Culture

Escherichia coli	Pseudomonas aeruginosa	Staphylococcus aureus	Neisseria catarrhalis	Streptococcus lactis

3. Sketch a few typical organisms from the gram-stained preparation of *S. lactis* and *P. aeruginosa.*

Streptococcus lactis   *Pseudomonas aeruginosa*

1. Which of the species used in this exercise is the most fastidious? Cite evidence for your statement.

_____

_____

_____

_____

_____

_____

_____

2. As this exercise was performed, would it be possible to determine whether any of the organisms used are autotrophs? Explain.

_____

_____

_____

_____

_____

_____

_____

3. If a large amount of inoculum (several loopfuls) were used to inoculate each of the media, might this affect the results? Explain.

_____

_____

_____

_____

_____

_____

4. What type of instrument is available for measurement of bacterial growth on the basis of turbidity? What advantages are associated with this method of measuring growth?

_____

_____

_____

_____

_____

_____

EXERCISE ELEVEN
SELECTIVE, DIFFERENTIAL, AND
ENRICHED MEDIA

Many special-purpose media are available to the microbiologist, the use of which facilitates the isolation of some specific group or type of organisms usually present with other species, i.e., a mixed culture.

MATERIALS

1. 2 sterile petri dishes
2. 1 tube each deoxycholate agar and phenylethyl alcohol agar
3. 1 blood-agar plate
4. Broth cultures of *Escherichia coli, Staphylococcus aureus,* and *Streptococcus durans*

PROCEDURE

1. Pour each tube of melted and cooled (45 to 50°C) agar medium into a separate petri dish. Allow the media to solidify.
2. With the wax marking pencil, mark the bottom of each petri dish of medium, including the blood-agar plate, into thirds

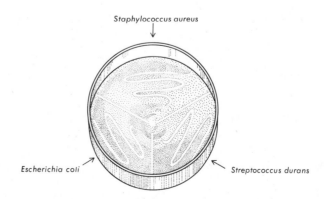

Staphylococcus aureus

Escherichia coli   Streptococcus durans

and enter the name of each species in this area. Inoculate (streak) each sector with the appropriate culture as illustrated.

3. Label each plate with your name and date and place them, in an inverted position, in the 35°C incubator for 48 hr.

4. Prepare and examine a gram stain of *S. durans*.

RESULTS

1. Examine carefully the growth on each plate. Record the relative amount of growth along the streak inoculation (e.g., abundant, moderate, meager, or none). Describe the appearance of the growth as well as the appearance of the medium adjacent to the growth.

MEDIUM	BACTERIAL SPECIES	AMOUNT OF GROWTH	DESCRIPTION OF GROWTH
Deoxycholate agar	Escherichia coli		
	Staphylococcus aureus		
	Streptococcus durans		
Phenylethyl alcohol agar	Escherichia coli		
	Staphylococcus aureus		
	Streptococcus durans		
Blood agar	Escherichia coli		
	Staphylococcus aureus		
	Streptococcus durans		

2. Sketch several cells from the gram-stain preparation of *S. durans* to illustrate their characteristic shape and arrangement.

QUESTIONS

1. For what practical purposes, e.g., routine laboratory procedures, would you use (a) deoxycholate medium, (b) phenylethyl alcohol medium, and (c) blood-agar medium?

_____

_____

_____

_____

_____

_____

_____

_____

2. Give one other example of (a) an enriched medium, (b) a selective medium, and (c) a differential medium.

_____

_____

_____

_____

_____

_____

_____

3. Might a single medium function for both differentiation and enrichment? Selection and differentiation? Explain.

_____

_____

_____

_____

_____

_____

_____

_____

A prerequisite to the characterization of a microbial species is that it be available for study as a pure culture. The term pure culture denotes that all the cells in the culture had a common origin and are simply descendants of the same cell. It is possible to obtain a pure culture by transferring a single cell to a sterile medium. This can be accomplished by using a micromanipulator in conjunction with a microscope. However, indirect methods are almost always used to achieve a pure culture; e.g., agar plate cultures are so inoculated that isolated colonies result.

The assumption is made that the microbial population of a colony develops from a single cell and hence represents a pure culture. This may not always be the case, and therefore it is necessary to examine what is presumed to be a pure culture by additional cultural and microscopic tests.

Once a pure-culture isolation has been made, it is desirable to maintain the culture, without change in its characteristics, in a viable condition for varying periods of time ranging from weeks to years. For short-term preservation of a culture, one simply makes periodic transfers to a fresh medium, e.g., nutrient-agar slants or cystine-trypticase-agar deep tubes. Long-term preservation is best accomplished by lyophilization—the culture specimen is dehydrated while in a frozen condition and then sealed under vacuum.

EXERCISE TWELVE
THE STREAK-PLATE
METHOD FOR ISOLATION
OF PURE CULTURES

Practically all specimens of material obtained from natural environments contain a mixed population of microorganisms. Before one can make a detailed study of the characteristics of the individual species constituting the mixture, it is imperative that each species be isolated in pure culture. The streak-plate technique provides a simple procedure for this purpose.

REFERENCE: Text, chap. 8.

MATERIALS

1. 4 sterile petri dishes
2. 4 tubes nutrient agar
3. Diluted broth cultures of *Serratia marcescens, Micrococcus luteus,* and *Arthrobacter globiformis*
4. Mixed culture of above bacteria

PROCEDURE

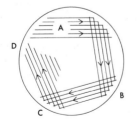

1. Pour each tube of melted and cooled (45 to 50°C) nutrient agar into separate petri dishes.
2. Allow the agar to become firmly solidified. *Never attempt to streak a plate until the medium is firm.*
3. Streak each bacterial suspension on a separate plate as shown in the illustration. Streak the initial inoculum over an area corresponding to A. Flame the loop and then make several streaks through area A to the side of the plate (B). Again flame the needle and make streaks through the lines at B to the side of the plate at C. Repeat the process from C to D. In each step, after the needle has been flamed, it is advisable to cool the needle by touching a portion of the sterile agar in the plate prior to the streaking process.
4. The fourth plate is to be streaked with a mixture of all three species. Place a small loopful of the mixed culture suspension on this plate in approximately position A in the sketch above. Proceed to streak this plate as directed in the sketch above.

5. Label plates with your name and date, and incubate them at 25°C (or room temperature) for 48 hr. *Inoculated plates are always incubated in an inverted position.*

RESULTS

1. Examine each of the streak plates, and make a sketch indicating the distribution of growth.

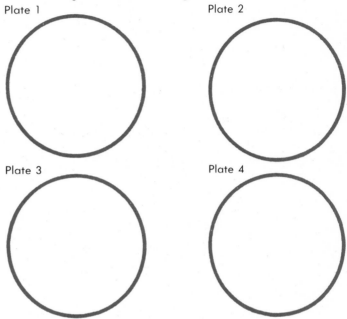

Plate 1

Plate 2

Plate 3

Plate 4

2. Describe the colonies that appear on the plates, i.e., size, color, elevation.
3. Prepare and examine gram-stained smears from each of the colonial types.

SPECIES	DESCRIPTION OF COLONIES	MORPHOLOGY OF BACTERIA
Serratia marcescens		
Micrococcus luteus		
Arthrobacter globiformis		
Mixture		

Laboratory Exercises in Microbiology

QUESTIONS

1. Define the following: colony, pure culture, axenic culture, mixed culture, normal flora, contaminant.

2. What is the rationale associated with the assumption that a colony represents a pure culture?

3. List several points of technique which should be carefully observed when streaking a plate.

4. Would a single bacterial colony appearing on a plate after 24 hr incubation eventually grow over the entire agar surface? Explain.

_____

_____

_____

_____

_____

_____

5. Why are inoculated petri dishes incubated in an inverted position?

_____

_____

_____

_____

_____

_____

EXERCISE THIRTEEN
THE POUR–PLATE
METHOD FOR ISOLATION
OF PURE CULTURES

Isolated colonies can be obtained from a mixed population of bacteria by diluting the specimen in a cooled (45 to 50°C) fluid-agar medium which is then plated. Since the magnitude of the microbial population is generally not known beforehand, it is necessary to make several dilutions to ensure obtaining at least one plate with colonies that are distinctly separated on, or in, the agar medium.

REFERENCE: Text, chap. 8.

MATERIALS

1. 1 10-ml tube of sterile saline solution
2. 4 tubes nutrient agar
3. 4 sterile petri dishes
4. Mixed bacterial suspension: freshly prepared mixture of broth cultures of *Staphylococcus aureus* and *Escherichia coli*

PROCEDURE

1. Melt the tubes of nutrient agar, cool them to 45 to 50°C, and maintain them at this temperature during the dilution manipulations described below.
2. With a sterilized inoculating loop, transfer one loopful of the bacterial suspension into a tube of sterile saline. Rotate this tube back and forth between the hands (10 times) to assure uniform distribution of bacteria.
3. Transfer two loopfuls of the suspension to a tube of melted nutrient agar. Label this tube 1 (see the diagram). Rotate this tube in the same manner as in step 2.
4. Transfer two loopfuls from tube 1 into another tube of nutrient agar labeled 2. Then pour the contents of tube 1 into a petri dish labeled 1.
5. Rotate tube 2 to distribute the inoculum, and transfer two loopfuls from tube 2 to a tube of agar labeled 3.
6. Pour the contents of tube 2 into a petri dish labeled 2.

7. Rotate tube 3 to distribute the inoculum and pour its contents into a plate labeled 3.

8. Pour a tube of sterile nutrient agar into a petri dish labeled control (petri dish 4).

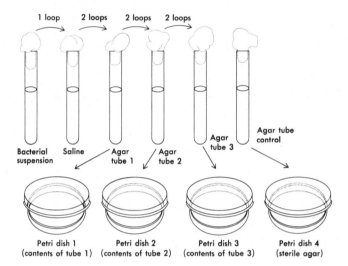

Dilution technique in pour-plate procedure.

9. Label plates with your name and date, and incubate all plates at 35°C for 48 hr.

RESULTS

1. Make a sketch from a section of each of the three inoculated plates to illustrate the amount of growth, distribution of growth, and size of colonies.
2. Prepare and examine gram-stained smears from each of the two colonial types.
3. Describe the appearance of subsurface colonies.

Distribution of Colonies on Pour Plates

PLATE 1   PLATE 2   PLATE 3

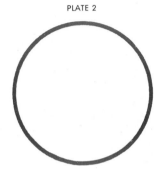
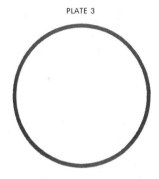

SPECIES	DESCRIPTION OF COLONIES	MORPHOLOGY
Staphylococcus aureus		
Escherichia coli		

QUESTIONS

1. Why do both surface and subsurface colonies appear in a pour plate?

_____

_____

_____

_____

2. What is the predominant shape of subsurface colonies? What accounts for this?

_____

_____

_____

_____

_____

_____

3. Compare the colonial characteristics of *Escherichia coli* and *Staphylococcus aureus* with those species used in Exercise 12.

_____

_____

_____

_____

_____

_____

_____

_____

4. Would anaerobic bacteria grow in a pour plate as inoculated and incubated in this experiment? Explain.

_____

_____

_____

_____

_____

_____

5. What is the purpose of the control plate (petri dish 4) in this exercise?

_____

_____

_____

_____

_____

_____

REFERENCES: Text, chap. 6; MMM, chap. 6; MCM, chaps. 32–36.

Certain bacteria (*aerobes*) grow only in the presence of free oxygen, whereas others (*anaerobes*) grow only in the absence of free oxygen. A third group (*facultative anaerobes*) are indifferent to this gas in the sense that they will grow under either aerobic or anaerobic conditions. The cultivation of anaerobic bacteria requires special techniques.

MATERIALS

1. Anaerobic equipment for demonstrations: anaerobic jar (BBL GasPak Anaerobic System)
2. 6 nutrient-agar slants
3. 3 tubes nutrient agar
4. 3 tubes nutrient broth
5. 3 tubes thioglycolate broth
6. Approximately 10 g pyrogallic acid
7. Approximately 10 ml 4% sodium hydroxide
8. Pipette to deliver approximately 2 ml and equipped with rubber bulb
9. 3 cork stoppers to fit smoothly and firmly into agar-slant tubes
10. Cultures of *Staphylococcus aureus* and *Bacillus subtilis* in nutrient broth and *Clostridium sporogenes* in thioglycolate broth

PROCEDURE

1. Demonstration of anaerobic culture jar (see illustration) for the cultivation of anaerobes. This jar is designed to be used with a disposable hydrogen + carbon dioxide generator envelope and eliminates the need for vacuum pumps, gas tanks, pressure regulators or manometers. It employs a room-temperature catalyst system and therefore does not use any electrical connections or other means of

heating the catalyst. The hydrogen produced reacts with the oxygen in the presence of the catalyst to produce an anaerobic atmosphere. The carbon dioxide generated helps to support growth of organisms requiring it.

"Courtesy of BioQuest, Division of Becton, Dickinson and Company."

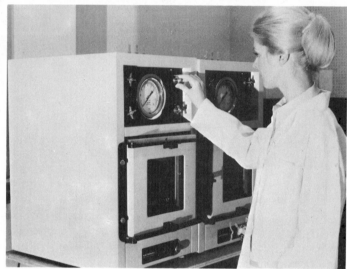

Modern anaerobic incubators being used by a microbiologist.

2. Streak duplicate sets of nutrient-agar slants with each of the three cultures. Select one of the duplicate sets and treat these tubes in the following manner:

   a. Push the cotton stopper into the tube until it nearly touches the end of the slant (see sketch).

   b. Fill the space between the top of the stopper and the open end of the tube with pyrogallic acid crystals.

   c. Select cork stoppers to close these tubes. Add approximately 2 ml sodium hydroxide to the pyrogallic acid contained in the tubes.

   d. *Stopper and invert the tubes immediately.*

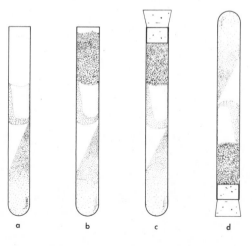

a   b   c   d

3. Melt the nutrient-agar deep tubes and cool them to 45 to 50°C. Transfer one loopful of each culture into separate nutrient-agar deep tubes. Roll these tubes between the palms of your hands to distribute the inoculum throughout the medium before it solidifies.

4. Inoculate each organism into nutrient broth and thioglycolate broth.

5. Incubate all the inoculated media at 35°C for 48 hr.

RESULTS

1. Observe all media for presence or absence of growth. Record results as $+++$, $++$, $+$, or 0.
2. By means of a sketch, illustrate the distribution of growth of each organism in the nutrient-agar deep tubes.

	BACTERIAL SPECIES		
	Staphylococcus aureus	Bacillus subtilis	Clostridium sporogenes
Nutrient-agar slants (aerobic)			
Nutrient-agar slants (anaerobic)			
Nutrient broth			
Thioglycolate broth			
Sketch of growth in nutrient-agar deep tubes			

QUESTIONS

1. Classify each of the organisms used in this exercise according to its oxygen relationship.

_____

_____

_____

_____

2. Describe the reaction between pyrogallic acid and sodium hydroxide that results in anaerobic conditions.

_____

_____

_____

_____

_____

_____

3. Why will a strict anaerobe grow in thioglycolate broth even though the medium is exposed to atmospheric oxygen?

_____

_____

_____

_____

_____

_____

4. An oats jar (moistened oats in a closed vessel) can be successfully used to grow cultures of anaerobes. What is the reaction by which anaerobiosis is produced in this system?

_____

_____

_____

_____

_____

EXERCISE FIFTEEN
CULTURAL CHARACTERISTICS

REFERENCES: Text, chap. 8; MMM, chap. 7.

The appearance of the growth or mass of cells of bacteria that develops on various media comes under the heading of cultural characteristics. Since various groups of bacteria manifest particular types of growth, this feature is useful as an adjunct in characterizing taxonomic groups.

MATERIALS

1.   100 ml nutrient agar in bottle
2.   6 nutrient-agar slants
3.   6 deep tubes nutrient agar
4.   6 tubes nutrient broth
5.   6 tubes nutrient gelatin
6.   6 sterile petri dishes
7.   Nutrient-agar slant cultures of *Streptomyces albus, Mycobacterium phlei, Bacillus subtilis, Pseudomonas aeruginosa, Sarcina lutea, and Escherichia coli.*

PROCEDURE

1.   Melt the bottle of nutrient agar, cool to 45 to 50°C, and dispense approximately 15 ml into each of six petri dishes. After the medium solidifies, prepare a streak plate from each culture so as to obtain isolated colonies (see Exercise 12).
2.   Using the transfer needle, inoculate each organism into the remaining media in the following manner:
     a.   *Agar slants:* one streak up the middle of the slanted surface
     b.   *Broth:* twirl the needle carrying the inoculum in the liquid
     c.   *Agar deeps:* stab inoculation, puncture of the agar column from top to bottom with withdrawal of the needle through the same path

d.   *Gelatin:* stab inoculation as above

NOTE: The gelatin tubes must be maintained at a temperature near 20°C so that the medium will remain solid.

3.   Incubate all the gelatin tubes at 20°C. The media other than gelatin inoculated with *S. albus* are to be incubated at room temperature, and all other media at 35°C. The tubes should be observed after 48 hr incubation and then further incubated for another observation between 4 and 7 days.

RESULTS

Make drawings and record descriptions of growth for each species on each medium as called for in the tables provided. Use the accompanying chart to facilitate description of the appearance of growth.

Cultural characteristics of bacteria.

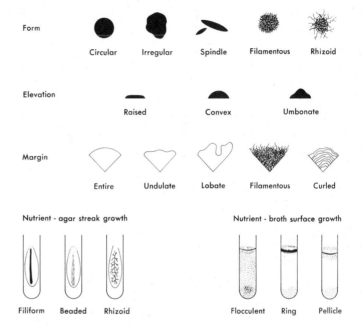

Form

Circular   Irregular   Spindle   Filamentous   Rhizoid

Elevation

Raised   Convex   Umbonate

Margin

Entire   Undulate   Lobate   Filamentous   Curled

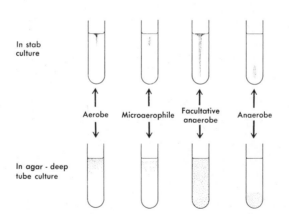

Nutrient - agar streak growth

Filiform   Beaded   Rhizoid

Nutrient - broth surface growth

Flocculent   Ring   Pellicle

Oxygen relationships shown.

In stab culture

Aerobe   Microaerophile   Facultative anaerobe   Anaerobe

In agar - deep tube culture

Cultural Characteristics of
Bacteria: Characterization
of Growth in Gelatin Stabs

BACTERIAL SPECIES						Sketch of growth	Amount of growth	Liquefaction, + or −	Degree of liquefaction	Nature of liquefaction
Streptomyces albus										
Mycobacterium phlei										
Bacillus subtilis										
Pseudomonas aeruginosa										
Sarcina lutea										
Escherichia coli										

Cultural Characteristics of
Bacteria: Characteristics of
Growth in Nutrient Broth

		BACTERIAL SPECIES					
	Streptomyces albus	Mycobacterium phlei	Bacillus subtilis	Pseudomonas aeruginosa	Sarcina lutea	Escherichia coli	
Sketch of growth							
Surface growth							
Degree of turbidity							
Odor							
Amount of sediment							
Nature of sediment							

Cultural Characteristics of
Bacteria: Characterization
of Growth on Nutrient-agar
Slants

BACTERIAL SPECIES	Streptomyces albus	Mycobacterium phlei	Bacillus subtilis	Pseudomonas aeruginosa	Sarcina lutea	Escherichia coli
Sketch of growth						
Amount of growth						
Form of growth						
Chromogenesis						
Odor						
Consistency						

Cultural Characteristics of
Bacteria: Characterization
of Growth in Nutrient-agar
Stab Culture

		BACTERIAL SPECIES					
		Streptomyces albus	Mycobacterium phlei	Bacillus subtilis	Pseudomonas aeruginosa	Sarcina lutea	Escherichia coli
Sketch of growth							
Amount of growth							
Distribution of growth:							
Top							
Middle							
Bottom							

Cultural Characteristics of
Bacteria: Characterization
of Colonies

	Streptomyces albus	Mycobacterium phlei	Bacillus subtilis	Pseudomonas aeruginosa	Sarcina lutea	Escherichia coli
Sketch of colonies						
Size, mm						
Form						
Elevation						
Margin						
Consistency						
Chromogenesis						

BACTERIAL SPECIES

QUESTIONS

1. Give an example to illustrate the use of cultural character-
    istics for assigning organisms to a taxonomic group.

    _____

    _____

    _____

    _____

    _____

    _____

2. Do pigment-producing bacteria always color the medium in
    which they are grown? Explain.

    _____

    _____

    _____

    _____

    _____

    _____

    _____

3. What cultural characteristic would enable you to distinguish
    between the genera *Clostridium* and *Bacillus*?

    _____

    _____

    _____

    _____

    _____

    _____

    _____

4. What is the taxonomic relationship between the genera *Streptomyces* and *Streptococcus*? Between *Streptomyces* and *Mycobacterium*?

_____

_____

_____

_____

_____

_____

_____

_____

EXERCISE SIXTEEN
MAINTENANCE AND
PRESERVATION OF CULTURES

A major aspect of microbiology involves techniques to keep cultures alive, in pure culture and in typical form (maintenance), and methods to retain cultures in this status over a long period of time (preservation). The choice of technique may be influenced by the length of time the cultures are to be maintained, e.g., months or years, and by the number of cultures in the collection.

REFERENCES: Text, chap. 8; MMM, chap. 5.

MATERIALS

1. 6 trypticase-agar slants in screw-cap tubes
2. 3 cystine-trypticase-agar deep tubes with screw caps
3. 30 ml sterile white mineral oil
4. Nutrient-agar slant cultures of *Bacillus subtilis, Neisseria perflava,* and *Chromobacterium violaceum*
5. Lyophilized specimen of bacterial culture

PROCEDURE

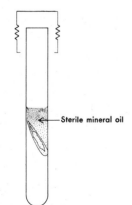
Sterile mineral oil

1. Transfer each culture to two agar slants and one tube of cystine-trypticase agar. Incubate *C. violaceum* at room temperature and the other two species at 35°C for 24 to 48 hr.
2. Following this incubation period, overlay one set of the agar slant cultures with sterile mineral oil. Be sure that the oil extends approximately 1/4 in. above the top of the agar slant as shown in the sketch.
3. Store all the cultures at room temperature for future testing for viability. Be sure that they are properly labeled, i.e., your name, date, and name of bacterial species.
4. At future times, as designated by the instructor (intervals of several weeks), make subcultures from each of the stored cultures to determine their viability.
5. Demonstration of technique for opening and culturing a typical lyophilized specimen. Steps in the procedure are illustrated.

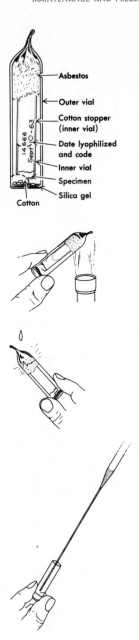

Lyophilized
specimen.

Procedure for opening
lyophilized specimen: Heat
top of outer vial; then,
allow a drop of water to
touch the heated region;
the top of the outer vial will
crack. Using a sterile
Pasteur pipette, introduce
sterile water or broth into
the vial containing the
dehydrated specimen. The
dry material goes into
suspension readily and is
transferred to suitable
media.

RESULTS   Following each subculture of the stored cultures, record whether they are viable.

METHOD	DATE TESTED	SPECIES		
		Bacillus subtilis	Neisseria perflava	Chromobacterium violaceum
Nutrient-agar slant				
Nutrient-agar slant (mineral-oil overlay)				
Cystine-trypti-case agar				

QUESTIONS   1.   Briefly describe what is meant by a "stock culture collection."

_____

_____

_____

_____

_____

_____

2. What is the function of the American Type Culture Collection?

_____

_____

_____

_____

_____

_____

3. What is the best method of preserving and maintaining bacterial cultures? Why?

_____

_____

_____

_____

_____

_____

Knowledge of the ability of bacteria to dissimilate certain substrates and to synthesize various products is indispensable for the adequate characterization of a species. It is not uncommon for two different bacterial cultures to be very similar in their morphological and cultural characteristics but to exhibit very striking differences in their metabolic reactions.

Routine qualitative tests designed to permit convenient detection of salient biochemical features generally consist of a nutrient medium plus substrate in which the organism is cultured. An "indicator" may also be included to reveal the accumulation of a product. In other instances, changes in the physical nature of the medium may be adequate evidence to conclude dissimilation of a substrate, e.g., liquefaction of gelatin, or synthesis of a substance, e.g., polysaccharides responsible for "stringy" milk.

More definitive measurements of metabolic products are often desired. Such data enable one to establish better criteria for a taxonomic group. For example, in the routine test to determine the ability of two cultures to ferment glucose, both are found to produce acid; the result for each is the same. However, if an experiment is performed to identify the acidic constituent, the results could quite possibly be very different. One culture may produce only a single acid, the other a different acid or even several different acids.

Knowledge of the biochemical activities or potential biochemical activities of a microbial culture has many applications in biology beyond that of characterizing a species. The role of microorganisms in man's environment is attributable to the ability of microorganisms to degrade various substrates and to synthesize new products.

EXERCISE SEVENTEEN
HYDROLYSIS
OF POLYSACCHARIDE,
PROTEIN, AND LIPID

Some microorganisms produce enzymes capable of splitting the large complex molecules of polysaccharides, proteins, or lipids. These enzymes are extracellular and accomplish the breakdown of their respective substrates via hydrolysis. *Carbohydrases* hydrolyze polysaccharides to sugars; *proteases* hydrolyze proteins to peptides and amino acids; *lipases* hydrolyze lipids (fats) to glycerol and fatty acids. When organisms are grown in a medium which contains one of these substrates, evidence of its degradation can be obtained.

REFERENCES: Text, chaps. 9 and 39; MMM, chap. 7.

MATERIALS

1. 1 tube each of starch agar, tributyrin agar, and milk agar
2. 3 petri dishes
3. 50 ml Gram's iodine solution in dropping bottle
4. Broth cultures of *Bacillus cereus*, *Escherichia coli*, and *Pseudomonas fluorescens*

PROCEDURE

1. With your glass-marking pencil, divide the outside bottom half of each petri dish into thirds.

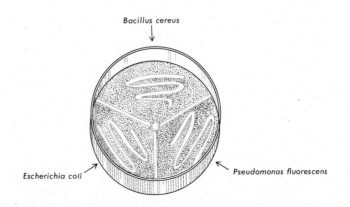

Bacillus cereus

Escherichia coli

Pseudomonas fluorescens

2. Pour a tube of each medium into a separate petri dish, and, upon solidification of the medium, inoculate (streak) each culture on the surface of each medium.

3. Incubate the inoculated plates at 35°C for 48 to 72 hr.

RESULTS

EVIDENCE OF STARCH HYDROLYSIS

Flood the surface of the starch agar plate with Gram's iodine solution. Iodine in the presence of starch results in the formation of a dark blue color; in the absence of starch, the blue color does not develop. Note the reaction surrounding each streak of growth. Sketch the appearance of growth and the surrounding medium for each organism, and record results in the table provided.

EVIDENCE OF LIPID HYDROLYSIS

The tributyrin, as you noted, is dispersed throughout the agar medium as an emulsion; the medium appears opaque. Hydrolysis of the lipid results in products (glycerol and fatty acid) which are soluble, and hence there is a clearing of the medium. Observe the appearance of the medium around each streak of growth, and record this in the table provided.

EVIDENCE OF PROTEIN HYDROLYSIS

Casein is the principal nitrogenous constituent of milk; it is a protein. It exists in a colloidal state and, as such, is responsible for the whiteness of milk. If the casein is hydrolyzed, the products of this hydrolysis are soluble; a clear zone surrounds the streak of bacterial growth. Record results of your observations in the table provided.

BACTERIAL SPECIES	STARCH AGAR		TRIBUTYRIN AGAR		MILK AGAR	
	SKETCH OF REACTION ON PLATE	STARCH HYDROLYSIS + OR −	SKETCH OF REACTION ON PLATE	LIPOLYSIS + OR −	SKETCH OF REACTION ON PLATE	PROTEOLYSIS + OR −
Escherichia coli						
Bacillus cereus						
Pseudomonas fluorescens						

QUESTIONS

1. Write a general equation for the enzymatic hydrolysis of each substrate used in this exercise.

_____

_____

_____

_____

_____

_____

2. Define the following: (a) lipolytic, proteolytic, saccharolytic; (b) amylase, lipase, protease.

_____

_____

_____

_____

_____

_____

_____

_____

_____

_____

3. What happens when butter turns rancid?

_____

_____

_____

_____

_____

4. Describe a procedure, other than the one you performed here, to demonstrate that a microorganism produces an extracellular hydrolytic enzyme.

_____

_____

_____

_____

_____

_____

_____

_____

FERMENTATION
OF CARBOHYDRATES

A wide variety of carbohydrates is fermented by bacteria, and the pattern of fermentation is characteristic of certain species, genera, or other taxonomic groups of organisms. Thus knowledge of the carbohydrates fermented by a particular organism aids in its identification. This characteristic can be determined by inoculating the organism into a tube of carbohydrate broth containing a Durham tube. The medium consists essentially of nutrient broth plus 0.5 percent of the particular carbohydrate plus an indicator. The Durham tube is a small inverted vial in the broth. Since the usual end products of carbohydrate fermentation are acid or acid and gas, the indicator will reveal production of acid and the inverted vial will trap gas if produced.

REFERENCES: Text, chap. 10; MMM, chap. 7.

MATERIALS

1. 6 each fermentation tubes containing phenol red–glucose broth, phenol red–lactose broth, and phenol red–sucrose broth
2. Broth cultures of *Bacillus subtilis, Escherichia coli, Proteus vulgaris, Alcaligenes faecalis,* and *Staphylococcus aureus*

PROCEDURE

1. Inoculate a series of the three different carbohydrate broths with *B. subtilis*. Use one loopful of the broth culture as inoculum.
2. Repeat this procedure with each of the remaining cultures.
3. Select one tube of each carbohydrate broth and keep it uninoculated as a control.
4. Be sure that each tube is labeled for carbohydrate and the organism inoculated. Label the uninoculated tube of carbohydrate as control.
5. Incubate all tubes at 35°C for 48 hr.

RESULTS

After the incubation period, compare each of the inoculated tubes with the control tube of the same medium to determine whether growth occurred and whether acid or gas was produced. Record results in the table below as follows: AG = acid and gas; A = acid; a = slight acidity; O = carbohydrate not fermented.

The sketch of the fermentation tubes shows one with gas and another without gas.

Sketch of
fermentation tubes.

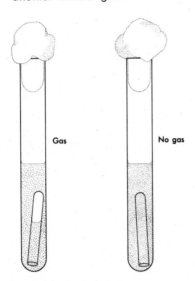

Gas   No gas

BACTERIAL SPECIES	CARBOHYDRATES		
	PHENOL RED–GLUCOSE BROTH	PHENOL RED–LACTOSE BROTH	PHENOL RED–SUCROSE BROTH
Bacillus subtilis			
Escherichia coli			
Proteus vulgaris			
Alcaligenes faecalis			
Staphylococcus aureus			

QUESTIONS

1. What are the essential ingredients of a carbohydrate broth?

_____

_____

_____

_____

_____

_____

_____

2. List several (a) acids, (b) neutral products, and (c) gases that may be produced during bacterial fermentation of glucose.

_____

_____

_____

_____

_____

_____

_____

3. What is the pH range of the indicator used in this experiment, and what colors denote a neutral, acid, or alkaline reaction?

_____

_____

_____

_____

_____

_____

4. How could you ascertain whether a particular bacterium fermented glucose if you used a glucose broth medium without a pH indicator?

_____

_____

_____

_____

_____

_____

_____

5. If the carbohydrate broth does not change color after it has been inoculated and incubated, how can one tell whether the unchanged color is due to failure of the organism to grow or failure to ferment the carbohydrate?

_____

_____

_____

_____

_____

6. Two different bacterial species are inoculated into glucose broth. After suitable incubation, the broth shows evidence of acid and gas. Does this mean that both species ferment glucose with the production of identical end products? Explain.

_____

_____

_____

_____

7. Use structural formulas to compare the molecular structures
of glucose, lactose, and sucrose.

EXERCISE NINETEEN
REACTIONS
IN LITMUS MILK

REFERENCES: Text, chaps. 10 and 39; MMM, chap. 7.

Milk, particularly skim milk, not only serves as an excellent culture medium but also is used extensively for biochemical characterization of bacteria. Protein and carbohydrate substrates, casein and lactose, respectively, are contained in skim milk, and microbial attack of either or both can be detected. The addition of the dye azolitmin to the milk provides an acid indicator as well as a reduction indicator.

MATERIALS

1. 6 tubes litmus milk
2. Trypticase-soy-broth cultures of *Streptococcus lactis*, *Streptococcus liquefaciens*, *Escherichia coli*, *Alcaligenes viscolactis*, and *Pseudomonas aeruginosa*.

PROCEDURE

Inoculate tubes of litmus milk with each of the cultures listed. Use an uninoculated tube as a control. Incubate the tubes at 35°C.

RESULTS

Observe and record the changes that appear at 48 hr and again at the end of 1 week's incubation. Listed below are the types of reactions that may be detected:

Lactose fermentation: acid, acid curd, gas (evidenced by breaks or bubbles in curd) may or may not be produced, litmus turns pink.

Proteolysis: casein solubilized; top portion of medium resembles a colored broth; litmus turns blue (alkaline reaction).

Reduction: litmus decolorized (white) except for colored ring at top.

Ropiness: abundant production of capsules or slime causes milk to become viscous.

Rennet coagulation (sweet curdling): coagulation of milk with little acid formation; action is due to a rennetlike enzyme.

BACTERIAL SPECIES	REACTIONS IN LITMUS MILK*			
	48 HR		7 DAYS	
	DESCRIPTION OF MEDIUM	TYPE OF REACTION	DESCRIPTION OF MEDIUM	TYPE OF REACTION
Streptococcus lactis				
Streptococcus liquefaciens				
Escherichia coli				
Alcaligenes viscolactis				
Pseudomonas aeruginosa				
Control				

*Abbreviations helpful for recording results: A = acid; AC = acid curd; AG = acid and gas; P = proteolysis; ALK = alkaline reaction; ACR = acid curd reduction; ACP = acid curd proteolysis; I = inert.

QUESTIONS

1. Why is milk a good culture medium?

_____

_____

_____

_____

_____

_____

_____

_____

_____

2. List some products of lactose fermentation that might occur in milk.

_____

_____

_____

_____

3. What are the products of proteolysis?

_____

_____

_____

_____

_____

_____

_____

4. What products are responsible for the development of an alkaline reaction in milk? For a viscous consistency?

_____

_____

_____

5. When a curd develops in a sample of milk, how could you determine whether it was a rennet or acid curd?

_____

_____

_____

_____

_____

_____

_____

_____

6. What constituent of milk provides buffering action? Explain the mode of action.

_____

_____

_____

_____

_____

_____

EXERCISE TWENTY
ADDITIONAL BIOCHEMICAL CHARACTERISTICS
A. HYDROGEN SULFIDE PRODUCTION

REFERENCES: Text, chaps. 10, 34; MMM, chap. 7.

Hydrogen sulfide is produced by certain bacteria through dissimilation of sulfur-containing amino acids, e.g., cystine and methionine, or through reduction of inorganic sulfur compounds such as thiosulfate, sulfite, or sulfate. The hydrogen sulfide liberated can be detected by incorporating a heavy-metal salt into the medium; hydrogen sulfide reacts with these compounds to form black metal sulfides.

MATERIALS

1. 3 tubes SIM (sulfide, indole, motility) agar
2. Nutrient-agar slant cultures of *Proteus vulgaris*, *Escherichia coli*, and *Serratia marcescens*

PROCEDURE

1. Inoculate each of the organisms into separate tubes of SIM agar. Use the transfer needle and make a stab inoculation along the outer edge of the medium.
2. Incubate tubes at 35°C for 48 hr.

RESULTS   Observe tubes for evidence of hydrogen sulfide production (blackening along the line of inoculation). Sketch each tube, illustrating the type of reaction exhibited.

	BACTERIAL SPECIES		
	Proteus vulgaris	*Escherichia coli*	*Serratia marcescens*
Sketch of reaction in tubes			
Hydrogen sulfide production, + or −			

QUESTIONS   1. Write the chemical reaction which illustrates hydrogen sulfide production and also the reaction responsible for the blackening of the medium in a positive test.

_____

_____

_____

_____

_____

_____

_____

_____

2. What are the constituents of SIM medium?

_____

_____

_____

_____

_____

_____

3. Information whether an organism ferments lactose or produces hydrogen sulfide is useful in characterizing bacteria of the coli-typhoid-dysentery group. Explain why this is so.

_____

_____

_____

_____

_____

_____

_____

_____

4. Under natural conditions, where might one expect to find hydrogen sulfide production by microorganisms?

_____

_____

_____

_____

5. Certain bacteria are capable of utilizing hydrogen sulfide. Give one example, and indicate the role of this compound in the metabolism of the organism.

_____

_____

_____

_____

_____

_____

6. Sulfur compounds may be oxidized or reduced by micro-organisms. Give an example of each, identifying the organism and the reaction in each example.

_____

_____

_____

_____

_____

_____

B. PRODUCTION OF INDOLE

Amino acids are produced as a result of hydrolytic degradation of proteins, peptones, and peptides. One of these amino acids, tryptophan, serves as a substrate for biochemical differentiation or characterization, since some species are capable of hydrolyzing this amino acid. One of the end products of this reaction is indole, which can be detected by a colorimetric test. The tryptophan in the test medium is supplied by the peptone.

REFERENCES: Text, chap. 10; MMM, chap. 7.

MATERIALS

1. 4 tubes trypticase broth
2. Kovacs' reagent
3. Nutrient-broth cultures of *Escherichia coli, Aerobacter aerogenes,* and *Proteus vulgaris*

PROCEDURE

1. Inoculate tubes of trypticase broth with each of the three cultures. Use the uninoculated tube as a control.
2. Incubate tubes at 35°C for 48 hr.

RESULTS

Add approximately 1.0 ml of Kovacs' reagent to each of the tubes. Gently shake the tubes and allow them to stand to permit the reagent to rise to the top. The presence of indole is indicated by a deep red color, which develops in the reagent layer. Compare each inoculated tube with the uninoculated control.

BACTERIAL SPECIES	DESCRIPTION OF REAGENT LAYER IN CULTURE TUBE	INDOLE PRODUCTION + OR −
Escherichia coli		
Aerobacter aerogenes		
Proteus vulgaris		
Control		

QUESTIONS

1. Write the structural formulas for tryptophan and indole.

2. A positive indole test, as performed here, is indicated by the cherry-red color of the surface layer. Why is the red color not distributed throughout the culture medium?

_____

_____

_____

_____

_____

3. Could any peptone serve satisfactorily to demonstrate production of indole? Explain.

_____

_____

_____

_____

_____

_____

4. How might the end products of tryptophan hydrolysis be further metabolized by microorganisms?

_____

_____

_____

_____

_____

_____

5. List the ingredients of Kovacs' reagent.

_____

_____

_____

_____

_____

_____

C. REDUCTION OF NITRATE

A biochemical characteristic of many bacteria is their ability to reduce certain compounds. Nitrate reduction is an example. This reaction can be detected by growing the organisms in a medium containing a nitrate and subsequently testing for the presence of its reduction product, nitrite.

REFERENCES: Text, chap. 34; MMM, chap. 7.

MATERIALS

1. 4 tubes trypticase-nitrate broth
2. Reagents for detection of nitrite: 5 ml sulfanilic acid solution and 5 ml dimethyl-α-naphthylamine solution
3. 2 1-ml pipettes
4. Zinc dust
5. Nutrient-broth cultures of *Pseudomonas aeruginosa, Bacillus subtilis,* and *Micrococcus luteus*

PROCEDURE

1. Inoculate tubes of trypticase-nitrate broth with each of the three cultures. Use the uninoculated tube as a control.
2. Incubate tubes at 35°C for 48 hr.

RESULTS

1. Add approximately 1.0 ml sulfanilic acid solution and 1.0 ml dimethyl-α-naphthylamine to each of the tubes, including the control. The development of a red, purple, or maroon color indicates the presence of nitrite.

2. A negative test (no development of color) is interpreted as follows:

   a. Nitrate not reduced.

   b. Nitrate reduction has occurred, but the reaction has gone beyond the nitrite stage to ammonia or gaseous nitrogen. Therefore, it is desirable to test further those tubes giving a negative reaction for the presence of nitrite. This can be done by the addition of a very small amount (a trace) of powdered zinc. The zinc reduces nitrate to nitrite, and the color characteristic of a positive nitrite test develops.

BACTERIAL SPECIES	TEST FOR NITRITE		RESULTS OF ZINC TEST IF NITRITE TEST IS NEGATIVE
	COLOR CHANGE AFTER ADDITION OF REAGENTS	INTERPRETATION, + OR −	
Pseudomonas aeruginosa			
Bacillus subtilis			
Micrococcus luteus			
Control			

3. Compare results obtained from inoculated tubes with those observed in the control.

QUESTIONS

1. Could the medium used in this exercise be employed for the detection of indole? Explain.

2. Is the reduction of nitrate to nitrite favored by aerobic or anaerobic conditions? Explain.

3. Explain why a negative test (lack of color development in the presence of test reagents) need not necessarily mean that the nitrate was not reduced.

4. It is preferable to perform this test by periodic testing of some of the culture over a period of several days. Why?

_____

_____

_____

_____

_____

_____

PART SEVEN
CHARACTERIZATION
OF UNKNOWN
CULTURES

Adequate characterization of a culture should enable one to establish the identity of the culture. However, one must ascertain that the culture is *pure* before proceeding to other tests.

Morphological characterization of the unknown should provide some clue to the group to which the unknown belongs. For example, if the unknown is found to be a gram-positive spore-former it most likely is a species of *Bacillus* or *Clostridium*. In this instance, results from cultural tests (aerobic or anaerobic growth) should provide information about the proper genus. Further differentiation (identification to the species level) requires biochemical and/or serological data. The number and kind of tests to be performed are determined by the type of organism with which one is working, e.g., gram-positive spore-forming rod, or gram-negative diplococcus, or gram-negative rod, etc. One needs to consult classification schemes or keys for guidance in the selection of appropriate tests.

The most widely used system of a conventional classification is that described in Bergey's "Manual of Determinative Bacteriology." In this conventional scheme, certain characters of bacteria are given more weight than others, e.g., flagellation. An alternative to such an approach is to assume that all observable characters or features are of equal importance and to assign them equal weight in the classification scheme. This principle was first proposed by Adanson in 1757. Furthermore, as many features as possible are examined to create natural groups; the relationship between the groups is a function of the similarities of the characters which are being compared. It is obvious that such an approach gives rise to voluminous data from the studies of bacterial properties. Since such data lend themselves to computer treatment, this kind of classification is now called *numerical taxonomy*. This, however, is not yet a routine technique. One of the shortcomings of this classification is that phylogenetic considerations are not taken into account in constructing taxonomic groups and the groups are constructed in an empirical manner.

Other modern approaches to characterization of organisms include the determination of the composition of their DNA for purposes of establishing a base ratio, i.e., ratio of adenine and thymine to guanine and cytosine. This gives some measure of the genetic relatedness between different microorganisms; closely related bacteria have similar base compositions, and these may reflect the phylogenetic relationships between different organisms.

Nucleic acid homology techniques can also be used to create taxonomic groups of microorganisms. These methods depend upon the ability of single-stranded nucleic acids obtained from genetically related organisms to form hybrids. This ability of two polynucleotide chains to interact and form a base-paired helical structure represents a sensitive test for complementarity in their base sequences. Since the base sequence of a poly-nucleotide is a chemical expression of its genetic information content, the test becomes a measure of the genetic relatedness of the two strands. Bacteria can thus be classified into taxonomic groups by the degree of hybridization between heterologous DNAs. Such hybridization data might even give clues to phylo-genetic relationships. Again, such modern approaches are not routine techniques, especially in the clinical diagnostic laboratory.

EXERCISE TWENTY-ONE
MORPHOLOGICAL, CULTURAL, AND BIOCHEMICAL CHARACTERIZATION OF UNKNOWN CULTURES

REFERENCES: Text, chap. 13; MMM, chap. 7.

The techniques performed in Exercises 5 to 20 are typical of the types of tests performed on bacteria to establish their identity in a conventional classification scheme. They do not, however, include all the tests required to identify bacteria of certain groups. For example, an organism found to be an aerobic gram-negative diplococcus can be identified as to species on the basis of its ability or inability to ferment the carbohydrates glucose, levulose, maltose, and sucrose. On the other hand, identification of an unknown gram-negative rod requires a much more elaborate scheme of testing. The purpose of this exercise is to characterize (not necessarily to identify) an unknown culture.

MATERIALS

1. Staining reagents for gram stain, acid-fast stain, spore stain
2. 1 tube each of motility-test agar, nutrient broth, nutrient gelatin, nutrient-agar deep, nutrient-agar slant, phenol red fermentation broths (glucose, lactose, sucrose), trypticase broth, trypticase-nitrate broth, SIM agar, litmus milk
3. Plating media, sufficient for one plate: nutrient agar, starch agar, tributyrin agar
4. Reagents for detection of starch hydrolysis, indole, nitrites
5. 3 sterile petri dishes
6. Unknown culture identified by code number

PROCEDURE

1. Review the headings in the tabular protocol provided for this exercise and familiarize yourself with the information to be obtained on the unknown culture.
2. Inoculate and incubate all the media provided in the manner described in the previous exercises where they were used.
3. Prepare and examine gram-, acid-fast-, and spore-stain smears.

RESULTS

Record results of microscopic examinations, the cultural characteristics, and the results of the biochemical tests, in the table provided:

CODE NUMBER:		
MORPHOLOGICAL CHARACTERISTICS	BIOCHEMICAL CHARACTERISTICS	
	TESTS	RESULTS, + OR −
Cell morphology and arrangement:	Fermentation of: Glucose	
	Lactose	
	Sucrose	
Staining reactions:	Gelatin liquefaction	
	Indole	
	Nitrate reduction	
Motility:	Hydrogen sulfide	
	Starch hydrolysis	
	Fat hydrolysis	
	Reactions in litmus milk	
CULTURAL CHARACTERISTICS		
Colonies:	Agar stab:	
Agar slant:	Gelatin stab:	
Nutrient broth:		

QUESTIONS

1. Name the organisms used in the laboratory to date that have characteristics similar to the unknown culture, insofar as tests were performed.

_____

_____

_____

_____

_____

_____

2. What additional information would you need to have before you could identify your unknown by species name?

_____

_____

_____

_____

_____

_____

Summary of Biochemical
Tests

TEST	MEDIUM	SUBSTRATE	POSITIVE TEST		
			END PRODUCTS	APPEARANCE	TYPE OF REACTION
Starch hydrolysis	Starch agar	Starch	Dextrins, maltose	Clear zone around growth in presence of iodine solution	Hydrolysis
Carbohydrate fermentation	Phenol red broth and carbohydrate, with Durham tube	Glucose, sucrose, or lactose, etc.	Acids, e.g., lactic, acetic, propionic; gases: carbon dioxide and hydrogen may or may not be produced	Indicator changes from red to yellow; gas collects in fermentation vial	Fermentation
Gelatin hydrolysis (liquefaction)	Nutrient gelatin	Gelatin	Peptones→ peptides→ amino acids	Failure of medium to gel at 20°C	Hydrolysis, proteolytic
Casein hydrolysis	Milk agar	Casein	(As above)	Clear zone around growth	Hydrolysis, proteolytic
Hydrogen sulfide production	SIM agar	Cystine (sulfur-containing amino acid)	*Hydrogen sulfide* + pyruvic acid + ammonia	Blackening of media as result of iron sulfide formation	Amino acid degradation
Indole production	Trypticase broth	Tryptophan	*Indole* + pyruvic acid + ammonia	Red color in presence of Kovacs' reagent	Hydrolytic, amino acid degradation
Nitrate reduction	Trypticase-nitrate broth	Potassium nitrate, KNO_3	Potassium nitrite, KNO_2	Red to maroon color develops in presence of sulfanilic acid and dimethyl-α-naphthylamine	Reduction
Lipid hydrolysis	Tributyrin agar	Tributyrin	Fatty acid and glycerol	Clear zone around growth	Hydrolysis, lipolytic

Summary of Biochemical
Tests (Continued)

TEST	MEDIUM	SUBSTRATE	POSITIVE TEST		TYPE OF REACTION
			END PRODUCTS	APPEARANCE	
Reactions in litmus milk	Litmus milk	Lactose	Acid(s); e.g., lactic, propionic, acetic, in various combinations; gases: carbon dioxide and hydrogen	Curd, coagulation of casein, litmus turns pink (acid curd); breaks or bubbles in curd	Fermentation
	Litmus milk	Casein	Calcium paracaseinate	Curd, coagulation of casein, neutral or alkaline reaction (litmus bluish), rennet curd	Coagulation
	Litmus milk	Casein	Peptones→ peptides→ amino acids	Clearing of milk (solubilization of casein) and development of blue color (alkaline reaction)	Proteolysis
	Litmus milk	Litmus	Leucolitmus (colorless compound)	Medium appears white except for ring at surface	Reduction

PART EIGHT
HIGHER PROTISTS:
MOLDS, YEASTS, PROTOZOA, AND ALGAE

Yeasts, molds, protozoa, and algae (except for the blue-green algae) are sometimes referred to as the *higher protists* (*eucaryotes*), while bacteria, rickettsiae, and blue-green algae are designated as *lower protists* (*procaryotes*). The laboratory study of the higher protists and blue-green algae is performed in essentially the same manner as that already described for the bacteria. In general, their cells are larger, and they exhibit more anatomical details and structures. Microscopic examinations are frequently made from microcultures or wet preparations; fixed, stained smears, commonly used for the observation of bacteria, are used infrequently here. Morphological characteristics are the most important single contribution to the identification and classification of most of these organisms.

Laboratory cultivation of the higher protists is likewise similar to that described for the bacteria. Broth and agar media are conventionally employed. As a group, the higher protists are less fastidious than the bacteria.

The routine biochemical tests used for the characterization of bacteria have less application to most of the higher protists. However, studies of the metabolic processes of yeasts, molds, protozoa, and algae are conducted by the same general procedures that are applicable for bacteria.

EXERCISE TWENTY-TWO
MORPHOLOGICAL AND
CULTURAL CHARACTERISTICS
OF MOLDS

REFERENCES: Text, chap. 14; MCM, chap. 44

The molds (filamentous fungi) are much larger and morphologically more complex than bacteria. They are characterized as *eucaryotic protists*, in contrast to bacteria, which are *procaryotic protists*. Morphological details can be differentiated in molds by microscopic examination of unstained specimens. In fact, identification of these fungi is dependent to a large extent on morphological descriptions. They are cultivated in the laboratory in the same general manner as bacteria. Unlike bacteria, which are either aerobic, facultative, or anaerobic, molds are strictly aerobic.

MATERIALS

1. 1 bottle (approximately 80 ml) Sabouraud's agar
2. 4 tubes (approximately 5 ml each) Sabouraud's agar
3. 8 sterile petri dishes
4. Absorbent cotton
5. 4 sterile dropping pipettes with narrow-bore opening (Pasteur pipettes)
6. 4 slides and 4 cover slips
7. 5-ml syringe containing paraffin-petrolatum mixture
8. Sabouraud's agar slant cultures of *Penicillium notatum*, *Aspergillus niger*, *Rhizopus stolonifer*, and *Mucor mucedo*

PROCEDURE

1. Melt the bottle of Sabouraud's agar, cool to 45 to 50°C, and pour four plates, approximately 20 ml of medium per plate.
2. Upon solidification of the medium, make a single streak inoculation, across the center of the plate, from each culture. Each mold is to be inoculated on a separate plate. Incubate plates at room temperature for 2 to 4 days.
3. Morphological characteristics of molds can best be observed

from slide cultures. The following technique (see sketch) will be used to prepare slide cultures:

a. Select a clean slide and pass it through the flame of the burner. Allow it to cool.

b. Make two ridges on the slide with paraffin-petrolatum (approximately 1 in. apart). The thin column of paraffin-petrolatum can be forced out of the syringe more effectively if the loaded syringe is warmed beforehand (kept in the 35°C incubator).

c. Select a clean cover slip, pass it through the flame, and then place it upon the ridges on the slide.

d. Inoculate a tube of melted, cooled (45 to 50°C) Sabouraud's agar with one of the mold cultures. Roll the tube between the palms of your hands to distribute the inoculum.

e. With a Pasteur pipette, transfer a small amount of the inoculated agar to the region between the cover slip and slide. Allow the medium to fill approximately one-half this space.

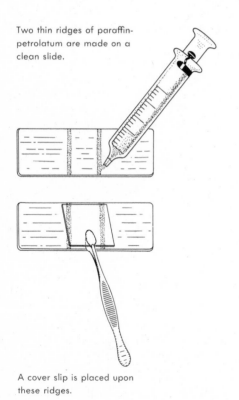

Two thin ridges of paraffin-petrolatum are made on a clean slide.

A cover slip is placed upon these ridges.

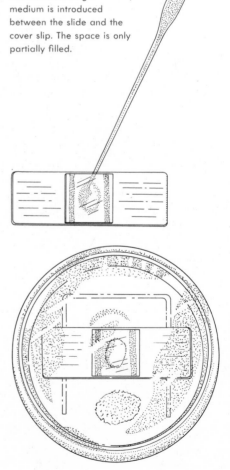

The inoculated agar medium is introduced between the slide and the cover slip. The space is only partially filled.

The slide culture is placed in a petri dish containing glass-rod support and a wet cotton plug.

f. Place the slide culture in a petri dish containing a bent glass rod and a small ball of cotton soaked with water. The wet cotton provides moisture to prevent drying of the medium. Incubate the preparation for 2 to 4 days at room temperature.

4. Prepare slide cultures for each of the four species.

NOTE: It is advisable to observe the inoculated plates and slide cultures daily to determine when the growth best exhibits the morphological structures. If detailed examinations cannot be performed at this time, the cultures can be placed in a refrigerator to retard growth until such examinations are made.

RESULTS

1. Examine the plate cultures macroscopically. Record the gross appearance of the growth.

2. Examine each of the slide cultures microscopically, using the low-power and high-dry objectives. Make drawings of typical structures found in each culture, identifying such structures as the following: mycelia, septate and nonseptate hyphae, conidia and conidiophores, sporangia and sporangiophores, and rhizoids. Refer to textbook drawings of these fungi for aid in identification of structures seen microscopically.

SPECIES	APPEARANCE OF CULTURES		
	MACROSCOPIC	MICROSCOPIC	
		LOW-POWER	HIGH-DRY
Penicillium notatum			
Aspergillus niger			
Rhizopus stolonifer			
Mucor mucedo			

QUESTIONS

1. Compare bacteria to molds with respect to the significance of the morphological characteristics used in assigning them to a taxonomic group.

_____

_____

_____

_____

_____

_____

2. What is the pH of Sabouraud's agar? How does this compare with the pH of media used for cultivation of bacteria?

_____

_____

_____

_____

3. List several distinguishing characteristics of each of the four molds studied in this exercise.

_____

_____

_____

_____

_____

_____

_____

_____

_____

4. Why should a person who is trained as a bacteriologist be familiar with molds?

_____

_____

_____

_____

_____

_____

5. Why are molds designated as eucaryotic protists?

_____

_____

_____

_____

_____

_____

EXERCISE TWENTY–THREE
SEXUAL REPRODUCTION
OF MOLDS

REFERENCE: Text, chap. 14.

Molds produce different kinds of sexual spores; e.g., phycomycetes produce *zygospores* or *oospores,* and ascomycetes produce *ascospores.* In this experiment, you will observe zygospore formation by *Phycomyces blakesleanus.*

MATERIALS

1. 3 tubes Sabouraud's agar
2. 3 sterile petri dishes
3. *Phycomyces blakesleanus* (+) strain and (−) strain.

PROCEDURE

1. Prepare three plates of Sabouraud's agar. Draw a line across the center of the outside bottom part of the dish. Inoculate the plates at opposite sides (at locations *A* and *B* in the sketch) with the *P. blakesleanus* strains as follows:

   Plate 1: strain (+) inoculated at *A;* strain (−) inoculated at *B*
   Plate 2: strain (+) inoculated at *A* and *B*
   Plate 3: strain (−) inoculated at *A* and *B*

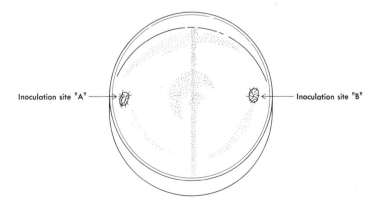

Sabouraud's agar plate Inoculation site "A" ──→ ←── Inoculation site "B"

2. Incubate the plates at room temperature in a container which can be humidified, e.g., a large enclosed can or jar containing a beaker of water.

3. Observe the plates at each subsequent laboratory period. Use the low-power objective to view the morphological structures, particularly at the converging margins of growth.

RESULTS

1. Describe the appearance of growth at each time of observation.
2. Diagram the structures associated with stages in the production of a sexual spore, i.e., suspensor, progamete, gamete, zygote.

DATE	AMOUNT OF GROWTH	DESCRIPTION AND SKETCHES OF MOLD STRUCTURES

QUESTIONS

1. Define the following: gamete, progamete, zygote, oospore, ascospore.

_____

_____

_____

_____

_____

2. How do mold spores compare with bacterial spores?

_____

_____

_____

_____

_____

3. Is the production of sexual spores the only mode of reproduction exhibited by the mold used in this experiment? If your answer is "no," list other modes of reproduction.

_____

_____

_____

_____

_____

EXERCISE TWENTY-FOUR
MORPHOLOGY
OF YEASTS

REFERENCE: Text, chap. 15;
MCM, chap. 42

Yeasts are fungi that do not form a mycelium, although a pseudomycelium* is formed by some species. They are single-celled organisms larger than bacteria but less complex morphologically than the molds. Laboratory study of yeasts is performed in essentially the same manner as for bacteria.

MATERIALS

1. 1 bottle (approximately 100 ml) Sabouraud's agar
2. 5 fermentation tubes each of carbohydrate broth (glucose, maltose, lactose)
3. 5 sterile petri dishes
4. 1 stoppered test tube with approximately 1 ml sterile water
5. Sabouraud's agar slant cultures of *Saccharomyces cerevisiae, Rhodotorula rubra, Geotrichum candidum,* and *Schizosaccharomyces octosporus*
6. Compressed yeast cake

PROCEDURE

1. Prepare five plates with Sabouraud's agar.
2. With the aid of the inoculating loop, transfer a small piece of the yeast cake to the tube with sterile water. Agitate the tube vigorously.
3. Prepare a streak plate (see Exercise 12) of this yeast-cake suspension. Prepare streak plates of each of the pure cultures of yeast provided. Incubate plates at room temperature for 2 to 4 days. Inoculate the carbohydrate-broth fermentation tubes and incubate them in a similar manner.
4. Make a "wet" preparation of each pure culture and the yeast-cake suspension. Mix a drop of methylene blue with the yeast cells to make the wet mounts. Examine these using the high-dry and oil-immersion objectives.

*A false mycelium; it is a series of cells adhering end to end to form a chain.

RESULTS

1. Make drawings of a few cells from each preparation. Observe the shape of individual cells and the characteristic arrangement of cells, and note particularly the presence of any intracellular structures. Attempt to identify the latter. Note also the presence of any ascospores in any of the cultures.

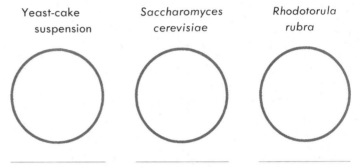

specimen:

Yeast-cake suspension	Saccharomyces cerevisiae	Rhodotorula rubra

magnification: _____   _____   _____

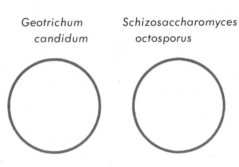

specimen:

Geotrichum candidum	Schizosaccharomyces octosporus

magnification: _____   _____

2. Observe the streaked plates, and describe the appearance of isolated colonies. Note the odor of the cultures. Record the changes in the fermentation tubes.

SPECIMEN	DESCRIPTION OF COLONIES	ODOR	FERMENTATIONS		
			G	M	L

QUESTIONS

1. Compare, in general terms, the morphological characteristics of bacteria, yeasts, and molds.

_____

_____

_____

_____

_____

_____

_____

2. How did the cells from the culture of *Saccharomyces cerevisiae* compare with those from the yeast cake? What distinctive features were exhibited by each of the species examined?

_____

_____

_____

_____

_____

_____

3. Would there be any advantages if the wet preparation of yeast were examined by phase microscopy rather than bright-field microscopy? Explain.

_____

_____

_____

_____

_____

_____

4. Compare laboratory techniques used for the study of yeasts with those used for the study of bacteria.

_____

_____

_____

_____

_____

5. The name *Saccharomyces* is derived from two Greek words. What are they and what do they mean?

_____

_____

_____

_____

_____

6. Which of the species studied in this exercise do not form ascospores?

_____

_____

_____

EXERCISE TWENTY-FIVE
ALCOHOLIC
FERMENTATION

Yeasts are the most important organisms involved in alcoholic fermentation, i.e., the anaerobic dissimilation of sugars to alcohol and carbon dioxide. Yeast fermentation of sugary materials, e.g., fruit juices, and, more specifically, grape juice, results in the production of wine. Grape juice contains 15 to 25 percent sugar, chiefly as glucose and fructose. Other nutrients, including amino acids, are present in the juice; thus it is capable of supporting growth of yeasts.

REFERENCES: Text, chaps. 15 and 40.

MATERIALS

1. Approximately 200 ml grape juice
2. 1 tube *Saccharomyces cerevisiae* var. *ellipsoideus* cultured in 10 ml sterile grape juice
3. Distillation apparatus (see figure)

PROCEDURE

1. Thoroughly rinse a 250-ml graduate cylinder several times with tap water and then use it to measure 150 ml grape juice. Add this to a sterile, cotton-stoppered 250-ml Erlenmeyer flask.

Distillation assembly for recovery of alcohol.

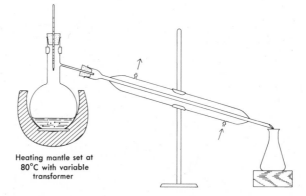

Heating mantle set at 80°C with variable transformer

2. Inoculate the flask with 5 ml of the yeast culture and incubate at 25°C (or room temperature) for 1 week.

3. Prepare and examine a wet preparation of the fermented juice.

4. After noting the characteristics of the fermented juice, decant 100 ml of it into the distillation flask of the apparatus shown. Distill approximately 10 ml. Compare this distillate with the alcohol used in the laboratory for staining, e.g., aroma and volatility of a drop placed in a glass dish.

RESULTS

1. Record the appearance of the contents of the flask. Was any foam evident?
2. Note any aroma of the contents. How did the distillate sample compare with the known alcohol sample?
3. Sketch a few cells from a typical microscopic field of the wet mount prepared above.

Saccharomyces cerevisiae
var. *ellipsoideus*

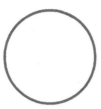

CHARACTERIZATION OF FERMENTED JUICE	CHARACTERIZATION OF DISTILLATE

QUESTIONS

1. Write the chemical equation illustrating the reaction involved in alcoholic fermentation by yeasts. What is the usual alcoholic content, in percent by volume, of commercially fermented grape juice (wine)?

_____

_____

_____

_____

_____

_____

2. Some yeasts are characterized as *fermentative*, others as *oxidative*. In terms of metabolic activity, characterize these two groups.

_____

_____

_____

_____

_____

_____

_____

3. What is meant by the term "wild yeast"?

_____

_____

_____

_____

_____

_____

_____

4. What is the taxonomic relationship between *Saccharomyces cerevisiae* and *S. cerevisiae* var. *ellipsoideus*?

_____

_____

_____

_____

_____

_____

_____

EXERCISE TWENTY-SIX
MORPHOLOGICAL
CHARACTERISTICS
OF PROTOZOA

Protozoa are primitive animals, the majority of which are microscopic. Many species are free-living (saprophytic) and may be found almost universally distributed in ponds and streams; others are parasitic and are the causative agents of disease. Many are sufficiently large for microscopic examination to demonstrate clearly the structures of a typical single cell. The method of locomotion is generally used to determine the group in which a protozoan is classified.

REFERENCE: Text, chap. 17; MCM, chap. 49

MATERIALS

1. Prepared permanent slides or living cultures of *Amoeba, Paramecium, Euglena* species
2. Pond water or hay infusion
3. Stained smear of human blood showing *Plasmodium vivax*
4. Chart showing stages of development of *Plasmodium vivax* in red blood cells
5. A few milliliters 10% methyl cellulose

PROCEDURE

1. Observe the prepared slides of *Amoeba, Paramecium,* and *Euglena,* using the low-power and high-dry objectives of the microscope. If living cultures are available, prepare wet mounts and examine similarly. The use of living cultures permits detection of the mode of locomotion or motility. If the organisms are very actively motile, making examination of cellular morphology difficult, they can be slowed down by the addition of a drop of the methyl cellulose solution.
2. After scanning several microscopic fields, select a field with a single organism in the center, and make a detailed drawing. Identify and label all parts. Use the illustrations in your text to assist in the identification of cellular structures.

3. Prepare a wet mount of the pond water or hay infusion and examine as above. Describe the protozoan types found in this specimen.

4. Review the chart provided showing the stages of development of *Plasmodium vivax* in red blood cells. Now examine the prepared smear and locate infected red blood cells. Make a sketch of several such cells.

RESULTS

1. Drawings of *Amoeba, Paramecium,* and *Euglena* should be made sufficiently large to permit differentiation of cellular structures. The drawing made from the blood smear should include some uninfected red blood cells.

Amoeba sp.   *Euglena* sp.

Paramecium sp.   Blood smear

2. Describe some of the protozoan types observed in the pond water or hay infusion, and note the manner in which each moves.

DESCRIPTION OF CELLS	TYPE OF MOTILITY

1. Define the following: cilium, flagellum, pseudopodium, vacuole, oral groove, gullet.

2. *Euglena* is grouped with the algae by some authors and with the protozoa by others. What are the characteristics of this organism that place it at the border line of plant and animal life?

3. What is the mode of locomotion in each of the four protozoa examined? To what class or group does each of these protozoa belong?

EXERCISE TWENTY-SEVEN
MORPHOLOGY AND CULTIVATION OF ALGAE

Laboratory Exercises in Microbiology

Algae contain the green pigment chlorophyll, which is characteristic of plants. They range in size from microscopic single cells to extremely large forms such as seaweeds and giant kelp. The most primitive of the algae are the Myxophyceae, or blue-green algae. These organisms, particularly the colorless members of this group, are very closely akin to bacteria; like bacteria, they are procaryotic protists.

REFERENCE: Text, chap. 16

MATERIALS

1. 6 tubes calcium nitrate—salts agar
2. 6 tubes nutrient agar with 0.5% glucose
3. Nutrient-agar slant cultures of *Chlorella* sp., *Chlamydomonas* sp., and *Nostoc* sp.

PROCEDURE

1. Pour six plates with each medium listed above.
2. After the media solidify, streak one plate of each medium with each algal culture. Incubate one set of plates, i.e., each of the algae on both media, in the *dark* (desk drawer) and the other set of plates in the *light* (near a window). Incubation should be at room temperature for 5 to 7 days.
3. Prepare a wet amount of each algal culture and examine the cells under low-power magnification and high-dry magnification. Observe cells for size, shape, and evidence of external and internal structures. Note particularly any similarities and/or differences with bacteria, yeasts, molds, and protozoa.

RESULTS

1. Make a drawing of cells as seen by high-power magnification and label all structures.

   Chlorella sp.   Chlamydomonas sp.   Nostoc sp.

2. After the required incubation time, observe the plates. Record presence or absence of growth and a description of growth.

MEDIUM	CONDITIONS OF INCUBATION	DESCRIPTION OF GROWTH		
		Chlorella sp.	Chlamydomonas sp.	Nostoc sp.
Calcium nitrate – salts agar	Light			
	Dark			
Nutrient agar with glucose	Light			
	Dark			

QUESTIONS

1. Were any differences observed with respect to the growth of the algae on the two different media? In the light and in the dark? What accounts for the differences?

_____

_____

_____

_____

_____

_____

_____

2. Are all algae procaryotic protists? Explain.

_____

_____

_____

_____

_____

_____

_____

3. Are all algae microorganisms? Explain.

_____

_____

_____

_____

_____

_____

_____

The laboratory propagation of viruses requires suitable viable host cells in which the viral agent multiplies. The host cells are bacteria for bacterial viruses (bacteriophages); molds for mold viruses (mycophages); animal-cell cultures, embryonated chicken eggs, or animals for animal viruses; and plant-cell cultures or plants for plant viruses.

The bacterium-bacteriophage system is the most convenient for investigating phenomena in the biological system of host-cell–virus relationship. Host cells (bacteria) can be produced in abundance, inexpensively, rapidly, and easily. Action of the bacteriophage can be assayed in broth cultures or upon surface growth on nutrient-agar plates. This system is amenable to many manipulations for experimental purposes.

Propagation of animal or plant viruses in tissue cultures requires the maintenance and cultivation of appropriate host-cell lines in nutrient solutions dispensed in shallow layers in bottles or special flasks or tubes. The embryonated chicken egg is suitable for the multiplication of many viruses.

Direct visualization of a virus is possible by means of electron microscopy. Some of the characteristic virus shapes are spheroidal, filamentous, polyhedral, and spermlike.

Measurement of the potency of virus preparations, particularly animal viruses, is performed through the use of a variety of serological tests wherein the virus functions as the antigen.

EXERCISE TWENTY-EIGHT
THE VIRUSES
A. BACTERIAL LYSIS
BY BACTERIOPHAGE

Filterable agents that attack bacteria, namely, bacteriophages (phages), are considered to be representative of viruses. They are very specific in action: a bacteriophage for one strain of bacteria within a species may not attack another strain of the same species. The bacteriophages lyse bacterial cells. This can be demonstrated in broth cultures (clearing) or on agar surface cultures (clear zones, or *plaques*).

REFERENCE: Text, chaps. 18-20; MMM, chap. 11; MCM, chap. 52

MATERIALS

1. Bacteriological filter
2. 40 ml trypticase agar
3. 2 sterile petri dishes
4. 10 tubes (9 ml each) trypticase broth
5. Sterile bent glass rod
6. 9 sterile 1.0-ml pipettes
7. Specimen of *Escherichia coli* bacteriophage adjusted to have a titer of approximately 10^{-5}
8. Trypticase-broth culture of 6- to 12-hr bacteriophage-sensitive strain of *E. coli*

PROCEDURE

The laboratory instructor will demonstrate the use of the bacteriological filter for obtaining bacteria-free phage filtrates. How the phage specimen for this exercise was prepared and the titer adjusted to approximately 10^{-5} will likewise be explained.

1. Pour two plates of trypticase agar, each to contain approximately 20 ml of the medium. As soon as the agar solidifies, place the plates in the 35°C incubator until ready for use. This is done to dry the surface of the medium.
2. Arrange in a line 10 tubes of trypticase broth in a test-tube rack; label them 1 to 10. Using aseptic precautions, transfer 1 ml of the phage specimen into tube 1. Gently agitate the

tube; then transfer 1 ml from tube 1 into tube 2. Agitate tube 2; then transfer 1 ml from tube 2 into tube 3. Continue this process until tube 9 is reached. (A different sterile pipette should be used for each transfer.) Discard the 1 ml removed from tube 9. Tube 10 does not receive any of the diluted phage. (See scheme illustrating preparation of the phage dilutions.)

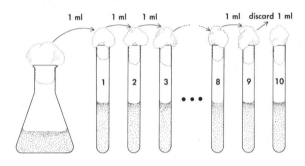

3. Remove the two plates from the incubator (see step 1 of procedure). Place one drop of E. coli culture on each of the two plates. Using a sterile bent glass rod, spread the inoculum over the entire surface of the plate. Extreme care must be exercised to ensure complete and uniform inoculation of the agar surface. Allow the inoculated plates to stand for several minutes to permit the agar surface to dry.

4. Invert the plates, draw five lines across the bottom of each, and label the lines as shown below.

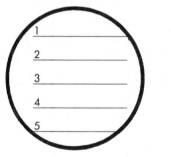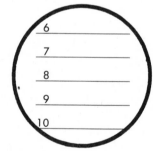

5. Now remove one loopful of material from tube 1 (see step 2 of procedure), and streak this on the surface of the agar plate following line 1. Do the same with each of the remaining tubes; one loopful from each tube is streaked along the line corresponding to the tube number. Incubate plates at 35°C.

6. Add 1 drop of the broth culture of E. coli to each of the 10 tubes prepared in step 2 of this procedure. Incubate these tubes at 35°C.

RESULTS

1. Observe the plates and tubes after 6 to 8 hr incubation and again after 12 to 18 hr. Compare the growth in each tube to that in tube 10. (Tube 10 is a positive control since it contains no phage.) Record growth in tube 10 as +++, lesser amounts of growth as ++ or +, and no growth as 0.

INCUBATION, HOURS	TUBE									
	1	2	3	4	5	6	7	8	9	10 CONTROL
6–8										
12–18										

2. Observe carefully the growth along each of the marked lines on the plate. Is there any evidence of clearing along any of these lines? Sketch one of the plates that exhibits clearing along one or more of the streaks.

QUESTIONS

1. What is meant by the term "titer of phage"? How much of the original phage specimen is contained in tube 5 of this exercise? (Refer to step 2 of the procedure.)

_____

_____

_____

_____

_____

_____

2. "Phage typing" is sometimes performed on strains of certain bacterial species, e.g., *Staphylococcus aureus*. What does this mean, and of what significance are the results of such a typing?

3. What is meant by the term "host strain"?

4. What is the role of phage in the process of transduction?

B. TISSUE–CULTURE TECHNIQUES AND VIRUS PROPAGATION (DEMONSTRATION)

The propagation of viruses takes place only within susceptible living host cells. These cells may be in the tissues of a living animal or in a culture vessel, where they are cultivated in a nutrient solution (tissue culture). Accordingly, propagation of the virus can be accomplished by inoculating a susceptible animal or susceptible cells in a tissue culture. The tissue-culture–virus system provides a very convenient system for the study of viruses.

MATERIALS

1. Samples of commercially prepared tissue-culture media and supplements, e.g., Eagle's amino acid concentrate, Hank's balanced salt solution; animal sera, etc.
2. Tissue-culture vessels, e.g., Leighton tube, tissue culture flask, and others as suggested in the illustration
3. If available, virus growing in tissue culture in which the cytopathogenic effect (CPE) is apparent
4. Normal, uninfected tissue culture (control)

PROCEDURE

1. Examine the tissue-culture media and the nutritional supplements. Note the composition of the various mixtures.
2. Examine the tissue-culture vessels on display. Several examples of tissue-culture vessels are shown on the next page.
3. Observe the inoculated tissue-culture specimen using low-power (10x) magnification and look particularly for areas showing destruction of tissue. Compare this with an un-inoculated tissue culture.

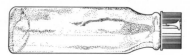

1 - ounce pharmaceutical bottle

Tissue-culture vessels.

Leighton tube

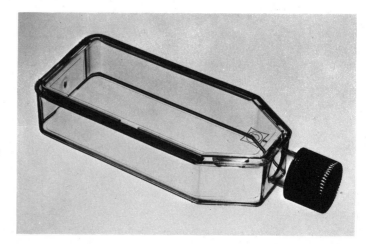

Tissue culture flask.
Courtesy of BioQuest,
Division of Becton, Dickinson
and Company.

Tissue culture tube/Tissue
culture dish. Courtesy of
BioQuest, Division of Becton,
Dickinson and Company.

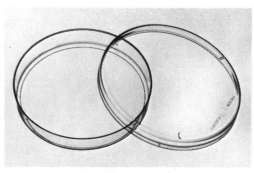

RESULTS

1. Make a sketch of the cells in the infected tissue culture and in the uninoculated tissue culture.

Infected tissue culture   Uninoculated tissue culture

QUESTIONS

1. Compare the media, i.e., type of ingredients, used for cultivation of tissue cells with those used for cultivation of bacteria.

_____

_____

_____

_____

_____

_____

_____

2. Compare the bacteria-bacteriophage system with the virus-propagation system of the type observed in this experiment.

_____

_____

_____

_____

_____

_____

3. Do you think it may be possible to propagate viruses in a system free of living host cells? Explain why.

_____

_____

_____

_____

_____

_____

_____

4. What is your opinion whether viruses are living entities? State some reasons in support of your opinion.

_____

_____

_____

_____

_____

_____

_____

5. What relationship, if any, is there between viruses and the organisms classified as Mycoplasmatales?

_____

_____

_____

_____

_____

6. Complete the summary table below, comparing the general characteristics of microorganisms. Consult text for data not obtained in laboratory exercises.

Comparison of Bacteria,
Viruses, Rickettsiae, Yeasts,
Molds, Algae, and Protozoa

| ORGANISM | SIZE | | CHARACTERISTICS | | |
	A*	B*	CELL SHAPES	DISTINGUISHING CELLULAR STRUCTURES	LABORATORY CULTIVATION
Bacteria					
Viruses					
Rickettsiae					
Yeasts					
Molds					
Algae					
Protozoa					

*A = dimensions of typical
organism, in micrometers
B = size range, in micrometers

PART TEN
CONTROL OF MICROBIAL POPULATIONS: PHYSICAL AGENTS

The physical environment has a profound influence on the growth and survival of microorganisms. As a group, microorganisms are capable of growing in a wide range of temperature, pH, osmotic pressure, and other physical conditions. However, members of a particular genus or species exhibit specific requirements.

Physical conditions or processes are commonly employed to kill, inhibit, or remove microorganisms from various materials or environments. The requirement may be complete destruction of all microbial life (sterilization) or a degree of reduction in the microbial flora where some survivors are permitted or can be tolerated (as in sanitization).

The autoclave, the hot-air oven, and the bacteriological filter are representative of the type of apparatus available in the microbiological laboratory for sterilization of media, reagents, glass petri dishes and test tubes, pipettes, etc. Various items are preferentially sterilized by one of these methods (bacteriological media are sterilized by autoclaving whereas dry glassware is generally sterilized in the hot-air oven).

Microbial species differ in their susceptibility to destruction by physical agents, bacterial spores being the most resistant group. Standardized bacterial-spore suspensions are often used to test the efficacy of a sterilization process.

EXERCISE TWENTY-NINE
THE EFFECT
OF TEMPERATURE
ON GROWTH

REFERENCES: Text, chap. 6;
MMM, chap. 7.

Microorganisms are capable of growing over a wide range of temperature. On the one extreme are bacteria that grow at a temperature of 0°C (*psychrophiles*); and at the other are those requiring high temperatures (*thermophiles*), some of which grow at 75°C. Intermediate between these two groups are the *mesophiles*, which grow between the temperatures of 20 and 45°C. Each type, i.e., psychrophile, mesophile, or thermophile, has a minimum, maximum, and optimum growth temperature.

MATERIALS

1. 16 nutrient-agar slants
2. 8 Sabouraud's agar slants
3. Nutrient-broth cultures of *Staphylococcus aureus, Micrococcus agilis, Pseudomonas fluorescens,* and *Bacillus stearothermophilus*
4. Sabouraud's agar slant cultures of *Saccharomyces cerevisiae* and *Aspergillus niger*

PROCEDURE

1. Inoculate four nutrient-agar slants with each of the bacterial cultures. Inoculate four Sabouraud's agar slants with *S. cerevisiae* and four others with *A. niger*.
2. Incubate an inoculated slant of each culture at the following temperatures: 4 to 6°C (refrigerator), 20 to 25°C (room), 35°C (incubator), 55°C (incubator).

RESULTS

Observe each of the tubes at the end of 24 to 48 hr and again after 5 to 7 days' incubation. Record the amount of growth as follows: 0 = no growth; + = scant growth; ++ = moderate growth; +++ = very good or profuse growth. Note any differences in appearance of growth, particularly pigmentation, at the different temperatures.

24 to 48 hr Incubation

ORGANISM (SPECIES)	AMOUNT AND APPEARANCE OF GROWTH			
	4−6°C	20−25°C	35°C	55°C
Staphylococcus aureus				
Micrococcus agilis				
Pseudomonas fluorescens				
Bacillus stearothermo- philus				
Saccharomyces cerevisiae				
Aspergillus niger				

5 to 7 Days' Incubation

ORGANISM (SPECIES)	AMOUNT AND APPEARANCE OF GROWTH			
	4–6°C	20–25°C	35°C	55°C
Staphylococcus aureus				
Micrococcus agilis				
Pseudomonas fluorescens				
Bacillus stearothermo- philus				
Saccharomyces cerevisiae				
Aspergillus niger				

QUESTIONS

1. What generalization can be made from the results of this experiment about temperature required for growth of bacteria vs. temperature required for growth of yeasts and molds? Are there exceptions to your generalization? Give examples.

_____

_____

_____

_____

_____

_____

_____

_____

2. What effect does temperature of incubation have on pigment production?

_____

_____

_____

3. Explain how temperature would influence (a) the rate of growth and (b) the cell crop from a particular culture.

_____

_____

_____

_____

_____

_____

_____

4. Is the occurrence of thermophilic microorganisms restricted to high-temperature environments? State some evidence to support your answer.

_____

_____

_____

_____

_____

5. What is a thermoduric bacterium?

_____

_____

_____

_____

Vegetative cells of microorganisms exhibit differences in their tolerance to heat. The spores of bacteria are extremely resistant to heat; many can survive prolonged exposure to boiling water. The degree of heat tolerance of an organism can be assessed in the laboratory by exposing the cells to a fixed temperature for increasing periods of time, subcultures being made at the end of each time interval; or the time may be fixed and the temperature varied. The latter procedure is referred to as the *thermal-death-point determination*. In the procedure to be performed, the organisms or spores will be exposed to increasing temperatures for a fixed time period, i.e., 10 min. Accurate information on the heat tolerance of various types of microorganisms is imperative in any practical process that employs high temperature as the means for destroying microorganisms.

REFERENCE: Text, chap. 23.

MATERIALS

1. 12 tubes trypticase-soy broth
2. Trypticase-soy-broth cultures of *Escherichia coli, Staphylococcus aureus, Microbacterium flavum, Bacillus subtilis* var. *globigii* (young culture, vegetative cells), and *B. subtilis* var. *globigii* (old culture, predominantly spores)
3. Water bath and thermometer

PROCEDURE

1. Set up a water bath and place seven tubes of trypticase-soy broth in the bath. The level of water in the bath should be above the level of the broth in the tubes.
2. Place a thermometer in one of the tubes of broth.
3. By gentle heating, bring the temperature up to 50°C. NOTE: Constant attention should be given to the temperature of the water bath so that adjustments in heating can be made before a serious fluctuation in temperature occurs.

4. Inoculate one of the tubes with one loopful of one of the nonsporeforming species and another tube with one loopful of *B. subtilis* var. *globigii* (either the spores or vegetative cells). Remove both these tubes, cool them under tap water, and place them in a test-tube rack. Label these "control." NOTE: Each student will use just two cultures, which will be assigned so that all cultures are tested by the laboratory section.

5. Inoculate one tube with the nonsporeformer selected in the preceding step and allow it to remain in the bath at 50°C for 10 min before it is removed and cooled.

6. Repeat step 5 at temperatures of 60, 70, and 80°C. Be sure that the water bath is at the desired temperature before the tube is inoculated.

7. Place one tube of trypticase-soy broth in the water bath at a temperature of 80°C.

8. Inoculate this tube with one loopful of *B. subtilis* var. *globigii* (spores or vegetative cells), and maintain the temperature for 10 min. After this time, remove the tube, and cool it *immediately* under tap water.

9. Repeat steps 7 and 8 at temperatures of 90, 95, and 100°C.

10. Incubate all inoculated tubes at 35°C for 48 hr.

RESULTS

Compare the inoculated tubes exposed to various temperatures with the control tubes. Record evidence of survival (growth) as + and kill (no growth) as 0. The results of the laboratory section will be tabulated on the blackboard. Record this summary of results together with your own.

BACTERIAL SPECIES	EFFECT OF HEAT TREATMENT							CONTROL
	50°C	60°C	70°C	80°C	90°C	95°C	100°C	
Escherichia coli								
Staphylococcus aureus								
Microbacterium flavum								
Bacillus subtilis var. globigii (cells)								
Bacillus subtilis var. globigii (spores)								

QUESTIONS

1. Are gram-negative bacteria generally more susceptible to high temperatures than gram-positive bacteria? Give examples in support of your answer.

_____

_____

_____

_____

_____

_____

_____

2. Several members of your laboratory section performed this experiment using the same cultures. Were there any discrepancies in results? If so, give examples.

_____

_____

_____

_____

_____

_____

3. What are some of the reasons given for the ability of spores to withstand unusually high temperatures? Compare the heat resistance of mold and yeast spores to the heat resistance of bacterial spores.

_____

_____

_____

_____

_____

_____

_____

_____

4. How could the isolation of sporeformers from a soil sample be facilitated?

_____

_____

_____

_____

_____

EXERCISE THIRTY-ONE
STERILIZATION
WITH AUTOCLAVE AND
HOT-AIR OVEN

The autoclave and hot-air oven are the two most widely used devices for sterilizing laboratory equipment. The conditions necessary for sterilization, particularly the time and temperature, are influenced by many factors, including the numbers and kinds of contaminating spores. This exercise should serve two purposes: (1) to acquaint you with the operation of the autoclave and hot-air oven and (2) to demonstrate that the number of bacterial spores, as well as the kind of bacterial spores, must be considered in establishing sterilization times and temperatures.

REFERENCE: Text, chap. 23.

MATERIALS

1. 12 tubes trypticase-soy broth
2. 4 9-ml dilution blanks
3. 12 sterile filter-paper strips 1.5 by 5.0 cm
4. 12 sterile stoppered test tubes
5. 5-ml spore suspensions of *Bacillus subtilis* var. *globigii* and *Bacillus stearothermophilus*, both 10^{10} spores/ml
6. 2 sterile petri dishes

PROCEDURE

1. Prepare a 1:10 and a 1:100 dilution of each spore suspension.
2. Observing aseptic technique, arrange 12 of the sterile filter-paper strips individually in glass petri dishes so that each strip can be identified. With a sterile pipette, impregnate two strips with 0.1 ml from each of the suspensions of *B. subtilis* var. *globigii*, including the original suspension (10^{10} spores/ml) and impregnate another series in a similar manner with the *B. stearothermophilus* spore suspensions.
3. Allow a brief period for the strips to dry and then transfer the strips into labeled sterile test tubes, one strip per tube. Arrange the tubes in two sets, each set to include strips

impregnated with the three spore suspensions of each species.

4. Autoclave one set at 15 lb pressure (121°C) for 10 min and place the other in the hot-air oven (adjusted to 160°C) for 60 min. (The laboratory instructor will demonstrate operation of this sterilizing equipment to the class.)

5. At the end of the exposure time, remove the tubes containing the strips, permit them to cool, and then place each strip in a tube of trypticase-soy broth. Incubate *B. subtilis* var. *globigii* at room temperature and *B. stearothermophilus* at 55°C for 24 to 48 hr.

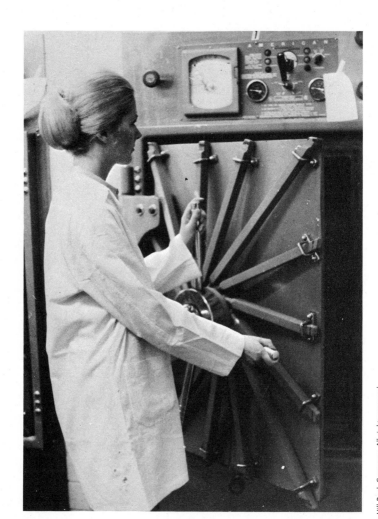

A large autoclave is being used for sterilization.

RESULTS

Observe each tube for the presence or absence of growth. Record growth as (+) and no growth as (0).

	SPECIES	DILUTION	GROWTH
Autoclave	Bacillus subtilis var. globigii	Original	
		1:10	
		1:100	
	Bacillus stearothermophilus	Original	
		1:10	
		1:100	
Hot-air oven	Bacillus subtilis var. globigii	Original	
		1:10	
		1:100	
	Bacillus stearothermophilus	Original	
		1:10	
		1:100	

QUESTIONS

1. Compare the heat resistance of the two sporeforming species used in this exercise.

_____

_____

_____

_____

_____

_____

_____

_____

_____

2. Outline a procedure by which a standardized suspension of bacterial spores can be produced. How could you be sure that the suspension was free of viable vegetative cells?

_____

_____

_____

_____

_____

_____

_____

_____

_____

3. Describe how spore strips are used as indicators for sterilization processes under practical circumstances, e.g., in a hospital.

_____

_____

_____

_____

_____

_____

4. Assume that you have a suspension of bacterial spores (1 × 10^9 spores/ml) and you expose them to a constant lethal temperature. It has previously been established that there is a 90 percent kill of these spores per unit of time (30 min). What is the minimal time required to kill *all* the spores in the suspension referred to above?

_____

_____

_____

_____

EXERCISE THIRTY–TWO
BACTERICIDAL EFFECT
OF ULTRAVIOLET
RADIATIONS

Radiations in the ultraviolet region of the spectrum are lethal to microorganisms. Their effectiveness is influenced by several factors, including the specific wavelength employed and the time and intensity of the exposure. Furthermore, these radiations have very little penetrating power; unless the microorganisms are directly exposed, they are likely to escape destruction.

REFERENCE: Text, chap. 23.

MATERIALS

1. 100-ml bottle nutrient agar
2. 5 sterile petri dishes
3. 1 sterile cotton swab
4. Ultraviolet (germicidal) lamp
5. Cardboard mask with design to cover bottom half of petri dish
6. Nutrient-broth culture of *Serratia marcescens*.

PROCEDURE

1. Pour nutrient agar into each of five petri dishes.
2. After solidification of the medium, inoculate the agar surface evenly and completely in each plate, using a cotton swab soaked with the broth culture of S. *marcescens*.
3. Label one plate as the control. It will not receive further treatment.
4. Expose the remaining four plates to the ultraviolet light as follows: Replace each cover from three of the dishes with a square piece of cardboard in which a narrow letter has been cut. The letter should be within the circumference of the dish (see sketch). Expose the dishes covered in this manner to the ultraviolet light source, one for 30 sec, one for 1 min, and the other for 3 min (or other time periods directed by the laboratory instructor). Remove the dishes after the exposure period, and replace their covers. Expose one petri dish with

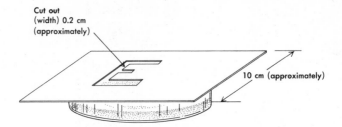

Cut out
(width) 0.2 cm
(approximately)

10 cm (approximately)

cover in place for 3 min. NOTE: Precautions should be observed during the performance of this exercise to shield the eyes from direct exposure to the ultraviolet radiations. This can be accomplished by housing the light source in a box with one side open, through which the petri dishes can be inserted.

5. Incubate all the petri dishes at 25°C or room temperature for 48 hr.

RESULTS

1. Sketch the pattern of growth on the petri dishes that were exposed with the cardboard-mask cover:

exposure time:

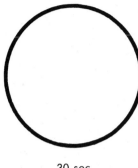 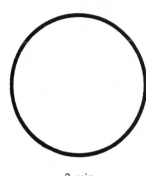

30 sec   1 min   3 min

2. Compare the growth on the control plate with that on the plate exposed with glass cover intact.

_____

_____

_____

_____

QUESTIONS

1. Are all wavelengths in the ultraviolet region equally germicidal? Explain.

_____

_____

_____

_____

2. What did the results of this exercise reveal about the penetrating ability of ultraviolet radiations? How do climatic and other conditions of our atmosphere influence the amount of ultraviolet radiations that reach the earth's surface?

_____

_____

_____

_____

3. List some radiations other than ultraviolet that are germicidal.

4. Which of the following conditions might be accomplished with ultraviolet radiation: sterilized, sanitized, disinfected? Explain.

5. Give an example of an industrial application of ultraviolet radiation to accomplish a reduction of the microbial flora.

EXERCISE THIRTY–THREE
EFFECT OF HIGH CONCENTRATIONS OF SALT AND SUGAR ON MICROBIAL GROWTH

High concentrations of dissolved substances, such as salts and sugars, in a liquid results in a solution that will exhibit a marked osmotic effect on cells. Many microorganisms in a medium or solution with abnormally large amounts of dissolved materials will be restricted in their growth since there will be a tendency for establishment of an equilibrium between the solution enclosed within the cellular membrane and the solution exterior to the membrane. Water will pass from the cell interior into the solution. In effect, the cells become dehydrated, which in turn prevents growth. However, some microorganisms are capable of tolerating very high concentrations of salt or sugar; others grow only in a medium which contains a relatively large amount of salt.

REFERENCE: Text, chap. 23.

MATERIALS

1. 1 tube (20 ml) trypticase-soy agar
2. 1 tube each of trypticase-soy agar with 5, 10, 15, and 20 percent sodium chloride (20 ml per tube)
3. 2 tubes (5 ml) malt-extract broth
4. 2 tubes each malt-extract broth with 5, 10, 15, and 20 percent sucrose (5 ml per tube)
5. 5 sterile petri dishes
6. Trypticase-soy-broth cultures of *Staphylococcus aureus, Halobacterium salinarium, Streptococcus liquefaciens,* and *Brevibacterium linens*
7. Sabouraud's agar slant culture of *Saccharomyces cerevisiae*
8. Spore suspension of *Aspergillus niger*

PROCEDURE

1. Melt the tubes of agar media, cool to 45°C, and pour the contents of each tube into a petri dish previously labeled to

indicate the salt concentration, i.e., 0, 5, 10, 15, and 20 percent.

2. After the medium solidifies, mark the bottom of each plate into quadrants, using the glass-marking pencil. Inoculate each of the bacterial cultures (streak inoculation) in one quadrant of a plate; repeat this process with all the plates. Incubate plates at 35°C for 48 hr.

3. Inoculate one set of the malt-extract-broth media (0, 10, 25, and 50 percent sucrose) with S. cerevisiae and another set with the spores of A. niger. Incubate at room temperature. Observe after 48 hr and 5 to 7 days' incubation.

RESULTS

1. Record the growth on the control plate (trypticase-soy agar without sodium chloride) as +++. Compare the amount of growth of each organism on the sodium chloride–agar plates with that of the control, and record as +++, ++, +, or 0.

BACTERIAL SPECIES	SODIUM CHLORIDE CONTENT OF MEDIUM, PERCENT				
	5	10	15	20	0 CONTROL
Staphylococcus aureus					
Halobacterium salinarium					
Streptococcus liquefaciens					
Brevibacterium linens					

2. Observe the tubes of malt-extract broth inoculated with the yeast and mold, and compare the growth in each tube containing sucrose with that of the control (no sucrose). Record results in the same manner as described above.

INCUBATION	ORGANISMS	SUCROSE CONTENT OF MEDIUM, PERCENT			
		10	25	50	0 CONTROL
48 hr	Saccharomyces cerevisiae				
	Aspergillus niger				
5–7 days	Saccharomyces cerevisiae				
	Aspergillus niger				

QUESTIONS

1. Distinguish between the terms "plasmolysis" and "plasmoptysis." Which of these processes occurs to cells placed in high concentrations of sugar?

_____

_____

_____

_____

_____

2. What is a "halophilic" organism? Where do they occur in nature?

_____

_____

_____

_____

_____

_____

3. What cytological structure of *Escherichia coli* might you identify through microscopic examination of the cells suspended in a solution of high salt concentration? Explain.

_____

_____

_____

_____

_____

4. Sucrose solution, approximately 10%, is used with protoplasts. What is the function of this solution?

_____

_____

_____

_____

_____

5. Is the absence of growth, as observed in some conditions of this experiment, due to a microbicidal or microbistatic effect? How could this be ascertained experimentally?

_____

_____

_____

_____

_____

_____

EXERCISE THIRTY–FOUR
STERILIZATION
BY FILTRATION

Bacteriological filters are designed to prevent the passage of objects as small as bacteria. The material passing through the bacteriological filter (filtrate) and collected in a previously sterilized vessel is free of microorganisms and hence sterile. Sterilization by filtration is required of many products such as animal sera, enzyme solutions, and other materials that are damaged by high temperatures or chemical agents.

REFERENCE: Text, chap. 23.

MATERIALS

1. Bacteriological filters (see sketches)
2. Bacteriological filter assembly (see sketch)
3. Dilute suspension of *Sarcina lutea*
4. 3 trypticase-soy-agar plates

PROCEDURE

1. The laboratory instructor will discuss and demonstrate several types of bacteriological filters such as those illustrated.

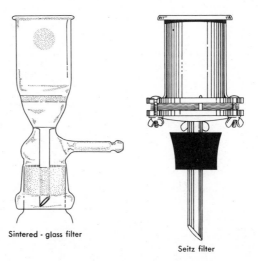

Sintered - glass filter

Seitz filter

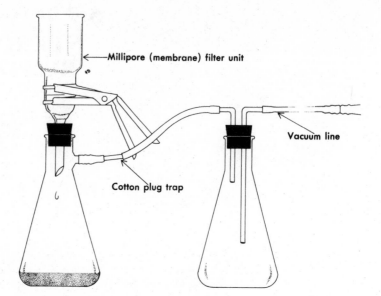

Bacteriological filtration
assembly.

2. Filter a sample from the S. *lutea* suspension, using a membrane-type filter.
3. After completion of the filtration, remove the membrane filter disk with sterile forceps and place the disk on the surface of a trypticase-soy-agar plate. Streak the surface of another trypticase-soy-agar plate with a loopful of the filtrate and a third trypticase-soy-agar plate with a loopful of the unfiltered suspension. Incubate these plates at 35°C for 48 hr.

RESULTS

Observe each of the inoculated plates and record the presence or absence of growth.

SAMPLE	EVIDENCE OF GROWTH

QUESTIONS

1. How does the mechanism of bacterial removal by a membrane filter differ from that accomplished by a Seitz or Berkefeld filter?

_____

_____

_____

_____

_____

_____

_____

2. What advantages does the membrane filtration technique provide over other filtration methods?

_____

_____

_____

_____

_____

_____

3. Assume that you have performed a filtration to sterilize 1 liter of horse serum. What tests would you have to perform to ascertain that the product is sterile?

_____

_____

_____

_____

_____

_____

4. Assume that you are conducting an experiment which involves growing a mold in a large volume of medium, for example, 10 liters, and that constant aeration of the medium is required. How would you provide for a constant flow of sterile air through the medium?

_____

_____

_____

_____

_____

_____

PART ELEVEN
CONTROL OF MICROBIAL POPULATIONS: CHEMICAL AGENTS

An extensive array of chemical substances is available for control of microbial populations. Some, for example, are prescribed for use on inanimate surfaces (disinfectants), while others are intended for use in treatment of infections (chemotherapeutic agents). The chemical characteristics of the substance, together with its intended application, are taken into consideration when tests are designed to determine antimicrobial activity. Laboratory in vitro testing of a chemical agent to determine its antimicrobial efficacy requires the use of designated test organisms. Specific strains of certain species have been selected for various assays, e.g., *Staphylococcus aureus* (ATCC 6538) for the phenol-coefficient technique and *Alternaria brassicicola* (ATCC 12251) for fungicide tests.

Quantitative assay of chemotherapeutic antibiotics by microbiological methods represents a special application of microbial inhibition. These tests have been so designed that a relationship exists between the degree of antimicrobial activity and the quantity of the antibiotic; i.e., within certain limits of antibiotic concentration, proportionality exists between the amount of antibiotic and the degree of inhibition.

Three general methods for determining bacterial susceptibility to antibiotics are currently in use:

1. Serial broth dilution
2. Agar diffusion (medicated disk)
3. Plate dilution

The first is considered more reliable, provided constant conditions and care are maintained. The second is most widely used because of its simplicity. The third equals the first and is chosen by some laboratories as a matter of individual preference.

The antimicrobial spectrum of any antibiotic is an important factor in its choice as a therapeutic agent. Unfortunately, great variations in sensitivity of microorganisms, not only from species to species but even from strain to strain, make it necessary to determine in vitro the effect of the available antibiotics upon the individual strain for optimum results. Development of resistant strains is frequent in some species, and possible cross resistance must also be considered. The correlation between the in vitro tests and the clinical responses, although not absolute, is usually good.

EXERCISE THIRTY-FIVE
COMPARATIVE EVALUATION
OF ANTIMICROBIAL
CHEMICAL AGENTS

REFERENCE: Text, chap. 24.

One of the basic techniques employed for assessing the anti-microbial capacity of a chemical agent is to add a "test" organism to a solution of the chemical agent and make periodic transfers from this mixture into a suitable medium to determine whether the test organism has been killed. Many refinements of this general procedure have been developed in order to provide tests suitable for the evaluation of the antimicrobial efficacy of a great variety of chemical substances.

MATERIALS

1. 18 tubes nutrient broth
2. Chemical agents: group A—0.5% phenol, 70% alcohol, 3% hydrogen peroxide, tincture of iodine; group B—several proprietary disinfectants and antiseptics
3. 4 1-ml and 4 10-ml sterile pipettes
4. 4 sterile stoppered test tubes
5. Nutrient-broth cultures of *Staphylococcus aureus* and *Bacillus subtilis*

PROCEDURE

1. Select one of the solutions from group A, and add 5 ml to a sterile test tube. To this, add 0.5 ml of the *S. aureus* culture and gently agitate the tube to distribute the organisms uniformly. Note the time; at intervals of $2^1/_2$, 5, 10, and 15 min, transfer one loopful of the mixture to a tube of nutrient broth (see sketch).
2. Repeat step 1, using one of the products from group B.
3. Repeat steps 1 and 2, using *B. subtilis* as the test organism. NOTE: By staggering the times of addition, e.g., every $2^1/_2$ min, of test organism to the chemical agent, it is possible to conduct the tests simultaneously.

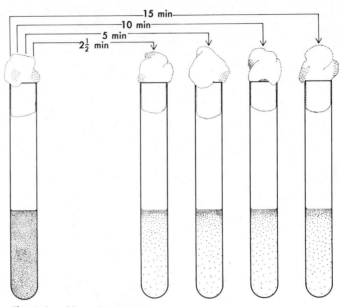

Chemical and bacteria

4. Inoculate a tube of nutrient broth with a loopful of S. *aureus* and another with a loopful of B. *subtilis* to serve as controls.
5. Incubate all tubes at 35°C for 48 hr.

RESULTS

Observe all the inoculated tubes for evidence of growth. Record presence of growth as + and absence of growth as 0. Record results in the table below. (Include results obtained by other members of the class who used different chemical agents.)

TEST ORGANISM	CHEMICAL AGENT	MINUTE INTERVALS				CONTROL
		2½	5	10	15	

QUESTIONS

1. How would you conduct an experiment to distinguish between bactericidal and bacteriostatic action of a chemical agent?

2. What is the phenol-coefficient technique? How does it differ from the procedure followed in this exercise?

3. List several reasons why the results of a test-tube evaluation of a disinfectant may not accurately reflect its performance in practical application.

4. Assume you have spilled a culture of *S. aureus* on the laboratory bench. How would you disinfect this area?

_____

_____

_____

_____

_____

_____

EXERCISE THIRTY-SIX
ANTIBIOTICS

REFERENCE: Text, chap. 25; MCM, chap. 37.

The susceptibility of microorganisms to many different antibiotics can be expediently determined by the disk-plate technique. This procedure consists of inoculating the organism in question on an agar plate, placing disks containing antibiotics on this inoculated surface, and, after incubation, observing zones of inhibition. The size of the zone of inhibition is influenced by a complex of factors such as the rate of diffusion of the drug through agar, the size of the inoculum, the rate of growth of the organism, and its susceptibility to the antibiotic.

MATERIALS

1. 100-ml trypticase-soy agar
2. Freshly prepared solutions (approximately 10 ml) of the following antibiotics: penicillin, 500 units/ml; tetracycline 1,500 μg/ml; streptomycin, 2,500 μg/ml; chloramphenicol, 1,500 μg/ml; Nystatin, 2,500 units/ml; Actidione (cycloheximide), 2,500 μg/ml
3. Absorbent paper disks ($^1/_4$ in.)
4. Small forceps
5. 5 sterile cotton swabs
6. 5 sterile petri dishes
7. Broth cultures of *Staphylococcus aureus*, *Escherichia coli*, *Mycobacterium smegmatis*, and *Saccharomyces cerevisiae*
8. Spore suspension of *Aspergillus niger*

PROCEDURE

1. Prepare five trypticase-soy-agar plates.
2. Inoculate the surface of each plate evenly and entirely, using a different organism for each plate. Use a cotton swab soaked in the culture (or spore suspension) to distribute the organisms over the agar surface.

3. Saturate a paper disk by touching the edge of the disk to the antibiotic solution. Place the impregnated disk near the periphery of the agar surface of an inoculated plate. See the sketches illustrating these manipulations. Place six disks (one of each antibiotic), evenly spaced, around the outer edge of the agar surface.

4. Incubate the plates inoculated with bacteria at 35°C for 48 hr and the yeast and mold plates 2 to 4 days at room temperature.

Impregnating disk with antibiotic solution.

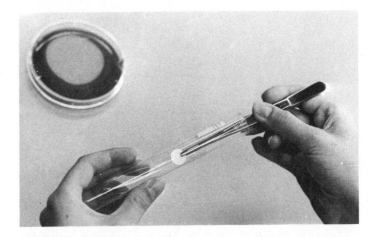

Placement of disk on inoculated agar plate.

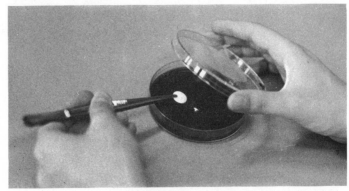

Examining a plate against background light to see whether there is inhibition of growth of microorganisms by antibiotics

RESULTS

1. Observe plates for zones of inhibition. Select two plates that exhibit sharp zones of inhibition, and sketch them.

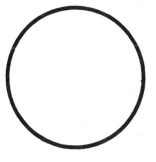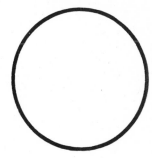

test organisms: _____   _____

2. With a millimeter rule, measure the diameter of all zones of inhibition and record in tabular form:

TEST ORGANISM	ANTIBIOTICS AND ZONES OF INHIBITION					
	PENI-CILLIN	TETRA-CYCLINE	STREPTO-MYCIN	CHLORAM-PHENICOL	NYSTATIN	ACTIDIONE
Staphylococcus aureus						
Escherichia coli						
Mycobacterium smegmatis						
Saccharomyces cerevisiae						
Aspergillus niger						

QUESTIONS

1. The absorbent disks used in this exercise absorb approximately 0.02 ml of solution. Calculate the number of micrograms (or units) of each antibiotic in the saturated disks.

_____

_____

_____

_____

_____

_____

2. Name the microorganism used to produce each of the antibiotics employed in this exercise.

_____

_____

_____

_____

3. What generalizations can be made with respect to the antimicrobial spectrum of each of these antibiotics?

_____

_____

_____

_____

_____

4. Assume that you have performed a susceptibility test using antibiotic A and antibiotic B against *Staphylococcus aureus*. The zone of inhibition produced by A is 15 mm; that produced by B is 30 mm. Does this mean that B is twice as effective as A? Explain.

_____

_____

_____

_____

_____

PART TWELVE
MICROORGANISMS
AND DISEASE

The procedures for the study of pathogenic microorganisms, particularly their characterization and identification, are no different from those used for other microorganisms. With pathogens, there is of course the additional test for virulence in animals or plants.

In medical microbiology diagnostic work, laboratory procedures are determined by the nature of the specimens and the pathogen suspected. For example, if a sputum specimen from a person suspected of having tuberculosis is submitted to the diagnostic laboratory, one of the first tests would be preparation and examination of an acid-fast smear. Additional tests would include inoculation of special media, e.g., Lowenstein-Jensen or Petragnani media, and inoculation of a guinea pig. On the other hand, if a fecal specimen from a suspected case of typhoid fever were received, the first test would be the inoculation of a selective medium. Following incubation, suspected colonies would be isolated in pure culture for subsequent biochemical and serological characterization.

When it is not possible to isolate the pathogen from the specimen, it is sometimes feasible to use an alternative approach, namely, a serological procedure. A specimen of blood is obtained from the patient, and the blood serum is used in serological tests with various antigens. The identification of a specific antibody in the patient's serum may reveal the agent responsible for his infection.

EXERCISE THIRTY–SEVEN
IMMUNOLOGY AND
SEROLOGY

Immunology is the study of properties of the host which confer resistance against specific infectious agents; serology is the study of antibodies which occur in serum. Specific acquired immunity or resistance may be natural or artificial, the former the result of disease and the latter of vaccination. In both cases antibodies against the antigens of the infecting or injected agent are formed. These antibodies can be measured by various serological tests. The three major tests used to measure antibody in clinical laboratories are precipitation, agglutination, and complement-fixation.

Precipitation is a reaction which occurs between a *soluble* antigen and its specific antibody. It can be demonstrated in several ways, one of the simplest being the ring test. A small amount of antibody or antiserum is placed in a capillary tube, and a small amount of antigen is carefully layered over the antibody. If the antibody is specific for the antigen, a fine line, or ring, of precipitate forms at the interface between the two within a few minutes. The ring test is very useful, particularly when only small amounts of either reagent are available, e.g., in medicolegal identification of bloodstains. In carrying out the precipitin reaction one uses a constant dilution of antibody and varying dilution of antigen because the bulk of the precipitate is formed by the antibody.

Agglutination, on the other hand, is the reaction which occurs between a *particulate* antigen and its specific antibody. Examples of such antigens include bacteria and erythrocytes. Agglutination reactions may be done in the test tube, where varying dilutions of antiserum are used with a constant amount of antigen, or on a slide. The former method gives a more quantitative measure of the amount of antibody present, whereas the latter gives a rapid answer to such questions as whether there is antibody in the serum to a particular antigen.

If the antibody is known, the latter method can be used to identify an unknown antigen. In agglutination reactions constant antigen and varying antibody are used because the bulk of the agglutinated material is formed by the antigen.

With some antigen-antibody systems no visible reaction occurs; in such cases complement-fixation may be used. Complement, which occurs in the serum of most warm-blooded animals, is a thermolabile complex made up of several components. It takes part in various serological reactions, and whenever an antigen-antibody combination occurs in the presence of complement, the complement is adsorbed or fixed. The fixation of complement (abbreviated C′) to an antigen-antibody complex is not necessarily visible and may have to be demonstrated by an indicator system. The most widely used indicator system is a combination of red blood cells and their specific antibody (hemolysin); this combination is known as a *sensitized* red-cell suspension. The sensitized cells, representing a specific antigen-antibody system, also fix complement, and in this case the combination of antigen-antibody and complement leads to *hemolysis,* or the dissolution of red blood cells with escape of the hemoglobin from the cell. The gross appearance changes from a turbid suspension of red blood cells showing a clear colorless super-

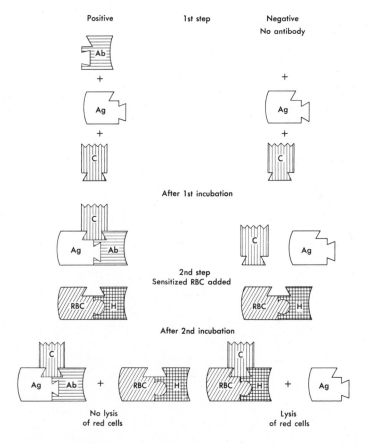

natant fluid after centrifuging to a transparent fluid when hemolysis has taken place with no change after centrifuging. In a complement-fixation test the antigen and antibody are allowed to react in the presence of C'. After the initial reaction period the indicator system is added and the mixture allowed to react. If the original antigen and antibody are homologous, i.e., specific for each other, no hemolysis is seen since the C' is bound. If the original antigen and antibody are heterologous, i.e., not specific, then hemolysis occurs since the C' is not fixed by the first system and is free to act on the sensitized cells of the indicator system. Thus, *failure* to obtain lysis denotes a *positive* reaction, while complete *hemolysis* indicates a *negative* reaction. The principle of complement fixation is shown in the accompanying diagram.

A. PRECIPITATION: RING TEST

This form of the precipitin test is widely used in forensic medicine in identifying blood stains and in detecting food adulteration. The suspected material is dissolved or infused in saline (0.85% sodium chloride), which is then serially diluted and tested with a variety of antisera. The appearance of a white ring of precipitate at the interface of antigen and antibody indicates a positive test.

REFERENCE: Text, chaps. 27 and 28.

MATERIALS

1. 1.0 ml extract A
2. 1.0 ml extract B
3. 2.0 ml antihuman rabbit serum (dispensed in two narrow tubes)
4. 2 Pasteur pipettes
5. Rack for narrow tubes

PROCEDURE

1. You are provided with two tubes labeled extract A and extract B, each containing a saline extract made from a different blood stain.
2. To determine whether either extract came from a human source you are provided with two narrow tubes containing antihuman rabbit serum (the blood serum of a rabbit immunized with human blood). Label these tubes A and B.
3. Using a fresh Pasteur pipette each time, carefully layer an equal amount of extract A over the antiserum in tube A and similarly an equal volume of extract B in tube B. (Avoid mixing; i.e., allow the extracts to run down the side.)
4. Place carefully in a rack without mixing and observe for at least 30 min.

RESULTS

Record the reaction of each tube with a + or −, i.e., ring or no ring:

Tube A (with extract A) = _____

Tube B (with extract B) = _____

QUESTIONS

1. Which extract was from a human source?

   _____

2. What disadvantages are there in precipitation tests carried out in solutions?

   _____

   _____

   _____

   _____

3. What other kinds of precipitation tests are there? Describe them briefly.

   _____

   _____

   _____

   _____

B. AGGLUTINATION: DETERMINATION OF BLOOD GROUPS

Serological tests are extensively used in diagnostic medical microbiology; they are highly sensitive and extremely specific. One kind of serological test is used to determine human blood groups; the groups, or types, that is, A, B, AB, and O, are established on the basis of the red-blood-cell antigens. Antibodies specific for the antigens cause the red blood cells to clump, or agglutinate.

REFERENCES: Text, chap. 28; MMM, chap. 9.

MATERIALS

1. Sterile disposable lancet
2. 70% isopropyl alcohol
3. Cotton sponge
4. Applicator stick
5. 1 drop of each per student of blood-grouping antisera anti-A and anti-B

PROCEDURE

1. Select a clean glass slide and mark off two circular areas with the wax marking pencil, each about the size of a dime. Label them A and B.
2. Wipe off the tip of your middle finger with a cotton sponge soaked with alcohol; allow this surface to dry, and then make a puncture through the skin with the sterile lancet.
3. Apply pressure along the finger in the direction of the puncture to facilitate obtaining droplets of blood; place one drop of blood within each circle made on the slide (step 1). Add a drop of anti-A serum to the circle labeled A and a drop of anti-B serum to the circle labeled B. Break an applicator stick in half and use a different half for each circle to mix the drops within the circles.
4. Examine the mixtures within each circle, macroscopically

and microscopically, for evidence of red-blood-cell clumping. The blood group can be determined from the following scheme of reactions.

REACTION OF RED BLOOD CELLS WITH ANTISERA		BLOOD GROUP
A	B	
None	None	O
None	Clumping	B
Clumping	None	A
Clumping	Clumping	AB

RESULTS

1. Sketch the appearance and arrangement of cells in each mixture.

2. Tabulate the number and percentage of each blood group in (a) your laboratory section and (b) in the entire class.

BLOOD GROUP	IN SECTION		IN CLASS	
	NUMBER	PERCENT	NUMBER	PERCENT
O				
A				
B				
AB				

QUESTIONS

1. Define the term "isoantibody" and explain its relevance to this exercise.

_____

_____

_____

_____

_____

_____

2. What is the practical significance of knowing your blood group?

    _____

    _____

    _____

    _____

    _____

    _____

3. What group or type of blood would the serum from your blood agglutinate? Why?

    _____

    _____

    _____

    _____

    _____

    _____

C. BACTERIAL AGGLUTINATION TESTS

The agglutination reaction is one of the most widely used serological tests for the identification of microorganisms. The procedure consists of mixing a suspension of the microorganism (agglutinogen) with serum containing antibody (agglutinin), incubating the mixture, and then observing for clumping of the bacterial cells. This procedure can be performed on a slide or in test tubes. Serological reactions are highly specific and are used very extensively for identification of bacterial species or "types" within a species. Many other applications are made of antigen-antibody reactions in biology and medicine.

REFERENCES: Text, chap. 28; MMM, chap. 9.

MATERIALS

1. Antiserum diluted for rapid slide-agglutination test
2. Antiserum for tube-agglutination technique
3. Normal serum
4. Heat-killed suspension of bacterial cells against which antisera were prepared
5. Physiological salt solution (0.85% sodium chloride)
6. 10 1.0-ml serological pipettes
7. 10 serological test tubes

PROCEDURE

SLIDE AGGLUTINATION

1. Using the glass-marking pencil, draw two circles about the size of a dime at opposite ends of a clean slide.

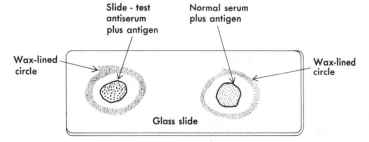

Slide - test antiserum plus antigen

Normal serum plus antigen

Wax-lined circle

Wax-lined circle

Glass slide

2. Within the area of one circle add one drop of antiserum (antiserum for slide test), and within the other add one drop of normal serum. To each of these drops, add one drop of the antigen (see sketch on preceding page).

3. Grasp the slide between the thumb and forefinger, and rock it gently back and forth. Observe the mixtures against a white background and in the presence of a good light source. Look for clumping (agglutination) of cells.

TUBE AGGLUTINATION

1. Arrange 10 serological test tubes in a line in a test-tube rack and label them 1 to 10.

2. Add 0.8 ml physiological saline to the first tube and 0.5 ml to all the rest (see protocol below).

Protocol

	TUBE NUMBER									
	1	2	3	4	5	6	7	8	9	10 (ANTIGEN CONTROL)
Saline, ml	0.8	0.5	0.5	0.5	0.5	0.5	0.5	0.5	0.5	0.5
Antiserum, ml	0.2									
Transfer to next tube, ml	0.5	0.5	0.5	0.5	0.5	0.5	0.5	0.5	*	
Antigen	0.5	0.5	0.5	0.5	0.5	0.5	0.5	0.5	0.5	0.5
Reciprocal of final serum dilution	10	20	40	80	160	320	640	1,280	2,560	

*0.5 ml from tube 9 discarded.

3. Pipette 0.2 ml of antiserum into the first tube. Using a clean pipette, mix the contents of the first tube by alternately sucking up and blowing back the mixture. Following this, transfer 0.5 ml from the first tube to the second tube. Mix the contents of tube 2 in a like manner, using a *clean* pipette, and then transfer 0.5 ml to the third tube. Continue this procedure through the ninth tube. The 0.5 ml removed from the ninth tube is discarded since the tenth tube serves as a control for the antigen suspension. This process of dilution (twofold-dilution series) is sketched.

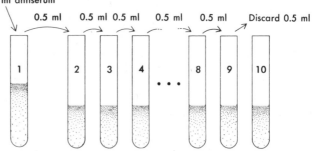

Initially contains
0.8 ml saline+
0.2 ml antiserum

Initially, all contain 0.5 ml saline

4. Add 0.5 ml of antigen suspension to each tube. Now grasp the rack containing the tubes with both hands and shake it vigorously back and forth in short abrupt strokes. Place the rack, with tubes, in a constant-temperature water bath (45°C) for 2 to 4 hr.

5. Observe each tube individually for evidence of clumping. NOTE: More pronounced reactions can be obtained by placing the tubes in a refrigerator overnight after the water-bath incubation.

RESULTS

1. Describe what occurred to the cells in each of the droplets in the slide-agglutination test.

2. Record the reaction observed in each tube by the following scheme: 4+ = complete clumping of all cells, fluid clear; 3+ = nearly complete clumping of all cells, fluid very slightly turbid; 2+ = moderate degree of clumping of cells, fluid moderately turbid; 1+ = slight degree of clumping of cells, fluid turbid; 0 = no clumping of cells, fluid reveals even suspension of cells.

DILUTIONS OF ANTISERUM AND DEGREE OF AGGLUTINATION								ANTIGEN CONTROL

QUESTIONS

1. Define the following: serum, antiserum, immune serum.

_____

_____

_____

_____

_____

_____

2. The titer of an antiserum is defined as the highest dilution at which clumping can be readily detected. What is the titer of the antiserum used in this exercise (tube-agglutination technique)?

_____

_____

3. How could you prepare an antiserum against a bacterial antigen?

_____

_____

_____

_____

_____

_____

_____

_____

_____

_____

_____

_____

4. How does an agglutination test differ from a precipitation test?

_____

_____

_____

_____

_____

_____

5. An antiserum produced against one species of *Salmonella* is likely to also agglutinate, at a lower titer, a different *Salmonella* sp. In light of the highly specific nature of antigen-antibody reactions, how can this be explained?

_____

_____

_____

_____

D. COMPLEMENT-FIXATION

Complement-fixation tests are widely used in the diagnosis of infectious diseases. Although they are considerably more elaborate and difficult to perform than agglutination or precipitation tests, they have a much wider range of application and can be carried out with antigens in soluble or particulate form and under conditions in which the antigen-antibody combination does not lead to visible reaction by any other method.

Careful standardization and titration of reagents used in the test are essential for valid results.

Four of the five components used in complement-fixation tests must be known, and only one component may represent the unknown factor. Either antigen or antibody is identified in the common complement-fixation tests.

MATERIALS

HEMOLYSIN TITRATION

*The saline used throughout the complement-fixation test contains 1.0 g magnesium sulfate per liter.

1. 1 ml hemolysin diluted 1:100 with 0.85% saline*
2. 5 ml complement diluted 1:10 with 0.85% saline
3. 5 ml 2% sheep red blood cells
4. 15 ml 0.85% saline
5. 4 1-ml pipettes
6. Rack with 9 serological test tubes
7. Water bath at 37°C

TITRATION OF COMPLEMENT

1. 6 ml hemolysin (2 MHD/ml)†
2. 15 ml 0.85% saline
3. 3.5 ml complement (1:10)
4. 6 ml 2% sheep red blood cells
5. Rack with 10 serological test tubes

DETERMINATION OF ANTIGENIC DOSE

†See Results for the definition of MHD.

1. 6.5 ml antigen solution in initial dilution
2. 5 ml antiserum (1:5 dilution)
3. 20 ml complement (4 MHD/ml)
4. 17 ml hemolysin (4 MHD/ml)

5. 17 ml 2% sheep red blood cells
6. Rack with 33 serological test tubes
7. 5 ml saline

**WASSERMAN TEST
(MODIFIED)**

1. 1.5 ml test serum (patient with suspected syphilis) heated at 56°C for 30 min to inactivate complement
2. 1.5 ml normal serum
3. 5 ml complement (appropriately diluted)
4. 2 ml Wasserman antigen (lipoidal extract of beef heart titrated and standardized)
5. 8 ml 0.85% saline
6. 5 ml hemolysin (against sheep red blood cells, appropriately diluted)
7. 6 ml 2% sheep red blood cells
8. 10 1.0-ml pipettes (use each only for its specific reagent)

PROCEDURE

Titrations of hemolysin and complement are preliminary to any complement-fixation reaction and in practice are set up each day complement-fixation tests are performed. The antigen used in any complement-fixation test must also be standardized and titrated. The antigen must be tested for anticomplementary and hemolytic activity, and the optimal concentration to be used must be determined. However, all these tests need be done only once for each batch of antigen, provided it is stable.

HEMOLYSIN TITRATION

1. Add 0.5 ml saline to each of nine tubes (see protocol below).
2. Add 0.5 ml hemolysin to tube 1, mix, and make halving dilutions of the hemolysin up to and including tube 8.
3. Add 0.5 ml complement to each tube.
4. Add 0.5 ml 2% red blood cells (RBC) to each tube.
5. Add 1 ml saline to each tube. (Saline is added here to bring the volume to 2.5 ml, the standard volume adopted for our purposes. A constant volume must be maintained in all tests.)
6. Shake the rack and place it in the water bath at 37°C for 1 hr.

Protocol for Hemolysin
Titration

TUBE	1	2	3	4	5	6	7	8	CONTROL 9
Saline	0.5	0.5	0.5	0.5	0.5	0.5	0.5	0.5	0.5
Hemolysin (1:100)	0.5				Halving dilutions				
Dilution of hemolysin	1:200	1:400	1:800	1:1,600	1:3,200	1:6,400	1:12,800	1:25,600	
Complement (1:10)	0.5	0.5	0.5	0.5	0.5	0.5	0.5	0.5	0.5

Protocol for Hemolysin
Titration (con't.)

RBC, 2%	0.5	0.5	0.5	0.5	0.5	0.5	0.5	0.5	0.5
Saline	1	1	1	1	1	1	1	1	1
Final dilution of hemolysin	1:1,000	1:2,000	1:4,000	1:8,000	1:16,000	1:32,000	1:64,000	1:128,000	

TITRATION OF
COMPLEMENT

1. Follow the protocol below after setting up 10 serological tubes in a rack.

TUBE	1	2	3	4	5	6	7	8	9	CONTROL 10
Saline	0.45	0.4	0.35	0.3	0.25	0.2	0.15	0.1	0.05	0.5
Complement (1:10)	0.05	0.1	0.15	0.2	0.25	0.3	0.35	0.4	0.45	
Hemolysin (2 MHD/ml)	0.5	0.5	0.5	0.5	0.5	0.5	0.5	0.5	0.5	0.5
RBC, 2%	0.5	0.5	0.5	0.5	0.5	0.5	0.5	0.5	0.5	0.5
Saline	1	1	1	1	1	1	1	1	1	1

2. Shake the rack, incubate for 1 hr in a 37°C water bath and read the results.

DETERMINATION OF
ANTIGENIC DOSE

1. Prepare a master titration of the antigen provided through six doubling dilutions (1:40 through 1:1,280) in 3-ml quantities.
2. Arrange five rows of serological tubes with six tubes in each row.
3. Pipette the antigen dilutions as follows:

> Tube 1 of each row: 0.5 ml 1:40 antigen
> Tube 2 of each row: 0.5 ml 1:80 antigen
> Tube 3 of each row: 0.5 ml 1:160 antigen
> Tube 4 of each row: 0.5 ml 1:320 antigen
> Tube 5 of each row: 0.5 ml 1:640 antigen
> Tube 6 of each row: 0.5 ml 1:1,280 antigen

4. Prepare a master titration of a strongly positive anti-serum through five doubling dilutions (1:5 through 1:80) in 4-ml quantities.
5. Pipette serum dilutions as follows:

> Add 0.5 ml 1:5 serum to each tube in first row
> Add 0.5 ml 1:10 serum to each tube in second row
> Add 0.5 ml 1:20 serum to each tube in third row
> Add 0.5 ml 1:40 serum to each tube in fourth row
> Add 0.5 ml 1:80 serum to each tube in fifth row

6. Add 0.5 ml complement (2 units) to each tube.
7. Prepare these controls.

a. Serum control: 0.5 ml 1:5 serum
      0.5 ml complement (2 units)
      0.5 ml saline

b. Antigen control: 0.5 ml antigen 1:40
      0.5 ml complement (2 units)
      0.5 ml saline

c. Hemolytic system control: 0.5 ml complement (2 units)
      1.0 ml saline

8. Incubate in a 37°C water bath for 30 to 60 min.
9. After incubation, add 0.5 ml hemolysin (2 units) and 0.5 ml 2% red blood cells to each tube.
10. Mix the contents by shaking the rack and incubate at 37°C for 30 min.
11. Read the results.

WASSERMAN TEST (MODIFIED)

The ingredients to be put into each tube are tabulated as follows:

PIPETTE	INGREDIENT	CODE	TUBE NUMBER 1	2	3	4	5	6	7	8	9*
A	Test serum, ml	a	0	0	0	0	0.5	0.5	0	0	0
B	Normal serum control, ml	b	0	0	0	0	0	0	0.5	0.5	0
C	Complement, ml	c	0	0.5	0.5	0.5	0.5	0.5	0.5	0.5	0.5
D	Antigen, ml	d	0	0	0	0.5	0	0.5	0	0.5	0
E	Saline, ml	e	1.5	1.5	1.0	0.5	0.5	0.0	0.5	0.0	1.0

*Tube 9 is to be heated at 56°C for 30 min instead of incubating to show inactivation of complement. Replace in your series.

Shake till mixed and place the tubes in the water bath at 37°C for 1 hr, after which add the following:

PIPETTE	INGREDIENT	CODE	TUBE NUMBER 1	2	3	4	5	6	7	8	9*
F	Hemolysin, ml	f	0.5	0	0.5	0.5	0.5	0.5	0.5	0.5	0.5
G	RBC suspension, ml	g	0.5	0.5	0.5	0.5	0.5	0.5	0.5	0.5	0.5

Replace the tubes in the water bath for 1 hr, shaking again halfway through this period. At the end of the hour read your results *without further shaking*. NOTE: The following are the contents of each tube and the results that should be obtained.

1. Hemolysin + RBC = no hemolysis (complement lacking)
2. Complement + RBC = no hemolysis (hemolysin lacking)
3. Complement + hemolysin + RBC = hemolysis

4. Antigen + complement + hemolysin + RBC = hemolysis (no antibody)

5. Positive serum + complement + hemolysin + RBC = hemolysis (no antigen)

6. *Positive serum + antigen + complement + hemolysin + RBC = no hemolysis

7. Normal serum + complement + hemolysin + RBC = hemolysis (no antigen, no antibody)

8. †Normal serum + antigen + complement + hemolysin + RBC = hemolysis

9. Complement inactivated by heat + hemolysin + RBC = no hemolysis

*This is a positive test for complement-fixation because there is present specific antibody which is reacting with the antigen and fixes the complement.

†This is a negative test for complement-fixation because there is no specific antibody present to react with the antigen and thus fix the complement.

For the test to be reliable it is necessary to be sure that:

Hemolysin (f) alone does not lyse the corpuscles (tube 1).

Complement (c) alone does not lyse the corpuscles (tube 2).

Complement (c) + hemolysin (f) + RBC (g) give complete hemolysis (tube 3).

Antigen (d) alone does not fix the complement (tube 4).

Positive serum (a) alone does not fix the complement (tube 5).

Normal serum (b) alone does not fix the complement (tube 7).

These are your controls

RESULTS
HEMOLYSIN TITRATION

Record your readings as follows: complete hemolysis (clear red fluid), 4+; partial hemolysis (red fluid but also cells in suspension), 2 +; no hemolysis (turbid cell suspension), 0.

	TUBE								
	1	2	3	4	5	6	7	8	9
Dilution of hemolysin	1:1,000	1:2,000	1:4,000	1:8,000	1:16,000	1:32,000	1:64,000	1:128,000	
Reading									

The highest dilution of hemolysin giving complete (100 percent) hemolysis represents 1 unit of hemolysin under the conditions of the test (volume of 2.5 ml, complement 1:10, 2% red blood cells, etc.). This unit is termed the *minimal hemolytic dose* (MHD). (A more accurate end point is obtained by determining the amount or dilution which will give 50 percent lysis. However, such determinations require more complex titrations and equipment and are not essential in the routine performance of complement-fixation tests.) In the actual test, 2 to 3 MHD of hemolysin is used per volume unit, for example, 1 MHD in 0.5 ml of 1:32,000 dilution; 0.5 ml of 1:16,000 = 2 MHD.

TITRATION OF COMPLEMENT

Read degrees of hemolysis as in hemolysin titration*. The *smallest* amount of complement giving hemolysis equals 1 MHD (2 to 3 MHD of complement is used in the actual test).

	TUBE									
	1	2	3	4	5	6	7	8	9	CONTROL 10
C' ml	0.05	0.1	0.15	0.2	0.25	0.3	0.35	0.4	0.45	
Reading										

*4+ = complete hemolysis
 2+ = partial hemolysis
 0 = no hemolysis

DETERMINATION OF ANTIGENIC DOSE

1. Record results in the table below. Be sure to inspect the controls first.

SERUM DILUTIONS	ANTIGEN DILUTIONS					
	1:40	1:80	1:160	1:320	1:640	1:1,280
1:80						
1:40						
1:20						
1:10						
1:5						

2. The dose of antigen to be employed in the complement-fixation test is the largest amount giving complete hemolysis with the smallest amount of serum.

WASSERMAN TEST
(MODIFIED)

1. Read the results and note in the table below, + for hemolysis and − for no hemolysis.

	TUBE								
	1	2	3	4	5	6	7	8	9
Reading									

2. Interpret your results as described in the procedure.

EXERCISE THIRTY-EIGHT
AIRBORNE INFECTIONS*
A. THE CORYNEBACTERIA AND
THE GRAM-POSITIVE
COCCI

The genus *Corynebacterium* comprises nonsporeforming gram-positive rods. There are many species in this genus, including species pathogenic to man, animals, and plants. The most important human pathogen is C. *diphtheriae*, the causative agent of diphtheria. C. *diphtheriae* produces a potent exotoxin which is antigenic and specifically neutralized by antitoxin.

The streptococci are chain-forming gram-positive cocci. They are for the most part parasites living on the mucous membranes of man and the lower animals. Some species are present on the mucous membranes, invading and causing infection only when the tissue resistance is low. Others, e.g., *Streptococcus pyogenes,* are very highly pathogenic, and, except in a small percentage of the population who are carriers, their very presence means infection. S. *pyogenes* is a pus-producing organism. Some of the streptococci are of very considerable importance in the dairy industry.

Diplococcus pneumoniae is characteristically a somewhat elongated gram-positive coccus which occurs in pairs with flattened opposed surfaces and pointed distal ends. Each pair is surrounded by a capsule. The organism may form short chains, in which case the entire chain is surrounded by a capsule with indentations between the pairs. Since this organism may form chains and the capsule may be lost on artificial cultivation, and since colonies on blood agar are surrounded by a zone of alpha hemolysis, it may be difficult to distinguish it from alpha-hemolytic streptococci. Two tests make the distinction, shown in the following scheme.

ORGANISM	BILE SOLUBILITY	INULIN FERMENTATION
D. pneumoniae	+	+
Alpha-hemolytic streptococci, e.g., S. salivarius	—	—

*Students are reminded to exercise proper care in the handling of the microorganisms used in "Microorganisms and Disease" exercises.

Laboratory Exercises in Microbiology

REFERENCE: Text, chap. 29; MCM, chaps. 5, 6, 7, and 10.

MATERIALS

1. 1 each of *Corynebacterium diphtheriae* and *C. xerosis* cultures on Loeffler's slopes (slants)
2. Gram stains
3. Neisser's stain (for metachromatic granules)
4. 2 tubes cystine trypticase agar (CTA) medium with glucose
5. 2 tubes CTA medium with sucrose
6. 2 tubes CTA medium with maltose
7. 2 tubes CTA medium with inulin
8. 1 blood-agar plate with a mixture of *S. salivarius*, *S. pyogenes*, and *S. faecalis*
9. 1 blood agar plate with a mixture of *S. salivarius* and *D. pneumoniae*
10. 1 blood-agar plate of *Staphylococcus aureus*
11. Brain-heart-infusion-broth cultures of *Streptococcus salivarius*, *S. pyogenes*, *S. faecalis*, and *D. pneumoniae*
12. 0.25 ml type I pneumococcal antiserum
13. 0.25 ml type II pneumococcal antiserum
14. 1 Todd Hewitt broth culture of *S. salivarius*
15. 1 Todd Hewitt broth culture of *D. pneumoniae*
16. 1.5 ml sodium deoxycholate solution
17. 1 narrow tube (0.5 ml) group A streptococcal antiserum
18. 1 narrow tube (0.5 ml) group B streptococcal antiserum
19. 2 tubes (1 ml each) of unknown streptococcal antigen
20. Methylene blue stain
21. Reagents for capsule stain
22. 1 1-ml pipette
23. 1 Pasteur pipette

PROCEDURE
THE CORYNEBACTERIA

1. Cultures of *C. diphtheriae* and *C. xerosis* are provided on Loeffler's slopes. Make two films and stain with Gram's stain and Neisser's stain.*
2. Inoculate *C. diphtheriae* and *C. xerosis* each into the following set of CTA medium sugars: glucose, sucrose, and maltose.
3. Incubate at 37°C for 24 hr and observe the results.

THE GRAM-POSITIVE COCCI

1. You are provided with three blood-agar plates. One has been inoculated with a mixture of three species of the genus *Streptococcus*: *S. salivarius* (alpha-hemolytic), *S. pyogenes* (beta-hemolytic), and *S. faecalis* (nonhemolytic, or gamma, type). The other has been inoculated with two species of the chain-forming cocci *S. salivarius* and *D. pneumoniae*, both of which produce the same change in blood agar, i.e., alpha hemolysis, but which can be differentiated nevertheless by subtle differences in colony form. The third plate has been inoculated with *Staph. aureus* so that you will have the opportunity of making a direct comparison between colonies of *Staphylococcus* and those of the chain-forming cocci.

*Neisser's stain method:
1. Mix 2 parts of Neisser A with 1 part of Neisser B and stain film for a few seconds.
2. Rinse rapidly in water.
3. Counterstain with Neisser C for 30 sec.
4. Wash rapidly in water, blot and dry. Observe for blue-black granules and yellowish-brown cytoplasm.

2. Note particularly any alterations that the various species have produced in the blood. Use transmitted light (daylight provides the best results). Be certain that you can recognize the different forms of hemolysis produced by the chain-forming cocci.

3. Stain *D. pneumoniae* and any of the cultures of streptococci for capsules from the blood-agar plates.

4. You are provided with brain-heart-infusion-broth cultures of *S. salivarius*, *S. pyogenes*, *S. faecalis*, and *D. pneumoniae*. Make gram-stained preparations to study particularly the arrangement of the cells. Note that chain formation in the streptococci is poorly developed when the organisms are grown on a solid medium but well marked in a fluid medium.

5. You are provided with two tubes of inulin CTA medium.

6. Inoculate one tube with *D. pneumoniae*, the other with *S. salivarius*. Incubate at 37°C and observe the results after 24 hr.

7. The most convenient test for determining types in the pneumococcus is the Neufeld quellung reaction. This test is based on the fact that if a suspension of encapsulated pneumococci, say type I, is admixed with homologous antiserum, a reaction occurs between the capsular antigen and its homologous antibody. This results in a marked swelling of the capsule, which is visible on microscopic examination. The advantage of the Neufeld reaction is that it can be performed directly on any specimen containing sufficient numbers of pneumococci to be detected on microscopic examination, e.g., sputum from a case of pneumonia. You are provided with types I and II pneumococcal antisera.

8. Place a loopful of the broth suspension of *D. pneumoniae* on a slide (broth suspension from step 4 above). Flame the loop and add 2 loopfuls of the type I antiserum. Flame the loop again and add less than a loopful of methylene blue as a stain for the organisms. Mix the suspension, serum, and dye with the loop. Drop on a cover slip and examine under oil immersion. Repeat the entire procedure, this time using type II antiserum. Capsular swelling is best observed if the light intensity is reduced.

9. You are given cultures in Todd Hewitt broth of *S. salivarius* and *D. pneumoniae*. To each of these cultures add 0.5 ml sodium deoxycholate, shake, and note in which the turbidity due to growth is cleared. This is the bile-solubility test. NOTE: A buffered broth like Todd Hewitt maintains the pH of the culture in the range of optimal activity of autolytic enzymes which account for the lysis of *D. pneumoniae*. The bile salts play their part in this test in that they speed up a process, for purposes of diagnosis convenience, that would actually occur spontaneously under prolonged incubation of the cultures.

10. Now carry out the Lancefield grouping of beta- and nonhemolytic streptococci (a precipitation reaction). The beta-hemolytic and nonhemolytic streptococci can be divided into groups on the basis of Lancefield's precipitation tests. In this exercise it is not possible to carry through the entire test, i.e., isolation of the organism, its preparation in pure culture, extraction of its antigen, etc. Instead you are provided with the antigen solution which has been extracted from a beta-hemolytic streptococcus.

11. You are also provided with two samples of stock anti-streptococcal sera, a group A serum and a group B serum, each contained in a precipitation tube. With the pipette provided, carefully overlay each serum sample with 10 drops of the antigen solution. Avoid mixing and take care not to touch the Pasteur pipette to the serum samples during the layering of the antigen.

12. Note the development, within a few minutes, of a distinct ring of precipitate at the interface between the two fluids in one of the tubes.

RESULTS

1. Describe the gram stain and Neisser's stain of C. *diphtheriae* and C. *xerosis*.

2. Record the sugar reactions of C. *diphtheriae* and C. *xerosis* with + for acid production (positive) and − for no reaction.

SPECIES	CTA MEDIUM WITH		
	GLUCOSE	SUCROSE	MALTOSE
Corynebacterium diphtheriae			
Corynebacterium xerosis			

+ = acid (yellow)
− = no acid produced (red)

3. Describe the hemolytic reaction of S. *salivarius*, S. *pyogenes*, and S. *faecalis*.

4. Note the results of the capsule stains with D. *pneumoniae* and other cultures of streptococci on the blood-agar plates.

5. Draw the cell arrangements:

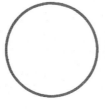
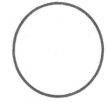

Streptococcus salivarius   Streptococcus pyogenes

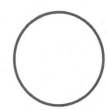

Streptococcus faecalis   Diplococcus pneumoniae

6. Give the results of inulin fermentation by

   D. pneumoniae: _____

   S. salivarius: _____

7. What was the type (I or II) of the pneumococcus in the suspension?

8. Describe the results of the bile-solubility test on

   S. salivarius: _____

   D. pneumoniae: _____

   How do these results correlate with the inulin-fermentation test?

9. What is the group of the streptococcus from which your antigen was extracted?

QUESTIONS

1. How is a blood-agar medium prepared?

   _____

   _____

   _____

   _____

   _____

2. Blood agar is regarded as both a differential and an enriched medium. Explain.

    _____

    _____

    _____

    _____

    _____

    _____

    _____

3. Describe a method, other than that used in this experiment, which would demonstrate hemolytic activity of bacteria.

    _____

    _____

    _____

    _____

    _____

    _____

    _____

B. THE MYCOBACTERIA, NEISSERIAS, AND BRUCELLAE

Laboratory Exercises in Microbiology

The genus *Mycobacterium* consists of acid-fast bacteria, including *M. tuberculosis* var. *hominis,* which causes tuberculosis primarily in man.

Members of the *Neisseria* group are gram-negative ellipsoidal cells occurring characteristically as paired cocci with the division line found along the axis of the paired cells. Some of the species are important human pathogens.

Another group of gram-negative rods are smaller in size than the bacteria you have seen during the first part of this course. They are grouped together in Bergey's manual, 7th edition, under the family Brucellaceae. Although they are smaller than organisms like *Escherichia coli,* there is a marked degree of pleomorphism characteristic of this group. Long, straight and curved filaments, balloon and stalked forms, and bipolar staining are seen in both the motile and nonmotile species. The group is predominantly and obligately parasitic and includes highly pathogenic organisms for man and other warm-blooded animals. The causative organisms of whooping cough, brucellosis, plague, and tularemia (as well as other serious infections) are found in this group of small gram-negative rods. They are generally parasitic in the respiratory tract or enter the body by inhalation or through some injured part of the skin. They are not enteric parasites or pathogens. The majority of the species require body-fluid enrichment or the incorporation of specific growth factors in a medium for isolation and subculture. Identification of genera and species depends upon cultural, biochemical, and serological characterization and, for the most important pathogenic species, upon a pathogenicity test in a suitable laboratory animal.

REFERENCE: Text, chap. 29; MCM, chaps. 8, 9, 14, 19, 20, and 23.

MATERIALS

1. Tube of tuberculous sputum (autoclaved) or culture of *Mycobacterium smegmatis*

2. 1 ascitic-agar slope of *Neisseria meningitidis*
3. 1 brain-heart-infusion-agar slope of *N. catarrhalis*
4. Gram stains
5. 1 18-hr culture of *N. meningitidis* on ascitic-agar plate
6. Freshly prepared tube of 1% tetramethyl-*p*-phenylenedia-mine dihydrochloride
7. 1 blood-agar plate of *Pasteurella multocida*
8. 1 Fildes agar plate of *Haemophilus influenzae*
9. Methylene blue stain

PROCEDURE
THE MYCOBACTERIA

Prepare and examine gram-stained and acid-fast stained films from the tuberculous sputum (or *M. smegmatis* culture) provided. This sample of sputum from an active case of tuberculosis has been sterilized by autoclaving to avoid the chances of infection.

THE NEISSERIAS

1. You are provided with *N. meningitidis* on an ascitic-agar slope and *N. catarrhalis* on a brain-heart-infusion-agar slope.
2. Note the cultural characteristics of the two species.
3. Make and study gram-stained films of each of the two species. Note the staining reaction, size, shape, and arrangement of the cells. Note particularly that there is no way of distinguishing between species in the genus on a morphological basis.
4. You are provided with an 18-hr culture of *N. meningitidis* grown on an especially enriched medium (ascitic-agar plate). Flood the plate with a 1% solution of tetramethyl-*p*-phenylenediamine dihydrochloride. This is a test for the presence of an *oxidase* in *Neisseria*. If positive, the colonies turn a bright purple. It is a useful test to detect the presence of *Neisseria* on plates inoculated from specimens which may contain a variety of contaminating organisms.

THE BRUCELLAE

A few representative species are offered for examination of colonial and microscopic morphology.

1. Examine the colonial morphology of *P. multocida* on blood agar and *H. influenzae* on Fildes agar.
2. Carry out gram-stain tests on each. Observe the gram reaction, size, and shape of the cells.
3. Carry out a methylene blue stain on each of the organisms and look for characteristic bipolar staining.

RESULTS

1. What are the gram stain and acid-fast stain reactions of *Mycobacterium?*

2. Describe the cultural characteristics of *N. meningitidis:*

   N. catarrhalis:

3. Illustrate the relative size, shape, and arrangement of cells of

   Neisseria meningitidis   *Neisseria catarrhalis*
   Gram reaction_____   Gram reaction_____

4. What is the result of the oxidase test on *N. meningitidis?*

5. Describe the colonial morphology of
   P. multocida:

   H. influenzae:

6. Illustrate the relative size and shape:

Pasteurella multocida
Gram reaction_____

Haemophilus influenzae
Gram reaction_____

7. Draw the appearance of the cells, after methylene blue staining:

Pasteurella multocida

Haemophilus influenzae

QUESTIONS

1. What is the "cord factor" packeting of virulent M. *tuberculosis* var. *hominis*?

_____

_____

_____

2. What is meant by the term BCG?

_____

_____

_____

3. What organism causes leprosy?

_____

4. How is Fildes enrichment agar prepared?

EXERCISE THIRTY-NINE
FOOD- AND
WATERBORNE
DISEASES

Among the gram-negative rods are species of bacteria commonly found in the intestinal tract of man and/or animal, including many well-known pathogens of the gastrointestinal and urinary tracts. These so-called enteric bacilli are all about 0.5 by 1.0 to 3.0 μm in size; some are motile, with peritrichous flagella, and others are nonmotile. Included among the enteric bacilli are intestinal commensals such as *Escherichia coli*. Examples of pathogenic enteric bacilli include species of *Salmonella*, which are the causative agents of typhoid and paratyphoid fevers, and of *Shigella*, which are the causative agents of bacillary dysentery.

Although not usually an enteric organism *Klebsiella pneumoniae* will be included in this exercise because certain cultural and biochemical characteristics are similar to those of enteric bacteria. Lesions due to *K. pneumoniae* may occur in any part of the body but are more frequent as a severe type of pneumonia.

Brucella is a genus of small gram-negative rods belonging to the family Brucellaceae mentioned earlier. There are three members in this genus, and man contracts the disease brucellosis either by direct contact with infected animals such as goats, cows, and swine or by consumption of their milk or milk products.

The family Micrococcaceae consists of several genera of the cluster-forming cocci. The most important genus in the family is *Staphylococcus*, of which there are two species, *Staph. aureus (pyogenes)*, which is pathogenic, and *Staph. epidermidis*, which is not.

Laboratory Exercises in Microbiology

REFERENCE: Text, chap. 30;
MCM, chap. 16.

MATERIALS

1. Trypticase-soy-agar plate containing a mixture of *Escherichia coli, Salmonella typhimurium* and *Salmonella* sp.

2. MacConkey agar plate with the same mixture as in item 1
3. Trypticase-soy-agar plate containing a mixture of *Shigella* sp., *K. pneumoniae*, and *Proteus* sp. (nonswarming strain)
4. MacConkey agar plate with the same mixture as in item 3
5. Capsule stains
6. Trypticase-soy-agar slope cultures of *E. coli, S. typhimurium, Salmonella* sp., *Shigella* sp., *K. pneumoniae, Proteus* sp., *Staph. aureus* and *Staph. epidermidis*
7. 5 tubes lactose tryptone water with Durham tube
8. 5 tubes glucose tryptone water with Durham tube
9. 7 tubes mannitol tryptone water with Durham tube
10. 5 tubes iron agar
11. 2 unknown cultures labeled A and B for *Salmonella* antiserum test
12. Test tube containing anti-*Salmonella* serum
13. Blood-agar plate containing a mixture of *Staph. aureus* and *Staph. epidermidis*
14. Gram stains
15. 2 tubes nutrient gelatin
16. 2 tubes oxalated rabbit plasma
17. 37°C water bath
18. Prepared slide of *Brucella abortus*

PROCEDURE
THE ENTERICS

1. You are provided with two sets of plates with trypticase-soy agar and MacConkey agar. Set A (one plate of each medium) contains the mixed culture of *E. coli, S. typhimurium,* and another *Salmonella* species. Set B contains the mixed culture of *Shigella* sp., *K. pneumoniae,* and a nonswarming strain of *Proteus.* Note and describe the growth characteristics of these organisms on both media.
2. Do capsule stains on films of *E. coli* and *K. pneumoniae.*
3. Cultures used in steps 1 and 2 above are provided on trypticase-soy-agar slopes. Make gram-stained films of all six cultures and do hanging-drop motility tests.
4. Use each of the agar slope cultures in step 3 above, with the exception of *K. pneumoniae,* to inoculate the following media: lactose, glucose, and mannitol in tryptone water and the tube of iron agar. Incubate at 37°C for 24 hr. (See the simplified key provided in this exercise for the identification of the enterics based on major physiological characters.)
5. You are provided with cultures labeled A and B and a test tube containing anti-*Salmonella* serum. Using the following procedure, determine which one of the two cultures is *S. typhimurium.* On the upper side of a clean glass slide make a circle with a grease pencil (about the size of a penny) in the central portion. To the center of this circle add a loopful of saline. Admix evenly a small portion of growth (antigen) from the slope. Add a drop of anti-*Salmonella* serum (anti-

body) provided. Slowly rock the slide several times and then observe for agglutination.

THE BRUCELLA

You are provided with a prepared slide of *Brucella abortus*. Observe the morphology of the organism.

THE STAPHYLOCOCCI

1. You are provided with a blood-agar plate which has been inoculated with a mixture of *Staph. aureus (pyogenes)* and *Staph. epidermidis*.

2. Study and record the colony form and pigmentation, etc., of the two species as they occur as discrete colonies on the blood-agar plate and as confluent growth on the trypticase-soy-agar slopes.

3. Prepare gram-stained films of each of the two species. Examine the films for gram reaction and the characteristic grouping of the cells (make your films from the slope cultures). Inoculate each of the two species into (a) tryptone water containing mannitol and (b) a tube containing nutrient gelatin. Incubate at 37°C for 24 hr.

4. You are supplied with two tubes of oxalated rabbit plasma. Add a heavy loopful of the *Staph. aureus* culture to one tube. Add a heavy loopful of *Staph. epidermidis* to the other tube. Distribute the growth in the plasma by shaking and place both tubes in the water bath at 37°C. Examine the tubes after 2 hr. The pathogenic *Staph. aureus* has the ability to clot citrated or oxalated blood plasma, whereas the non-pathogenic species does not.

. RESULTS

1. Describe the growth characteristics of the following organisms on trypticase-soy agar:

   E. coli: _____

   _____

   S. typhimurium: _____

   _____

   Salmonella sp.: _____

   _____

   Shigella sp.: _____

   _____

   K. pneumoniae: _____

   _____

   Proteus sp.: _____

   _____

2. Describe the growth characteristics of the following organisms on MacConkey agar:

   E. coli: _____

   _____

   S. typhimurium: _____

   _____

   Salmonella sp.: _____

   _____

   Shigella sp.: _____

   _____

   K. pneumoniae: _____

   _____

Proteus sp.: _____

3. Draw the appearance of the cells after capsule staining:

 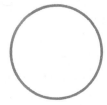

Escherichia coli   *Klebsiella pneumoniae*

4. Note the results of gram staining and motility testing on the species tabulated below. (Use + or —.)

SPECIES	GRAM REACTION	MOTILITY
Escherichia coli		
Salmonella typhimurium		
Salmonella sp.		
Shigella sp.		
Klebsiella pneumoniae		
Proteus sp.		

5. Record the results of fermentation on the organisms tabulated.

ORGANISM	TRYPTONE WATER WITH		
	LACTOSE	GLUCOSE	MANNITOL
Escherichia coli			
Salmonella typhimurium			
Salmonella sp.			
Shigella sp.			
Proteus sp.			

Do these results agree (or disagree) with the simplified key provided for the identification of the enterics?

6. Which culture, A or B, was *S. typhimurium*?

7. Draw the morphology of the prepared slide of *B. abortus*:

8. Describe the colonial growth characteristics (margin, eleva-
    tion, pigmentation, etc.) on blood agar:
    Staph. aureus: _____

    _____

    Staph. epidermidis: _____

    _____

    How do these characteristics compare with the confluent
    growth on trypticase-soy-agar slopes?

    _____

9. Report the gram-stain reaction and cell arrangement:

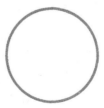

Staphylococcus aureus   *Staphylococcus epidermidis*
Gram reaction_____   Gram reaction_____

10. Note the results of the biochemical activities of *Staph.
    aureus* and *Staph. epidermidis* in the following table:

SPECIES	MANNITOL IN TRYPTONE WATER	NUTRIENT GELATIN
Staphylococcus aureus		
Staphylococcus epidermidis		

11. Give the results of the coagulase test on:

Staph. aureus: _____

_____

Staph. epidermidis: _____

_____

Simplified key based on
major physiological
characters of the enteric
bacilli.

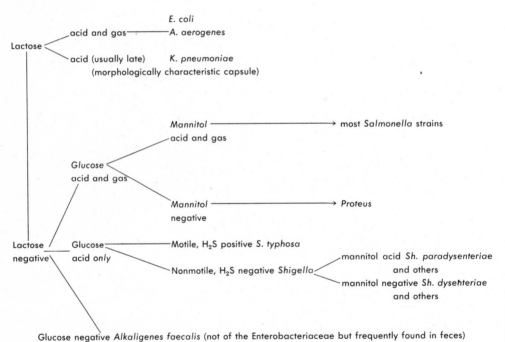

QUESTIONS

1. *Staph. aureus* is a "pyogenic" organism. What do we mean by this?

_____

_____

_____

2.   Define the term "virulence."

_____

_____

_____

3.   What is the Widal test?

_____

_____

_____

_____

4.   What is phagocytosis?

_____

_____

_____

_____

EXERCISE FORTY
CONTACT DISEASES

In this exercise examples of microorganisms causing the so-called contact diseases will be studied. Contact diseases is used in a broad sense and includes not only diseases transmitted by direct contact with an infected individual but also infections which occur through trauma or injury or diseases transmitted by means of a vector, usually an arthropod.

A large number of pathogenic microorganisms are capable of causing contact diseases in man. Some you have already studied because they can also be transmitted in other ways, and some will be new to you.

One family of microorganisms, Treponemataceae, is responsible for a number of diseases in this category. The bacteria in this family are spiral; most cannot be readily cultivated and are difficult to stain. Most are parasitic in vertebrates, and some are pathogenic. There are three genera: *Borrelia, Leptospira,* and *Treponema*. One of the prime examples of a direct contact disease, syphilis, is caused by *T. pallidum*. This is a tightly coiled organism with pointed ends and 8 to 14 spirals.

Gonorrhea is another example of a direct contact disease. It too is a venereal disease and is caused by *Neisseria gonorrhoeae,* a gram-negative coccus.

Many organisms can enter the body and cause infection through wounds or abrasions in the skin and mucous membranes. They include the hemolytic streptococci, the staphylococci, and the clostridia. The latter, normally found in the soil, are anaerobes. When wounds are contaminated with species of the clostridia, such conditions as gas gangrene and tetanus may result.

A number of diseases are transmitted by arthropods and include plague, caused by *Pasteurella pestis,* which is transmitted by the bite of infected rat fleas; yellow fever, caused by a virus transmitted by bites of the mosquito *Aedes aegypti;* the virus encephalitides, transmitted by insect vectors; and malaria, caused by a protozoan transmitted by a mosquito.

Many superficial mycotic infections, known as the dermatophytoses, are frequently transmitted by direct contact with infected individuals.

REFERENCE: Text, chap. 31; MCM, chaps. 9, 20, 28, 29, and 30.

MATERIALS

1. 5 toothpicks
2. Hollande's stain reagents
3. Dilute carbolfuchsin
4. Nigrosin solution
5. Permount (or equivalent mounting fluid)
6. Chocolate-agar slope culture of *N. gonorrhoeae*
7. Gram-stain reagents
8. 1 each brain-heart-infusion-agar slope culture of *Clostridium tetani* and *C. perfringens*
9. Spore-stain reagents
10. Starch-broth culture of *C. perfringens*
11. Capsule-stain reagents

PROCEDURE
SPIROCHETES

1. Due to the difficulty of culturing these bacteria, you will work with spirochetes found in the mouth. The numbers of these organisms present in the mouth of healthy individuals vary, but most people have some spirochetes at the gum margins. Make at least three films with scrapings removed from between your teeth near the gums. Use the toothpicks provided to obtain the scrapings.
2. Stain one film by Hollande's method:
   a. Fix with absolute alcohol for 1 to 2 min.
   b. Drain off the alcohol but do not let the preparation dry and do not wash it off.
   c. Flood with the mordant, warming it to steaming point for 1 min.
   d. Wash thoroughly with tap water holding the slide horizontally.
   e. Stain with pyridine-silver solution warming gently for 2 to 3 min. (Repeat this step if necessary.)
   f. Wash thoroughly and dry.
   g. Mount with Permount or similar mounting fluid.
3. Stain one film with dilute carbolfuchsin with warming for 30 sec.
4. Emulsify scrapings from between your teeth in nigrosin and spread the mixture in a thin film; dry rapidly.
5. Examine all stained preparations. In the microscopic examination of the specimens *Borrelia vincenti* will be the predominant spirochete present, but careful examination may disclose occasional nonpathogenic treponemata.

NEISSERIA GONORRHOEAE

You are provided with a chocolate-agar slope of *N. gonorrhoeae*. Make a gram stain and observe the morphology of this organism.

THE CLOSTRIDIA

1. You are provided with brain-heart-infusion-agar slope cultures of *C. tetani* and *C. perfringens* and a starch-broth culture of *C. perfringens*, which have been grown anaero-

bically in an anaerobic culture jar. Do a gram stain and a spore stain from each culture. Note that C. *perfringens* forms very few if any spores when grown on brain-heart-infusion agar slopes and requires special cultural conditions, such as starch broth, to sporulate.

2. Using the capsule-stain reagents provided, stain C. *perfringens* for capsules. Examine. (This is the only encapsulated member of the pathogenic clostridia.)

RESULTS

1. Draw the appearance of any spirochetes from the teeth scrapings stained by

Hollande's method

Dilute carbolfuchsin

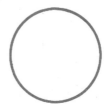

Nigrosin

2. Draw the morphology of *N. gonorrhoeae.*

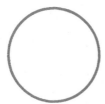

Gram reaction _____

3. Draw the gram-stain morphology:

Clostridium tetani
Gram reaction _____

Clostridium perfringens
Gram reaction _____

4. Draw the appearance of C. *perfringens* grown in starch broth after spore staining.

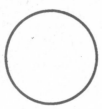

5. Draw the cells of C. *perfringens* after capsule staining.

QUESTIONS

1. Write an essay on syphilis under the following headings:
   a. History
   b. Causative organism
   c. Disease process
   d. Laboratory diagnosis

EXERCISE FORTY-ONE
BACTERIAL INFECTION
OF A PLANT

One of the pathological conditions resulting from bacterial infection of plants is the development of a tumor, or gall, on the stems. *Agrobacterium tumefaciens* is a pathogen of this kind. It causes an overgrowth of plant cells (enlargement or tumor) in the region it invades.

REFERENCES: Text, chap. 33; MMM, chap. 12.

MATERIALS

1. 2 potted tomato plants approximately 6 weeks old
2. 2 sterile disposable 1- or 2-ml syringes
3. 1 tube nutrient agar
4. 5-ml tube of sterile water
5. Broth culture of *Agrobacterium tumefaciens*
6. 1 sterile petri dish

PROCEDURE

1. Prepare one nutrient-agar plate. Streak it with A. *tumefaciens* in a manner to produce isolated colonies. Incubate for 48 hr at room temperature. Then characterize the colonies and make and examine a gram-stained preparation.
2. Draw a small amount of the broth culture into the sterile syringe and use it to inoculate the tomato plant in the following manner: puncture the tissue near a stem node and inject a small amount of the culture into the "cut." Repeat in two or three different locations. Using a second syringe in which you have drawn sterile water, make similar punctures and inoculations into a second tomato plant (control). NOTE: An incubation period of 2 or 3 weeks is required for the symptoms (tumors) to become evident on the plants. Accordingly, the plants must be maintained in a suitable environment, e.g., light, temperature, and humidity, for this period of time.
3. When tumors form on the plant, cut one off, using a sterile blade. Place this specimen in a sterile flask (250 ml) and

wash it with several changes of sterile water. Following the last washing, crush the tumor with a sterile glass rod. After the tissue is adequately macerated, remove a loopful, and streak a nutrient-agar plate; incubate the plate for 24 to 48 hr. Prepare and examine a gram stain from this macerated tissue.

RESULTS

1. Tabulate the characteristics of the colonies and the organisms observed from the original culture and from those obtained from the tumor.

CULTURE	MORPHOLOGY	COLONY CHARACTERISTICS
Original		
Isolated		

2. Sketch the plant showing the location and size of tumor(s) at the time the experiment was terminated.

QUESTIONS

1. What is the morphology and gram reaction of most bacterial plant pathogens? List several species with these characteristics.

_____

_____

_____

_____

_____

_____

_____

2. As this experiment was performed, did it satisfy Koch's postulates for establishing the causative agent of an infection? Explain.

_____

_____

_____

_____

_____

_____

_____

3. How does the bacterium *A. tumefaciens* incite tumor formations?

_____

_____

_____

_____

_____

_____

_____

4. What symptoms are produced in a plant infected with *Erwinia carotovora*?

_____

_____

_____

_____

_____

The microbial population of naturally occurring materials is frequently very large and extremely complex. Fertile soil, for example, may contain billions of microorganisms per gram — bacteria, yeasts, molds, algae and protozoa. Most, if not all, laboratory procedures used to isolate microorganisms from soil recover only a very small fraction of the total population. The great diversity of physiological types present precludes the possibility of major recovery of the population under a given physical environment on a single medium. The same situation exists with water and sewage. To a lesser degree, similar complications are associated with the microbiological analysis of milk and other foods when one wants to reveal the entire microbial flora.

Frequently, the microbiological analysis is directed toward the enumeration and isolation of a particular physiological group of organisms. For example, if our purpose is to isolate sporeforming anaerobic bacteria from soil, we can establish suitable cultural conditions to accomplish this. The standard procedure for the enumeration of bacteria in milk is described in great detail, and strict adherence to this procedure is required of laboratories engaged in this work. The bacteria detected by this technique can be characterized as aerobic or facultatively anaerobic, heterotrophic, nutritionally nonfastidious, and mesophilic.

One of the fascinating aspects of natural microbial flora is the extent to which interactions occur among the various species and the effect which this has on their combined physiological activities.

EXERCISE FORTY-TWO
ENUMERATION OF BACTERIA
BY THE PLATE-COUNT
TECHNIQUE

One of the routine procedures for determining the bacterial content of many different materials is the plate-count technique. This procedure is based upon the assumption that each viable cell will develop into a colony; hence, the number of colonies on the plate reveals the number of organisms contained in the sample which are capable of growing under the specific conditions of incubation. Several of the exercises which follow include making a plate count; consequently, the technique is outlined here so that details need not be repeated in later exercises.

GENERAL TECHNIQUE
DILUTION OF SPECIMEN

The specimen is diluted in order that one of the final plates will have between 30 and 300 colonies. Numbers of colonies within this range give the most accurate approximation of the microbial population. Since the magnitude of the microbial

Use of 9-ml dilution blanks.

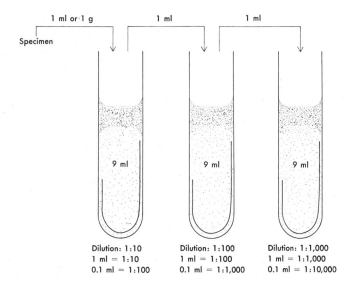

Specimen

1 ml or 1 g   1 ml   1 ml

9 ml   9 ml   9 ml

Dilution: 1:10
1 ml = 1:10
0.1 ml = 1:100

Dilution: 1:100
1 ml = 1:100
0.1 ml = 1:1,000

Dilution: 1:1,000
1 ml = 1:1,000
0.1 ml = 1:10,000

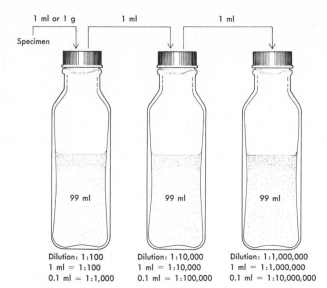

Use of 99-ml dilution blanks.

Dilution: 1:100
1 ml = 1:100
0.1 ml = 1:1,000

Dilution: 1:10,000
1 ml = 1:10,000
0.1 ml = 1:100,000

Dilution: 1:1,000,000
1 ml = 1:1,000,000
0.1 ml = 1:10,000,000

population in the original specimen is not known beforehand, a range of dilutions must be prepared and plated to obtain one within the above colony range.

The initial dilution is usually prepared by placing 1 ml or 1 g into a 9- or 99-ml dilution blank.* This dilution is shaken vigorously to obtain uniform distribution of organisms. Further dilutions are made by pipetting measured aliquots (usually 1 ml) into additional dilution blanks. Each dilution must be thoroughly shaken before removing an aliquot for subsequent dilution.

*Dilution blanks are tubes or bottles containing a known volume of sterile diluent. The 9- or 99-ml blank refers to the amount of sterile diluent (usually a physiological saline solution) in the container.

The procedure is illustrated diagrammatically.

PLATING OF DILUTION

Sterile petri dishes should first be labeled with your name, the specimen, and dilution. From the appropriate dilution blank(s), 1 ml or 0.1 is pipetted into a petri dish. NOTE: If 0.1 ml is plated, the dilution is increased 10 times.

Samples from each dilution are plated in duplicate or triplicate.

The accompanying sketch illustrates the manner of delivering the inoculum (material from dilution blank) into the petri dish.

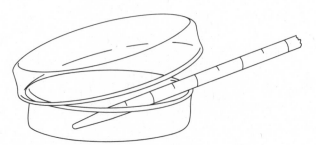

Technique for addition of inoculum into petri dish.

ADDITION OF PLATING
MEDIUM TO PETRI DISH

The agar medium to be used must first be melted and then cooled in a water bath adjusted to 45°C. Add approximately 15 ml of the cooled liquid medium to each petri dish. Immediately thereafter, rotate the plate gently to distribute the inoculum throughout the medium. This is the pour-plate method. (In the spread-plate method, the inoculum or dilution sample is placed on top of a prepoured nutrient-agar plate and is spread with a sterile glass spreader.)

INCUBATION OF
PLATED SPECIMENS

Upon solidification of the medium, *invert* the plates and place in an incubator.

COUNTING COLONIES

After the prescribed period of incubation, select a plate that contains a number of colonies in the 30 to 300 range. Make an accurate count of these colonies by placing the plate on the platform of a colony counter, e.g., a Quebec colony counter. This instrument facilitates the counting process, since the colonies are illuminated, magnified, and seen against a ruled background.

CALCULATION OF PLATE
COUNT

The number of colonies counted on a plate multiplied by the dilution of the specimen that the plate represents equals the plate count per milliliter (or gram) of the specimen. For example, if 180 colonies were counted on the 1:1,000 dilution of a milk sample, the calculation is

$$180 \times 1,000 = 180,000 = \text{plate count per milliliter of milk sample}$$

It is generally desirable to make duplicate or triplicate platings of each dilution and to average the resulting counts.

REFERENCE: Text, chap. 7.

MATERIALS

1. Bacterial suspension (faintly turbid suspension of *Escherichia coli*)
2. 4 99-ml dilution blanks
3. 9 sterile petri dishes
4. 2 bottles trypticase-soy agar
5. 6 sterile 1-ml pipettes

PROCEDURE

1. Prepare the following dilutions from the bacterial suspension supplied: 1:1,000,000 (10^{-6}), 1:10,000,000 (10^{-7}), and 1:100,000,000 (10^{-8}). Plate each of these dilutions in triplicate.
2. Following their incubation for 24 to 48 hr, observe the plates and describe the distribution of colonies from each dilution.
3. Select plates made from the appropriate dilution, make a plate count, and calculate the number of bacteria per milliliter of the original suspension.

RESULTS   1.   Description of plates from each dilution:

DILUTION	DESCRIPTION OF COLONY DISTRIBUTION
1×10^{-6}	
1×10^{-7}	
1×10^{-8}	

2. Record the colony count of each plate in the triplicate series counted. Calculate the average and from this the population of the original suspension.

3. Record the results (population of the suspension) of other class members. From these data, determine the *mean* and *median* result.

Plate-Count Data

RESULTS OF CLASS MEMBERS (POPULATION OF SUSPENSION)		
_____	_____	_____
_____	_____	_____
_____	_____	_____
_____	_____	_____
_____	_____	_____
_____	_____	_____
_____	_____	_____

YOUR RESULTS:
Plate counts 1×10^{-6}: _____ 1×10^{-7}: _____ 1×10^{-8}: _____

Your average (population of suspension): _____

CLASS MEAN: _____

CLASS MEDIAN: _____

QUESTIONS

1. Did each of the plates in the triplicate series counted have the same number of colonies? How might deviations be accounted for?

   _____

   _____

   _____

   _____

   _____

2. How much variation was noted in the results obtained by various classmates? How can this be explained?

   _____

   _____

   _____

   _____

   _____

3. What dilutions would you consider appropriate if you were to perform a plate count on a 24-hr nutrient-broth culture of *E. coli?*

   _____

   _____

   _____

   _____

   _____

4. Compute the average error in the triplicate plates of the dilution containing 30 to 300 colonies.

   _____

   _____

   _____

EXERCISE FORTY-THREE
BACTERIOLOGICAL
EXAMINATION OF WATER

Natural waters contain a wide variety of microorganisms. In fact, it is not unlikely that one might find representatives of each of the major categories of microorganisms in a specimen from such sources. A single medium, inoculated and placed under specific conditions of incubation, will reveal only a fraction of the total microbial population. It is necessary, therefore, to employ different procedures for the enumeration and isolation of different microbial types. The method that has been developed to determine the sanitary quality of drinking water is an example of a procedure designed to detect a certain category of bacteria, viz., those of fecal origin.

REFERENCES: Text, chap. 37; "Standard Methods for the Examination of Water and Waste Water," 12th ed., American Public Health Association, Inc., New York, 1965.

MATERIALS

1. 2 tubes nutrient agar
2. 10 tubes lactose broth, single-strength, with Durham tubes
3. 5 tubes lactose broth, double-strength, with Durham tubes
4. 15 ml eosin-methylene blue (EMB) agar
5. 1 nutrient-agar slant
6. 3 sterile petri dishes
7. 1 sterile 10-ml pipette
8. 2 sterile 1-ml pipettes
9. Water samples: tap water, tap water contaminated with sewage, tap water contaminated with *Escherichia coli* and *Aerobacter aerogenes*.

PROCEDURE

Since the bacteriological analysis of water to determine its sanitary quality requires performing certain procedures on successive days, this exercise is outlined in such a fashion.

STANDARD PLATE COUNT AND PRESUMPTIVE TEST FOR COLIFORMS

1. Select one of the water samples, and plate 1.0- and 0.1-ml quantities. Incubate plates at 35°C for 24 hr.
2. With the same sample, inoculate tubes of *single-strength* lactose broth with 1.0 and 0.1 ml (five tubes each volume)

and five tubes of *double-strength* lactose broth, each with 10 ml. Incubate these tubes at 35°C for 24 to 48 hr. After incubation, proceed as follows.

3. Count and record the number of colonies on the plates.

4. Observe the lactose-broth tubes for evidence of gas production. If no gas is present, incubate the tubes for another 24 hr; if gas is still absent at this time, the test for coliforms is considered *negative*. The presence of gas within 48 hr in any of the fermentation tubes constitutes a *positive presumptive test*. NOTE: If the water sample with which you are working gives a *negative presumptive test*, obtain a lactose-broth tube showing gas production from another member of the class and continue the examination.

CONFIRMED TEST

1. Streak an EMB plate from one of the tubes of lactose broth showing gas formation. Incubate this plate at 35°C for 24 hr.

2. Observe this plate, after incubation, for colonies of coliform organisms. *Escherichia coli* colonies appear bluish black by transmitted light and have a greenish metallic sheen by reflected light. *Aerobacter aerogenes* colonies are brownish and often convex and mucoid; they may tend to coalesce. If typical coliform colonies are present on the EMB plate, the result of the *confirmed* test is considered *positive*.

COMPLETED TEST

1. Inoculate a tube of lactose broth and an agar slant from a typical coliform colony. Incubate these tubes at 35°C for 24 to 48 hr.

2. Observe lactose broth for evidence of gas formation. Prepare and observe a gram-stain preparation from the agar slant culture. If gas appears in the lactose-broth tube and microscopic examination of the smear reveals gram-negative nonsporeforming bacilli, the test is considered *completed* and the presence of coliform organisms demonstrated.

RESULTS

Tabulate results of this exercise in the table provided below:

TEST PROCEDURES	RESULTS		
Standard plate count per milliliter of sample			
Presumptive test	NUMBER OF POSITIVES IN LACTOSE-BROTH TUBES WITH		
	10 ML	1 ML	0.1 ML
Confirmed test	Description of colonies on EMB		
Completed test	Lactose broth		
	Morphology and gram reaction from agar slant culture		

QUESTIONS

1. Does the standard plate count reveal all the microorganisms present in the water sample? Explain.

_____

_____

_____

_____

_____

_____

2. What circumstances might be responsible for a positive presumptive test on a sample which, on subsequent testing, does not yield a positive confirmed test?

_____

_____

_____

_____

_____

_____

_____

3. In the type of analysis performed, why would it be unsatis-
    factory to streak the water specimen directly onto an EMB
    plate?

    _____

    _____

    _____

    _____

    _____

    _____

4. Define the term "coliforms." What is their significance in
    sanitary bacteriology?

    _____

    _____

    _____

    _____

    _____

5. Name some differential and/or selective media, other than
    the ones used in this exercise, which are employed in the
    examination of water to determine potability. What does
    the use of each medium accomplish?

    _____

    _____

6. The bacteriological examination of water can also be performed using the membrane-filter technique. What advantages does this technique provide?

7. Determine the most probable numbers (MPN) of coliforms per 100 ml of your water sample.

EXERCISE FORTY-FOUR
THE BACTERIAL FLORA
OF RAW AND
PASTEURIZED MILK

Milk has an initial microbial flora at the time it is drawn from the cow. Furthermore, all utensils employed in handling the milk serve as potential sources of additional microorganisms. Information on the bacterial content of a milk sample may reflect the state of health of the cow and the conditions under which the milk was produced and stored. The standard plate count is one of the routine procedures widely used to enumerate the number of organisms in milk.

REFERENCES: Text, chap. 39; "Standard Methods for the Examination of Dairy Products," 12th ed., American Public Health Association, Inc., New York, 1967.

MATERIALS

1. 100 ml milk-protein-hydrolysate agar
2. 6 tubes litmus milk
3. 6 sterile petri dishes
4. 6 sterile 1.1-ml pipettes
5. 1 sterile 10-ml pipette
6. 3 99-ml dilution blanks
7. 1 9-ml dilution blank
8. 1 sterile test tube
9. Water bath and thermometer
10. Colony counter
11. Approximately 20-ml raw-milk sample in screw-cap tube

PROCEDURE
PASTEURIZATION OF
MILK SAMPLE

1. Adjust a water bath to a temperature of 63°C. (The temperature used in commercial pasteurization is 62.8°C.)
2. Shake the sample of raw milk vigorously to obtain uniform distribution of microorganisms. Use a sterile 10-ml pipette to transfer 10 ml of the raw-milk sample into a sterile tube and place this in the water bath maintained at 63°C. Allow this sample to remain in the water bath for 30 min. During this time, make sure that the temperature is held at 63°C and occasionally shake the tube of milk. At the end of 30

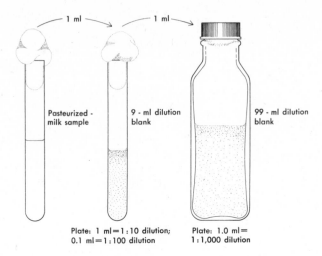

Pasteurized - milk sample

9 - ml dilution blank

99 - ml dilution blank

Plate: 1 ml = 1:10 dilution; 0.1 ml = 1:100 dilution

Plate: 1.0 ml = 1:1,000 dilution

min, remove the tube of milk and cool it immediately by holding it under cold running tap water.

THE STANDARD PLATE COUNT

3. Prepare and plate 1:10, 1:100, and 1:1,000 dilutions of the milk sample pasteurized above. Follow the plan sketched for making dilutions and plating the samples.

4. Add approximately 15 ml melted, cooled agar medium to each plate. Immediately upon addition of the medium, rotate each plate gently to effect uniform distribution of the inoculum.

5. Prepare and plate 1:100, 1:1,000, and 1:10,000 dilutions of the raw-milk sample as sketched.

Add medium to each of these plates as described in step 4.

6. Incubate all plates at 35°C for 48 hr.

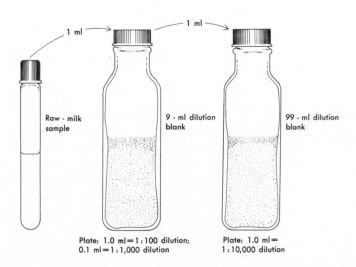

Raw - milk sample

9 - ml dilution blank

99 - ml dilution blank

Plate: 1.0 ml = 1:100 dilution; 0.1 ml = 1:1,000 dilution

Plate: 1.0 ml = 1:10,000 dilution

RESULTS

1. Examine the plates, and select those plated from the dilution(s) which contain a suitable number of colonies for counting. Use a colony-counting device to facilitate the counting. Calculation of the standard plate count per milliliter should be made from that dilution of the sample which yields a colony count between 30 and 300.

SAMPLE	COLONY COUNTS FROM VARIOUS DILUTIONS			CALCULATION OF STANDARD PLATE COUNT PER MILLILITER

2. Select one plate from the raw-milk series and one from the pasteurized-milk series that have well-isolated colonies. Draw circles on the bottom of each plate enclosing two or three representative colonial types. Describe these colonies. Make and examine a gram-stain preparation from each colony. Transfer a portion of each colony into a tube of litmus milk. Incubate these for 2 to 4 days, and record the changes that occur.

Raw-milk Sample

COLONIAL TYPE	MORPHOLOGY AND GRAM REACTION	REACTION IN LITMUS MILK

Pasteurized-milk Sample

COLONIAL TYPE	MORPHOLOGY AND GRAM REACTION	REACTION IN LITMUS MILK

QUESTIONS

1. Calculate the percentage reduction of microorganisms accomplished by pasteurization of the milk sample.

_____

_____

_____

_____

_____

_____

2. Describe the predominant types of organisms recovered from the raw-milk sample. Pasteurized sample.

_____

_____

_____

_____

3. Assume that a milk sample was suspected of containing beta-hemolytic streptococci. Outline a laboratory procedure which could provide confirmation of this.

_____

_____

_____

_____

_____

_____

EXERCISE FORTY-FIVE
MICROBIOLOGICAL
EXAMINATION OF FOODS

Results of microbiological analyses of foods provide information on the quality of the raw material, the cause of spoilage if it has occurred, or the present condition of the food. The nature of the food and the process by which it is preserved will have a bearing on the predominant types of organism that may be found. A single method of examination, i.e., one medium and one condition of incubation, is not suitable for all samples. The procedure to be performed will therefore not necessarily reveal the total flora of each sample.

REFERENCE: Text, chap. 38.

MATERIALS

1. 150 ml milk-protein-hydrolysate agar
2. 1 tube litmus milk
3. 1 tube lactose broth
4. 1 tube nutrient gelatin
5. Scalpel, forceps, and spatula
6. Sterile squares of weighing paper in a petri dish
7. Balance
8. Dilution blank: 9 ml sterile saline in 100-ml screw-cap bottle containing enough small glass beads to form about two layers over the bottom
9. 2 99-ml dilution blanks
10. 4 sterile 1.1-ml pipettes
11. 9 sterile petri dishes
12. Food samples, e.g., fresh hamburger, ham, fresh fish, frozen food, canned food

PROCEDURE

1. Select one of the food samples for analysis. NOTE: Before any manipulations are started, be sure that all necessary equipment is at hand for sampling of the specimen. Aseptic precautions must be observed. The scalpel, forceps, and

spatula should be flamed and cooled before they are used to obtain your sample.

2. Weigh a 1-g portion of the food specimen, and transfer it to the 9-ml dilution blank, which contains the glass beads. Shake vigorously to disintegrate the sample.

3. Prepare and plate further dilutions of 1:1,000, 1:10,000, and 1:100,000 as follows:

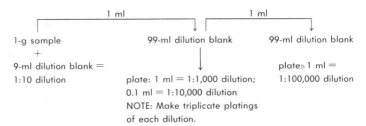

1-g sample
+
9-ml dilution blank =
1:10 dilution

1 ml → 99-ml dilution blank

plate: 1 ml = 1:1,000 dilution;
0.1 ml = 1:10,000 dilution
NOTE: Make triplicate platings
of each dilution.

1 ml → 99-ml dilution blank

plate: 1 ml =
1:100,000 dilution

4. Incubate one set of plates in a refrigerator (approximately 7°C) for 7 days; one set at 35°C for 48 hr; and one set at 55°C for 24 to 48 hr.

5. Inoculate the tubes of litmus milk, lactose broth, and gelatin with a loopful of material from the 1:10 dilution. Incubate at 35°C for 2 to 4 days.

RESULTS

1. Make colony counts from each of the plates which have isolated colonies. Calculate the standard plate count per gram of the food sample. Note changes produced in the tubes of litmus milk, gelatin, and lactose broth.

INCUBATION	DILUTIONS	COLONIES PER PLATE	STANDARD PLATE COUNT PER GRAM	CHANGES PRODUCED IN		
				LITMUS MILK	LACTOSE BROTH	GELATIN
7°C 7 days	1:1,000					
	1:10,000					
	1:100,000					
35°C 48 hr	1:1,000					
	1:10,000					
	1:100,000					
55°C 24–48 hr	1:1,000					
	1:10,000					
	1:100,000					

2. Prepare and examine gram stains of representative colonies that developed at each temperature. Record descriptions of the organisms.

SOURCE OF COLONY	DESCRIPTION OF COLONY	GRAM STAIN AND MORPHOLOGY OF ORGANISMS

QUESTIONS

1. Why is it more accurate to report the results of the plate count as "standard plate count per gram" than as "number of organisms per gram"?

_____

_____

_____

_____

_____

_____

2. What incubation conditions would be appropriate for micro-biological examination of a spoiled canned-food sample?

_____

_____

_____

_____

_____

_____

3. In the microbiological examination of shellfish, the detection of coliforms is stressed. Why?

_____

_____

_____

_____

_____

4. A can of food is suspected of containing *Clostridium botulinum*. Outline a laboratory experiment to obtain results to confirm or deny this assumption.

_____

_____

_____

_____

_____

_____

_____

_____

5. What genera of microorganisms would most likely be sought from each of the following materials?
   a. Chicken salad incriminated in an outbreak of food poisoning
   b. A can with bulged ends containing creamed corn
   c. Spoiled frozen orange juice
   d. A supply of sugar alleged to be heavily contaminated and responsible for spoilage of soft drinks

_____

_____

_____

_____

_____

_____

EXERCISE FORTY-SIX
MICROBIOLOGY OF SOIL
A. QUANTITATIVE
ENUMERATION OF
MICROORGANISMS

REFERENCE: Text, chap. 34.

Soil harbors microorganisms of all varieties. Special media and conditions of incubation are necessary to isolate the numerous species. This microbial flora performs a vast array of biochemical changes in soil that constitute essential links in the cycles of matter in nature. In this exercise, several different experiments will be performed, the results of which will reveal something of the soil microflora and its biochemical potential.

MATERIALS

1. 3 tubes nutrient agar
2. 3 tubes Czapek-Dox agar
3. 3 99-ml dilution blanks
4. 6 sterile 1.1-ml pipettes
5. 6 petri dishes
6. Balance and spatula
7. Sterile paper squares in petri dish
8. Soil sample: finely pulverized garden soil
9. 1 water bath at 45°C

PROCEDURE

1. Weigh out 1 g of soil and add to a 99-ml dilution blank.
2. Prepare and plate the following dilutions by the pour-plate method, using nutrient agar as the plating medium:

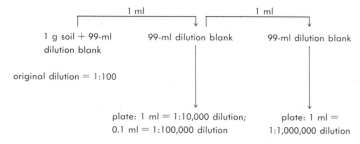

3. Prepare another set of plates of the following dilutions, using Czapek-Dox agar as the plating medium: 1:1,000, 1:10,000, and 1:100,000. (Use 0.1 ml from the 1:100 dilution for plating the 1:1,000 dilution.)

4. Incubate all plates at room temperature for 4 to 7 days.

RESULTS

Count and record the number of colonies on each plate. Describe the predominant colonial types that appear on each of the media.

MEDIUM	DILUTION	COLONY COUNTS	PLATE COUNT PER GRAM	DESCRIPTION OF PREDOMINATING COLONIES
Nutrient agar				
Czapek-Dox agar				

QUESTIONS

1. What types of microorganisms would be missed in the culturing procedure employed?

_____

_____

_____

_____

_____

_____

2. What differences were noted between the types of micro-organisms recovered on the two plating media?

_____

_____

_____

_____

_____

_____

3. What advantages does a direct microscopic count of organisms in soil have over a cultural procedure?

_____

_____

_____

_____

_____

_____

B. AMMONIFICATION, THE LIBERATION OF AMMONIA FROM NITROGENOUS COMPOUNDS

MATERIALS

1. 2 tubes casein solution
2. 2 tubes peptone solution
3. Nessler's reagent (for ammonia test)
4. Spot plate
5. Soil sample from previous experiment

PROCEDURE

1. Inoculate one tube of each medium with the soil sample. Make the inoculations by first wetting the loop transfer needle, e.g., by touching the sterile needle to the casein solution and then touching the soil sample. The soil adhering to the loop is sufficient inoculum.
2. Incubate the inoculated tubes and an uninoculated tube of each medium for 7 days.
3. After 2 to 4 days' incubation and again at 7 days' incubation, test contents of each tube for ammonia as follows. Place a drop of Nessler's solution in the depression of a spot plate and add a loopful of material from one of the tubes. Observe for any color changes. A *faint yellow* color is indicative of a small amount of ammonia; *deep yellow* indicates more ammonia; and a *brown* color or *brownish* precipitate signifies a large quantity of ammonia.

RESULTS   Record the results of the ammonia determination in tabular form.

SOLUTION	INCUBATION TIME	COLOR CHANGES WITH NESSLER'S REAGENT	
		INOCULATED TUBES	UNINOCULATED TUBES (CONTROL)
Casein			
Peptone			

QUESTIONS

1. Outline the biochemical changes that occur in the formation of ammonia from the two substrates employed.

_____

_____

_____

_____

_____

_____

2. What is the significance of ammonification in relation to soil fertility?

_____

_____

_____

_____

C. REDUCTION OF NITRATES AND DENITRIFICATION

MATERIALS

1. 3 Durham fermentation tubes nitrate-salts medium
2. Nessler's reagent (for ammonia test)
3. Trommsdorf's reagent and a 1:3 dilution of sulfuric acid (for nitrite test)
4. Diphenylamine reagent (for nitrate test)
5. Spot plate and glass rods
6. Broth culture of *Pseudomonas fluorescens*
7. Soil sample from previous experiment

PROCEDURE

1. Inoculate one tube of the nitrate-salts medium with soil, using a wet loop transfer needle. Inoculate another tube with a loopful of *P. fluorescens* culture.
2. Incubate the inoculated tubes and an uninoculated control at room temperature for 7 days.
3. After incubation, observe tubes for evidence of gas formation. Test the medium in each tube in the following order:
   a. *Nitrite test:* add 2 drops 1:3 dilution of sulfuric acid solution to a depression in the spot plate. To this add 1 drop of Trommsdorf's reagent. Dip a glass rod in the culture to be tested and touch the end of this to Trommsdorf's reagent mixture. Do not mix. Nitrates are indicated by the immediate appearance of a deep bluish color. If the nitrite test is negative, test for nitrates.
   b. *Nitrate test:* add 3 drops diphenylamine reagent to a depression on the spot plate. Place a drop of the culture to be tested at the surface of this solution as described above (a). If nitrates are present, a light blue color develops within a few minutes. NOTE: Nitrites also give a blue color with diphenylamine. However, if a negative test was demonstrated with Trommsdorf's reagent, nitrites can be excluded.
   c. *Ammonia test:* test with Nessler's reagent as described in experiment B (ammonification).

RESULTS   Record results of these tests in tabular form.

TEST	SPECIMEN	GAS FORMATION
Nitrite	Soil	
	Pseudomonas fluorescens	
	Control	
Nitrate	Soil	
	Pseudomonas fluorescens	
	Control	
Ammonia	Soil	
	Pseudomonas fluorescens	
	Control	

QUESTIONS   1. Distinguish between denitrification, nitrate reduction, nitrate utilization, and nitrification.

_____

_____

_____

_____

_____

_____

_____

2. When the test for nitrite is negative, why is it necessary to retest the inoculated medium (nitrate broth) for presence of nitrate?

_____

_____

_____

_____

_____

_____

3. What conditions in soil favor microbial reduction of nitrates?

_____

_____

_____

_____

_____

_____

D. SYMBIOTIC AND NONSYMBIOTIC NITROGEN FIXATION

Soon after seeds of leguminous plants germinate in the soil, certain bacteria (*Rhizobium* if a specific plant host is involved) invade the roots and stimulate the formation of root nodules, where the bacteria populate. These root-nodule species fix atmospheric nitrogen in symbiosis with the leguminous partner. Many soils, however, in which legumes are not growing and to which nitrogen is not added in the form of fertilizers, still increase in nitrogen content thanks to the presence of nonsymbiotic, free-living nitrogen-fixing species of bacteria. There are free-nitrogen fixers which are aerobic, e.g., *Azotobacter* spp.; and free-nitrogen fixers which are anaerobic, e.g., certain species of *Clostridium*.

MATERIALS

1. 1 125-ml Erlenmeyer flask with 100 ml nitrogen-free medium
2. Soil sample from previous experiment
3. Balance
4. Petri plate of nitrogen-free azotobacter medium
5. Gram stains
6. 2 microscope slides

PROCEDURE

1. You are provided with a 125-ml Erlenmeyer flask containing 100 ml of sterile nitrogen-free salt solution
2. Pour into the medium 1 g of soil (a heavy inoculum is required for the demonstration of nitrogen fixation by the anaerobic nitrogen fixers present in the sample).
3. Incubate the flask at room temperature for 1 week; then observe for the presence and growth of anaerobic nitrogen fixers.

4. Sprinkle soil over the surface of a nitrogen-free agar plate provided.

5. Incubate at room temperature for a week; then examine the surface for the presence of colonies of aerobic free-nitrogen fixers.

RESULTS

1. Examine the flask of nitrogen-free salt medium. Gas bubbles and a rancid odor are evidence of the activity of *Clostridium pasteurianum*. Make gram stains of films from the bottom of the medium. *C. pasteurianum* is a sporeforming bacillus with a terminal or central bulging spore.

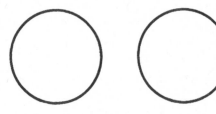

2. Examine the nitrogen-free agar plate. Describe the colonies. Make and examine stained films using gram staining. *Azotobacter* cells are large ovoid cells and are gram-negative.

    Description of colonies: _____

    _____

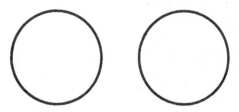

QUESTIONS

1. What species of microorganisms are symbiotic nitrogen fixers? Nonsymbiotic nitrogen fixers?

    _____

    _____

    _____

    _____

    _____

    _____

2. Can all legumes be successfully inoculated with the same species of symbiotic nitrogen-fixing bacteria? Explain.

    _____

    _____

_____

_____

_____

_____

3. Describe a laboratory experiment that would illustrate the effect of symbiotic nitrogen fixation on plant growth.

_____

_____

_____

_____

_____

_____

PART FOURTEEN
MICROBIOLOGICAL
PROBLEMS

The exercises in this section provide an opportunity to investigate selected microbiological topics in more depth and with more variation in experimental approach than was possible with preceding experiments. The topics include cytology of protists, production of an enzyme and measurement of its activity, analysis of a mixed microbial flora, use of the enrichment culture technique for the isolation of a specific biotype, and the isolation of a drug-resistant mutant. These exercises are not likely to be completed in the usual one or two laboratory periods; successive steps in the experiment may require or depend upon preliminary preparations or tests. The results of examinations performed on one day may influence subsequent steps in the procedure. Some steps in an exercise may need to be done outside the regularly scheduled laboratory; some reagents or media may have to be prepared in advance. Consequently, it is not possible to present in detail all the materials required or to prescribe a rigid set of directions. Thus it becomes the responsibility of the student to assume the initiative for performance of the experiment. This will require coordination of planning between student and instructor.

It is anticipated that these exercises will impart to the student some concept of the scientist's approach as he engages in research. During the performance of each of these exercises, the student will have the opportunity to use his initiative and ingenuity in coordinating much of the knowledge acquired earlier in the course.

EXERCISE FORTY-SEVEN
COMPARATIVE ANATOMY
OF SOME PROTISTS

Organisms included in the kingdom Protista (of Haeckel) lack definite cellular arrangement. Although some may be colonial in habit, the individual cells are identical and there is no specialization in terms of function or purpose. The objective of this exercise is to observe and compare cellular anatomy of several representative protists (see Introduction).

REFERENCE: Text, chaps. 5 and 14 to 17.

MATERIALS

1. Cultures of *Chlamydomonas* sp., *Tetrahymena pyriformis*, *Bacillus megaterium*, *Saccharomyces cerevisiae*, and *Aspergillus niger*
2. Phase microscope
3. Staining solutions for nuclear material and nuclei: Bouin's fluid, Giemsa stain, toluidine blue, 1N hydrochloric acid, 2% osmic acid, N/10 potassium hydroxide, 10 and 40% ethyl alcohol, methyl alcohol

PROCEDURE

1. Prepare wet mounts of each of the cultures provided and examine them by phase microscopy. (If a phase microscope is not available, make your examinations with a bright-field instrument. Exercise extreme care in the adjustment of light.) Observe several individual cells from each specimen, using the high-dry and oil-immersion objectives. Pay particular attention to details of cell structure such as the rigidity of the cell wall, presence or absence of appendages, cytoplasmic inclusions, etc. Your microscopic examinations must be performed in a critical and meticulous fashion in order to obtain maximum information about the cytological features of each species. Consult illustrations in your textbook and other reference material provided by the instructor to assist in identification of cellular structures.

Other illustrations for reference purposes may be made available.

2. Prepare and examine nuclear-stained films of each culture by the procedures outlined below.

BACILLUS MEGATERIUM*

*Taken from V. B. D. Skerman, "A Guide to the Identification of the Genera of Bacteria," The Williams & Wilkins Company, Baltimore, 1959.
†A cover slip can be used in place of a slide; the cover slip preparation would finally be mounted on a slide.

Gently press a slide to the growth of a very young culture on a nutrient-agar plate, thus making an impression on the glass surface.† Place the slide in a small glass chamber containing freshly prepared 2% osmic acid solution for 2 to 3 min. Remove the slide and immerse it in a solution of 1 N HCl at 60°C for 10 min, thoroughly wash with distilled water, and then stain with dilute Giemsa solution for 30 to 60 min. Wash thoroughly, mount in water, and examine using the oil-immersion objective. The nuclear substance stains a darker color than other protoplasmic material.

CHLAMYDOMONAS SP.

†Preparation of mount is accomplished by placing a drop of balsam or similar mounting fluid on the stained film and covering this with a cover slip.

Prepare a film of algal cells on a clean slide and fix it by flooding with Bouin's fluid for 4 to 6 hr. Wash off with distilled water, then immerse slide in dilute Giemsa stain (1:20) for approximately 40 hr. Wash slide with tap water, allow to dry, mount preparation, and examine.† The nuclei appear dark blue against a lighter background.

SACCHAROMYCES CEREVISIAE

Prepare a film from a very young (6- to 8-hr) yeast culture and allow to air-dry. Flood with 40% ethyl alcohol for 2 min. Wash with tap water. Flood with N/10 potassium hydroxide solution for 1 hr and then wash thoroughly with tap water. Apply toluidine blue solution for 2 min, wash off with 10% ethyl alcohol, blot dry, mount, and examine. The nuclei stain dark blue, the background pink.

ASPERGILLUS NIGER

Prepare a slide culture of this mold in the following manner. Place a sterile slide in a humidified petri dish (see Exercise 22). Inoculate a tube of malt-extract broth with spores from the mold culture and place a drop of this inoculated medium on the center of the slide. Incubate for 18 to 24 hr. Flood the slide culture (the drop of medium should have dried by this time) with Bouin's fluid for 4 to 6 hr to fix the film. Wash thoroughly with tap water; stain with dilute Giemsa stain (1:20) for 24 to 48 hr. Wash, mount, and examine. The nuclei appear dark blue, the background pink.

TETRAHYMENA PYRIFORMIS

Prepare a film from the culture of *T. pyriformis*, allow to air-dry, then fix by flooding with methyl alcohol for 3 min. Stain with Giemsa solution (diluted 1:10) for 1 hr. Wash with buffered distilled water (pH 7.0) for 30 to 60 sec, dry, and examine. The nuclei appear dark blue against a light background.

RESULTS

Record the details of cell structure for each species as seen in wet preparations. Sketch the nuclei of representative cells as revealed by the nuclear-stain techniques.

SPECIES	CHARACTERISTIC ANATOMY OF CELL	SKETCH OF CELLS SHOWING NUCLEI
Bacillus megaterium		
Chlamydomonas sp.		
Saccharomyces cerevisiae		
Aspergillus niger		
Tetrahymena pyriformis		

QUESTIONS

1. Compare the nuclear structures of procaryotic and eucaryotic protists.

_____

_____

_____

_____

_____

2. Which of the two cell dimensions, width or length, is more significant in distinguishing bacteria from other protists?

3. Bacteria are sometimes treated with ribonuclease in nuclear-staining techniques. Why is this done?

4. Name the various kinds of cytoplasmic granules which may appear in protists. Describe how you might identify the chemical nature of each type of granule.

EXERCISE FORTY-EIGHT
PROTOPLAST FORMATION
BY BACILLUS MEGATERIUM

REFERENCE: C. Weibull,
The Isolation of Protoplasts
from *Bacillus megaterium*
by Controlled Treatment
with Lysozyme, *J. Bacteriol.*
66:688–695 (1953).

Microbial cells devoid of the cell-wall structure but otherwise intact and metabolically active are called *protoplasts*. Bacterial protoplasts can be produced experimentally by dissolving the bacterial wall with lysozyme or by growing bacteria in the presence of penicillin, which inhibits cell-wall formation. Protoplasts are extremely delicate and will burst upon formation unless a stabilizing condition, e.g., high-concentration sucrose solution, is provided.

MATERIALS

1. 12- to 18-hr trypticase-soy-broth culture of *Bacillus megaterium*
2. Stock solution of egg-white lysozyme containing 4.0 mg/ml
3. Approximately 10 ml 15% sucrose solution in trypticase-soy broth
4. Formaldehyde
5. Gram-stain reagents
6. 1.0-ml serological pipettes and clean test tubes
7. Phase microscope

PROCEDURE

1. Mix 1.0 ml of culture with 1.0 ml trypticase-soy-broth sucrose solution to produce a "stabilizing" medium; the sucrose concentration of this mixture is 7.5%. (It is not necessary to use sterile solutions or glassware in this exercise since the reaction to be observed occurs before contamination would become significant.)
2. Add 0.1 ml (400 μg) lysozyme to the sucrose-culture mixture prepared above. Mix thoroughly and proceed immediately to step 3.
3. Place 1 drop of the suspension from the above mixture on a slide; cover with a cover slip, and observe this preparation under the oil-immersion objective (phase microscope).

The bacilli should lose motility in approximately 10 min or less. This is followed by a transition of cells from rods to spheres; protoplast formation should occur within 30 min. Frequent examination of the specimen at intervals of a few minutes is required.

4. After you have observed the presence of protoplasts, add 0.5 ml formaldehyde to the sucrose-culture-lysozyme mixture prepared in step 2. Prepare a smear for gram staining by mixing two loopsful of the formalinized protoplasts with one loopful of B. megaterium culture. Observe the gram reaction of bacilli and protoplasts.

RESULTS

1. Make a sketch of a few cells at regular intervals, 5 min, say, during the time they are exposed to lysozyme.

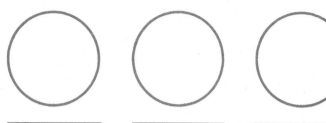

time: _____   _____   _____

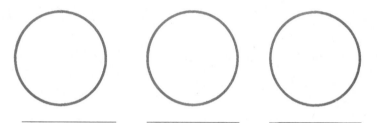

time: _____   _____   _____

2. Record the gram reaction of the cells and protoplasts.

QUESTIONS

1. Distinguish between protoplast, spheroplast, and "L" form.

_____

_____

_____

_____

_____

_____

2. What is mucopeptide?

_____

_____

_____

_____

_____

3. Can protoplasts survive in normal ecological environments? Explain.

_____

_____

_____

_____

_____

_____

4. Where does lysozyme occur? What is its function?

_____

_____

_____

_____

_____

_____

5. What difference was observed between the gram reaction of the bacilli and the protoplasts? How can this difference be accounted for?

_____

_____

_____

_____

_____

EXERCISE FORTY-NINE
BIOLOGICAL SUCCESSION
IN A MIXED MICROBIAL
FLORA

The laboratory study of microorganisms is conventionally done with pure cultures. The initial specimen, e.g., soil, water, or sputum, contains a variety of species. The routine techniques are directed toward isolating certain predetermined types in pure culture; the pure cultures are then characterized. In most natural environments, a multitude of microorganisms representing numerous species grow in a close physical association with each other. This intimate association of organisms may account for changes which reflect interactions among the species. This exercise will serve to illustrate the fluctuation in numbers and the sequence of predominant physiological types of microorganisms that develop in raw milk.

REFERENCE: Text, chaps. 39 and 41.

MATERIALS

1. 500 ml raw milk in a 1-liter flask
2. Milk-protein-hydrolysate agar*
3. Gelatin agar
4. Milk agar
5. Tributyrin agar
6. Dilution blanks
7. Sterile pipettes and petri dishes
8. Reagents for preparation of stained films of milk (xylol, alcohol, methylene blue)

*Amounts of media are not specified since procedural details are left to the instructor and student.

PROCEDURE

1. Place 500 ml raw (unpasteurized) milk in a clean 1-liter Erlenmeyer flask. Place a cotton plug in the mouth of the flask; store at room temperature for several weeks. Perform the following examinations on the fresh raw milk on the first day of this exercise.
   a. Prepare a stained film as follows. Spread a loopful of milk on a clean slide over an area about the size

of a dime. Allow it to dry without heating. Cover the milk film with xylol for 1 min to remove fat. Drain off the xylol, allow the slide to air-dry, and then cover film with alcohol for 1 min. Drain off alcohol, allow film to air-dry, and then stain film with methylene blue for approximately 5 min. Examine the film using the oil-immersion objective. Record the various morphological types and the approximate percentage of each.

b. Perform a standard plate count (see Exercise 44). Plate each dilution in triplicate, and incubate one set of plates at each of the following temperatures: 5, 35, and 50°C. Incubate the plates at 5°C for 7 days and the others for 48 hr. At the end of the incubation time, and after plate counts are made, transfer several colonies, of different types, to trypticase-soy-agar slants. Incubate each slant at the same temperature at which the original colony grew, that is, 5, 35, or 50°C. Subsequently, test each agar slant culture for its ability to hydrolyze fat, protein, and carbohydrate (see Exercise 17).

2. At intervals of approximately 3 to 5 days, over a period of 2 or 3 weeks, repeat all the examinations outlined in step 1 above. In addition, record the physical appearance of the milk at each of these times.

RESULTS

Tabulate results of the various examinations in the following table.

| DATE | DESCRIPTION OF MILK | MICROSCOPIC EXAMINATION | PLATE COUNTS | | | CHARACTERISTICS OF CULTURES ISOLATED |
			5°C	35°C	50°C	

QUESTIONS

1. Which of the major substrates of the milk was first utilized? What is the experimental evidence in support of your answer?

_____

_____

_____

_____

_____

_____

_____

2. What generalizations can you make about the succession of (a) morphological types and (b) physiological types of microorganisms during prolonged incubation of the milk?

_____

_____

_____

_____

_____

_____

_____

_____

_____

_____

_____

3. What interactions among various microbial species may have occurred during the incubation of the milk?

_____

_____

_____

_____

_____

_____

_____

_____

_____

_____

EXERCISE FIFTY
THE PRODUCTION AND ASSAY OF A MICROBIAL ENZYME (PENICILLINASE)

REFERENCE: Text, chap. 9.

Penicillinase is an extracellular enzyme produced by many microorganisms. Some species of bacteria produce extremely large quantities of this enzyme. In this experiment, penicillinase will be produced by *Streptomyces albus*, and you will determine its potency for inactivating penicillin.

MATERIALS

1. 200 ml nutrient broth in 1,000-ml Erlenmeyer flask
2. 1- and 10-ml sterile pipettes
3. Membrane-filter apparatus, e.g., Millipore filter
4. Fluid thioglycolate broth, 15 ml per tube
5. 1% phosphate buffer, pH 7.0
6. Freshly prepared penicillin solution, 50,000 units/ml
7. Trypticase-soy-agar culture of *Streptomyces albus*
8. Broth culture of *Staphylococcus aureus* (ATCC 6538P)
9. Rotary or reciprocating shaker
10. pH meter.

PROCEDURE

1. Wash the growth off a 1-week-old trypticase-soy-agar slant culture of *Strep. albus* with 3 to 5 ml sterile trypticase-soy broth. Use to inoculate the 1-liter flask containing 200 ml nutrient broth. Incubate the flask at 25°C on a shaking device.
2. Each day, over a 3-day period, remove a 10-ml sample from the flask culture; refrigerate the samples. On the fourth day, remove the flask from the shaker, and take another 10-ml sample. (Refrigerate the remaining culture in the flask.)
3. Prepare samples for estimation of penicillinase activity. Determine the pH (use a pH meter) of each of the four samples; adjust pH to 7.2 if necessary; sterilize each sample by filtration. You may have to centrifuge first if the filter gets clogged easily.

4. Assay for penicillinase activity.* The method for determining enzyme activity in the culture filtrates can be summarized as follows:

   a. Sterile culture filtrate (source of penicillinase) and penicillin are added simultaneously to a tube of culture medium.

   b. This mixture is held for a time to allow enzyme action.

   c. The tube containing this mixture is then inoculated with *Staph. aureus* (ATCC 6538P), which is sensitive to about 0.1 unit of penicillin per milliliter; hence growth indicates no residual penicillin, and no growth indicates residual penicillin. Experimental details for testing the sterile culture filtrates for the ability to inactivate penicillin are as follows (see sketch for outline):

   a. Add 1.0, 0.5, and 0.1 ml of each sterile sample to individual tubes of fluid thioglycolate broth.

*The procedure described here will provide only a relative approximation of the penicillinase in each sample. For a quantitative assay procedure, see F. W. Bowman and S. Holdowsky, Production and Control of a Stable Penicillinase, *Antibiotics Chemotherapy,* 10:508–514 (1960).

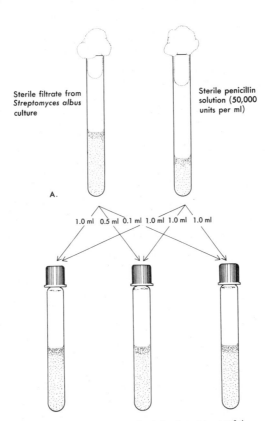

Sterile filtrate from *Streptomyces albus* culture

Sterile penicillin solution (50,000 units per ml)

A.

1.0 ml 0.5 ml 0.1 ml 1.0 ml 1.0 ml 1.0 ml

Schematic outline of procedure for estimation of penicillinase activity of culture filtrates.

B. Tubes of thioglycolate broth (incubate 2 hr at 25°C)

1.0 ml   1.0 ml   1.0 ml

C. 1:100 dilution of *Staphylococcus aureus*

b. Prepare a sterile solution of sodium- or potassium-benzyl penicillin in 1% phosphate buffer, pH 7.0, to contain 50,000 units/ml. (This solution must be prepared just before use.)

c. Add 1 ml of this penicillin solution to each tube of thioglycolate broth which previously received culture filtrate.

d. Shake the tubes vigorously to mix thoroughly. Allow to incubate at 25°C for 2 hr. At the end of the 2-hr period, inoculate each tube with 1 ml of a 1:100 dilution of a 24-hr culture of *Staph. aureus;* incubate tubes at 37°C for 24 to 48 hr; then observe for presence or absence of growth. NOTE: The following controls should be included in this experiment: a tube of medium inoculated with each filtrate to ascertain sterility and a tube of medium inoculated with *Staph. aureus* (culture control).

5. If time is available, additional experiments, as suggested below, may be performed using the culture fluid remaining in the 1-liter flask (step 2 above).

a. Remove the growth of *Strep. albus* by filtration; precipitate the penicillinase by adding ammonium sulfate to saturation. Recover the enzyme, which is in the precipitate, by redissolving it in pH 7.0 phosphate buffer. Assay this enzyme preparation.

b. The enzyme so recovered can be studied for its activity at various pH's and temperatures. To perform such experiments, one might allow the enzyme to be in contact with graded amounts of penicillin under specific conditions wherein temperature and/or pH would be the variable factor. The residual penicillin, after a period of exposure to the enzyme, could be determined as described in step 4 above.

RESULTS

1. Describe the appearance of the *Strep. albus* culture in the shake flasks on each of the four days of incubation.

INCUBATION TIME	DESCRIPTION OF GROWTH

2. Tabulate results of the penicillinase assay as suggested below. Report growth (penicillin inactivation) as +; no growth as 0.

SAMPLE	AMOUNT OF CULTURE FILTRATE			CONTROLS	
	1.0 ml	0.5 ml	0.10 ml	A	B

A =

B =

QUESTIONS

1. Assume that one of the inoculated penicillin-penicillinase culture tubes, as used in this experiment, showed no evidence of growth at 48 hr but on further incubation, namely, after 7 days, growth of *Staph. aureus* did occur. How could this be explained?

_____

_____

_____

_____

_____

_____

2. Name other species of bacteria that produce penicillinase. Are any of these pathogens? If so, what does this mean in terms of their susceptibility to penicillin chemotherapy?

_____

_____

_____

_____

_____

_____

3. Discuss the importance and necessity of employing various controls in an experimental procedure such as the ones performed here.

_____

_____

_____

_____

_____

_____

4. Why was a specific strain of *Staph. aureus* used in this experiment?

EXERCISE FIFTY-ONE
ENRICHMENT CULTURE TECHNIQUE:
ISOLATION OF PHENOL-OXIDIZING MICROORGANISMS

Natural environments are generally inhabited by numerous physiological types of microorganisms; the population of each type may vary considerably. In some instances, species of a biotype of particular interest to the investigator are present in such minority that it is difficult, if not impossible, to isolate them by the routine techniques, i.e., a streak plate or pour plate of the specimen. When the desired organisms are suspected of being few in number, the use of the enrichment technique greatly improves the prospect of their isolation. In principle, this technique provides an environment, i.e., media composition and physical conditions, which is preferentially selective for the biotype being sought. Consequently, on successive transfers in such an environment, the particular biotype will emerge as the predominant, if not exclusive, population. Using this principle, an attempt will be made to isolate microorganisms capable of utilizing phenol as their source of energy (phenol-oxidizing organisms).

REFERENCES: Text, chap. 8; MMM, chap. 3.

MATERIALS

1. Ingredients for mineral-salts medium: $(NH_4)_2SO_4$, K_2HPO_4, KH_2PO_4, $CaCl_2$, $FeSO_4 \cdot 7H_2O$, $MnCl_2 \cdot 4H_2O$
2. Phenol*
3. Agar
4. 250-ml Erlenmeyer flasks
5. Sterile petri dishes
6. 1- and 10-ml sterile pipettes
7. Soil samples

*This exercise can be adapted for enrichment culture isolation of other biotypes by substituting the available energy source, e.g., hydrocarbon, cellulose, etc.

PROCEDURE

Several different media are required for this exercise. They should be prepared in advance and stored in a refrigerator until required.

PREPARATION OF MEDIA

1. Phenol—mineral-salts medium.
   a. *Basal medium ingredients solution:* Prepare three separate solutions of the basal medium ingredients as indicated below. Sterilize them by autoclaving (15 min at 121°C).
      Solution A: $(NH_4)_2SO_4$, 1.0 g; K_2HPO_4, 1.0 g; KH_2PO_4, 0.5 g; H_2O, 700 ml.
      Solution B: $CaCl_2$, 0.01 g; $FeSo_4 \cdot 7H_2O$, 0.005 g; H_2O, 100 ml.
      Solution C: $MgSO_4 \cdot 7H_2O$, 0.2 g; $MnCl_2 \cdot 4H_2O$, 0.10 g; H_2O, 100 ml.
   b. *Phenol solution:* Prepare a solution to contain 7.5 g phenol per 100 ml H_2O.
   c. *Combination:* The phenol—mineral-salts medium is prepared by combining the above solutions in the following proportions: 7 parts solution A; 1 part solution B; 1 part solution C; and 1 part phenol solution. Place 40 ml of this medium into sterile stoppered 250-ml Erlenmeyer flasks; three such flasks will be required for each soil sample. Also dispense 10 ml per tube into 10 sterile test tubes.
2. Double-strength phenol—mineral-salts solution: Prepare as above, but double the concentration of each ingredient. Approximately 100 ml will be needed.
3. Sterile agar solution: Dissolve 3 g of agar in 100 ml of water and sterilize by autoclaving.

Enrichment culture procedure.

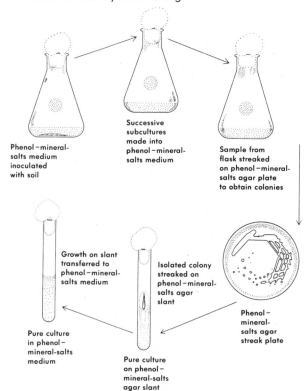

Phenol—mineral-salts medium inoculated with soil

Successive subcultures made into phenol—mineral-salts medium

Sample from flask streaked on phenol—mineral-salts agar plate to obtain colonies

Growth on slant transferred to phenol—mineral-salts medium

Isolated colony streaked on phenol—mineral-salts agar slant

Phenol—mineral-salts agar streak plate

Pure culture in phenol—mineral-salts medium

Pure culture on phenol—mineral-salts agar slant

4. Phenol–mineral-salts agar medium: Add the agar solution (100 ml) aseptically to the 100 ml double-strength phenol–mineral-salts solution; mix thoroughly and dispense into petri dishes and sterile test tubes (about six of each). Slant the tubed medium.

ENRICHMENT OF INOCULUM

Inoculate three flasks containing phenol–mineral-salts medium, each with a different sample of soil. Use approximately 0.5 g of soil for inoculum. Incubate these flasks at 25°C for 3 days (preferably on a shaking device) then make a transfer of 0.1 ml from each flask into another flask of phenol–mineral-salts medium. Repeat the same procedure after the second set of flasks has incubated 3 days.

ISOLATION OF PHENOL–UTILIZING MICROORGANISMS

See the sketch illustrating the scheme.

Prepare streak plates on phenol–mineral-salts agar from each of the last series of enrichment culture flasks (see illustration of scheme). Incubate plates at 25°C; then observe them for the presence of any colonies. Transfer representative colonies to phenol–mineral-salts agar slants. Test each pure culture in the fluid phenol–mineral-salts medium to ascertain that it does grow in this medium.

Characterize each culture isolated, following the schemes suggested in Exercises 17 to 20.

RESULTS

1. Describe the predominant morphological types of micro-organisms during each stage of the enrichment culture procedure.

2. Summarize the characteristics of phenol-utilizing micro-organisms isolated.

CULTURE IDENTIFICATION	SOURCE	CHARACTERISTICS

QUESTIONS

1. How might you account for the following experimental results? A colony is transferred from the phenol—mineral-salts agar into the fluid phenol—mineral-salts medium, and after appropriate incubation no growth occurs.

2. Name some of the products which may result from the microbial oxidation of phenol.

3. As this experiment was performed, is it likely that organisms from the original inoculum (soil) became adapted to the utilization of phenol? How might you proceed experimentally to acquire evidence to confirm or deny this assumption?

EXERCISE FIFTY-TWO
BACTERIAL GENETICS

The study of bacterial genetics has advanced rapidly in recent years. The use of bacteria and bacteriophage for investigating many fundamental problems in genetics has contributed greatly not only to our understanding of genetics but also to our understanding of bacteria. Microbial genetics has become a very specialized subject; only a few experiments are carried out in this exercise to illustrate genetic changes in bacteria.

Changes in bacteria may be either phenotypic or genotypic. The phenotype of a bacterium is a result of the interaction of its genetic constitution (genotype) and its environment. Thus changes brought about by altering the environmental conditions are not of a permanent nature; e.g., pigment production with *Serratia marcescens* and such changes are seen in virtually the whole population.

Genotypic changes in bacteria affect only small numbers of organisms in a bacterial population and are permanent. Changes in genotype may occur by mutation of the bacterial genetic material, i.e., DNA, or by recombination. The latter has been defined as any alteration of genotype resulting from the interaction of one microorganism with another or with genetic material derived from another microorganism. This broad definition of recombination thus includes such processes as transformation, transduction, conversion, conjugation, and the transfer of episomes such as the fertility factor and the colicines.

REFERENCE: An excellent manual on microbial genetics is "Experiments in Microbial Genetics," R. C. Clowes and W. Hayes (eds.), Blackwell, Oxford, 1968.

MATERIALS
PHENOTYPIC CHANGES

1. Nutrient-agar slopes of *Serratia marcescens* and *Proteus vulgaris*
2. Gram-stain reagents
3. 1 nutrient-agar plate
4. Nutrient-agar plate with 0.1% phenol incorporated
5. 2 nutrient-agar slopes

GENOTYPIC CHANGES
FERMENTATION MUTANTS

1. *Escherichia coli* ATCC 15939 on nutrient agar
2. 3 MacConkey's agar plates

NUTRITIONAL MUTANTS

1. Nutrient-agar slopes of *E. coli* strains ATCC 23716, 23717, 23718, 23719, and 23720
2. 20 minimal-agar-medium plates
3. 10 ml sterile 1% acid-hydrolyzed casein hydrolysate
4. Sterile glass spreaders
5. 10 ml sterile tryptophan, 2 mg/ml
6. 10 ml sterile anthranilic acid, 2 mg/ml
7. 10 ml sterile indole, 2 mg/ml
8. 5 tubes of liquid minimal medium of 5 ml each

RECOMBINANTS

1. *E. coli* strains ATCC 23590 and 23724 grown in 10 ml heart-infusion broth for 18 hr
2. 100 ml sterile saline
3. 2 centrifuge tubes
4. Bench centrifuge
5. 10 minimal-medium-agar plates
6. 4 heart-infusion-agar plates
7. Sterile 1-ml pipettes

PROCEDURE
PHENOTYPIC CHANGES

1. You are provided with an agar slope inoculated with *S. marcescens* and incubated at 37°C. Subculture this organism on two nutrient-agar slopes; incubate one at room temperature and the other at 37°C.
2. Examine after 24 hr for pigment production.
3. Make a gram stain from the growth obtained at each temperature to satisfy yourself that the same bacteria are present on both slopes.
4. You are provided with an agar slope culture of *P. vulgaris* and two petri plates, one containing nutrient agar and the other nutrient agar plus 0.1% phenol.
5. Make a hanging-drop preparation to check the motility of the culture.
6. Streak both plates for isolated colonies with *P. vulgaris* and incubate at 37°C for 24 hr.
7. Examine the type of growth obtained (look for surface growth with a background light).
8. Make a hanging-drop preparation for motility examination from each plate.

GENOTYPIC CHANGES
FERMENTATION MUTANTS

One type of bacterial mutant is the fermentation mutant, where one or more changes in the fermentation pattern of the organism are seen. One mutant strain of *E. coli* is lactose-negative; i.e., it has lost the ability to ferment lactose. However, it is not a very stable mutant and frequently reverts to its original state; in other words, back mutation to the lactose-positive characteristic occurs.

1. You are provided with a mutant strain of *E. coli* grown on a nutrient-agar slope.
2. Streak the organism on MacConkey's agar for isolated colonies and incubate at 37°C overnight.
3. Examine the plate and look for both lactose-positive and lactose-negative colonies. (On MacConkey's agar lactose-positive colonies appear red and lactose-negative colorless.)
4. Pick one lactose-positive and one lactose-negative colony and streak on MacConkey's agar plates.
5. Incubate at 37°C and examine the next day.

NUTRITIONAL MUTANTS

Nutritional mutants are bacteria which have lost their ability to synthesize a substance essential to their growth. They can therefore grow only when that substance is provided in the medium. Such mutants have one or more enzyme deficiencies preventing the synthesis of the essential substance, e.g., an amino acid.

The following experiment has been designed to show that a number of mutants, all derived from the same wild type able to synthesize tryptophan and now requiring its addition to minimal medium for growth to occur, are blocked at different steps in the synthesis of this amino acid. The pathway of tryptophan bio-synthesis (simplified) is as follows:

$$\overset{A}{\rightarrow} \text{anthranilic acid} \overset{B}{\rightarrow} \text{indole} \overset{C}{\rightarrow} \text{tryptophan}$$

If the mutant is blocked in the conversion of indole to tryptophan, i.e., at point C, it will grow only when tryptophan is added to the medium. If, however, the mutant is blocked at point B, it cannot convert anthranilic acid to indole and will grow when either indole or tryptophan is added to the minimal medium but not when anthranilic acid is added. The reason for this, of course, is that the enzyme which converts anthranilic acid to indole has been lost as a result of the mutation. If the mutation has caused a block at A, the mutant will grow in the presence of all three substances. By the method outlined below, it is possible to es-tablish at which point a mutation has occurred in the biosyn-thesis of tryptophan.

1. You are provided with four mutants blocked at various points in the tryptophan pathway and also with the wild-type parent organism, all grown for 24 hr on nutrient-agar slants. Inoculate heavily into liquid minimal medium overnight before use.
2. Prepare the minimal-medium plates in the following manner. Add 3 to 4 drops of 1% casein hydrolysate (acid-hydrolyzed) to each of 20 plates. Spread these drops over the surface with a clean sterile glass spreader. The small amount of casein hydrolysate, which contains no tryptophan, helps to get the organisms started on simple glucose-salts medium.

3. To five of the above plates spread in a similar manner anthranilic acid; to another five, indole; and to another five, tryptophan. The remaining five serve as controls and will detect the wild type.

4. Streak a loopful of each organism on one of each of the four different plates, i.e.,
   a. Minimal medium plus casein hydrolysate
   b. Minimal medium plus casein hydrolysate plus anthranilic acid
   c. Minimal medium plus casein hydrolysate plus indole
   d. Minimal medium plus casein hydrolysate plus tryptophan

5. Incubate at 37°C for 24 to 48 hr.

6. Locate the block in each mutant and indicate which strain is the wild type.

RECOMBINANTS

Two mutants cannot grow on a minimal-agar medium which contains only glucose and salts. If after the cultures have been mixed and incubated for a short time they are then plated on minimal medium and growth occurs, conjugation must have taken place.

1. You are provided with two strains of *E. coli* grown overnight in 10 ml of heart-infusion broth at 37°C.

2. Centrifuge each culture and wash twice with sterile saline. After the final centrifugation resuspend the cells in 3 ml sterile saline.

3. Combine 2 ml from each culture, retaining the other 1 ml for control plates.

4. Incubate at 37°C for 15 to 20 min.

5. Plate samples from each culture and from the mixture on minimal-agar medium as follows:

   Mixture: 0.05 ml on two minimal-agar-medium plates
              0.10 ml on two minimal-agar-medium plates
              0.20 ml on two minimal-agar-medium plates

   Pure cultures (separately):   0.2 ml on two minimal-agar-medium plates
                                 0.2 ml on two heart-infusion-agar plates

6. Incubate at 37°C for 24 to 72 hr and examine periodically for the growth of prototrophs from the mixed culture plated on minimal agar. There should be no growth on the minimal medium with the original pure (unmixed) cultures.

RESULTS
PHENOTYPIC CHANGES

1. Describe the pigmentation of *S. marcescens* after incubation at 37°C:

    25°C (room temperature):

2. Gram stain of
    37°C culture: _____
    25°C culture: _____

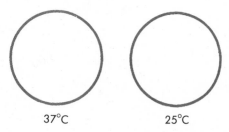

37°C   25°C

3. Describe the type of growth obtained with *P. vulgaris* on:
    Nutrient-agar plate:

    Nutrient-agar plate with 0.1% phenol:

4. Describe the motility of the cultures examined.

GENOTYPIC CHANGES
FERMENTATION MUTANTS

1. Describe the appearance of the colonies on the initial MacConkey's plate.

2. What kind of results did you obtain upon subsequent transfer of the lactose-positive and lactose-negative colonies?

NUTRITIONAL MUTANTS

1. Locate the block in each mutant and designate which strain is the wild type:
   E. coli ATCC 23716:
   E. coli ATCC 23717:
   E. coli ATCC 23718:
   E. coli ATCC 23719:
   E. coli ATCC 23720:

RECOMBINANTS

1. Report the growth obtained in the following table.

CULTURE	MEDIUM	INOCULUM, ml	GROWTH (+ OR −)
Mixed	Minimal		
		0.05	
		0.1	
		0.2	
Pure (ATCC 23590)	Minimal	0.2	
	Infusion		
		0.2	
Pure (ATCC 23724)	Minimal	0.2	
	Infusion		
		0.2	

EXERCISE FIFTY-THREE
ISOLATION OF STREPTOMYCIN-RESISTANT MUTANTS OF ESCHERICHIA COLI

REFERENCE: Text, chap. 12.

During the normal growth of a bacterial culture some cells develop with an aberration in their DNA; it is likely that some alteration occurred in assembling the nucleotide sequence. Such cells are *mutants,* and if they are able to grow in the environment provided, the altered DNA is reproduced in successive generations; consequently, these organisms exhibit some characteristics different from those of the parent strain. In normal populations, the incidence of mutants is very low, for example, 1 in 10,000 or 1 in 1,000,000. Nevertheless, since bacterial cultures ordinarily reach populations in the hundreds of millions or billions, an appreciable number of mutants are produced. The fate of the mutant is determined by its ability to survive in the environment in which it occurs; in many instances, the environmental conditions are less favorable for the mutant than for the parent strain, and the mutant is crowded out.

In the following experiment, you will attempt to isolate streptomycin-resistant strains (mutants) of *Escherichia coli* from a parent strain that is streptomycin-sensitive.

MATERIALS

1. Trypticase-soy agar, 15 ml per tube
2. Sterile petri dishes
3. Sterile streptomycin solution, 10 mg/ml
4. 18- to 24-hr broth culture of *E. coli*
5. Trypticase-soy broth, 9 ml per tube
6. Media for the performance of cultural and biochemical tests on parent strain and isolated mutant(s) (see Exercises 15, 17 to 20)

PROCEDURE

1. Prepare three streptomycin gradient plates as follows. Pour one tube of melted, cooled (45°C) trypticase-soy agar into a petri dish; elevate one side of the plate so that the

A. Trypticase-soy agar poured into petri dish elevated on one side.

B. Petri dish removed to flat surface and trypticase-soy agar containing streptomycin added

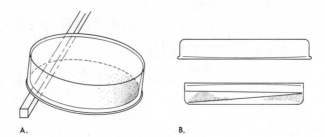

A.

B.

medium is in a thin layer on one side and a thick layer on the other (see sketch).

2. When this layer of medium solidifies, place the plate on a horizontal surface and pour in a tube of trypticase-soy agar to which you previously added 1 ml sterile streptomycin solution. The plate should now appear as shown in the sketch. The streptomycin will establish a concentration gradient across the plate; the high concentration of streptomycin will be where the streptomycin agar is thick, and the low concentration on the opposite side. Mark your plate accordingly.

3. Place the agar plates in the 35°C incubator for approximately 1 hr to reduce surface moisture.

4. Inoculate each plate by placing a single drop of the *E. coli* culture on the agar surface and then spreading it out uniformly over the entire surface with a sterile bent glass rod. It is important that the surface be uniformly and completely inoculated.

5. Incubate the plates 2 to 4 days; then observe for the presence of isolated colonies in the region of the high streptomycin concentration. Transfer one or more of these colonies to a trypticase-soy-agar slant, label them adequately, and incubate, along with a transfer from the parent strain, for 24 to 48 hr.

6. Determine streptomycin resistance of parent strain and mutant strains. Liquefy several tubes of trypticase-soy agar (20 ml per tube) and add decreasing amounts of streptomycin to each tube. NOTE: The laboratory instructor will suggest the concentrations to use. Pour the contents of each tube into separate labeled petri dishes. When the medium solidifies, make a single streak of each culture across each plate. Be sure that the plate is labeled so you can identify the culture used for each streak. You will, in effect, have each culture inoculated on media ranging from a high level to a low level of streptomycin. Incubate plates at 35°C and observe them for growth after 24 to 48 hr.

7. At the same time that step 6 above is performed, characterize each of the strains morphologically (gram stain), culturally (see Exercise 15), and biochemically (see Exercises 17 to 20).

RESULTS

1. Sketch one of the streptomycin gradient plates showing distribution of growth.

2. Tabulate the results you obtained on the streptomycin resistance of isolated strains (mutants) and the original culture. Indicate as follows: $+$ = growth; 0 = no growth.

STRAINS	STREPTOMYCIN CONTENT OF MEDIUM, MICROGRAMS PER MILLILITER			

3. Tabulate the morphological, cultural, and biochemical characteristics of the original culture as well as of each strain isolated.

QUESTIONS

1. Define mutant, mutation, and mutagen.

_____

_____

_____

_____

_____

2. Did any of the strains that you isolated exhibit characteristics different from the parent strain in addition to greater streptomycin resistance? How can this be explained in terms of DNA?

_____

_____

_____

_____

_____

_____

3. Genetic experiments with bacteria frequently employ strains with "markers." What does this expression mean? What is the significance of using such strains in genetic studies?

_____

_____

_____

_____

_____

_____

_____

4. Outline an experiment by which you could isolate nutritional mutants of *E. coli*.

_____

_____

_____

_____

_____

_____

_____

_____

_____

_____

EXERCISE FIFTY-FOUR
GROWTH OF CELLS

In discussing growth of cells with reference to unicellular micro-organisms, one should distinguish between growth (which may be defined as an increase in total protoplasm) of the individual cell and the increase in the number of cells in the population or culture. In general, unless otherwise specifically stated, physiological studies on growth of microorganisms entail manipulations that incorporate a culture or a population of cells.

It is possible to follow the growth of a culture by measurement of a number of parameters. Such measurements include the following:

1. Direct microscopic counts of numbers of individual cells in a population, using a counting device such as the Petroff-Hauser counting chamber
2. Viable counts using plate counts of appropriate dilutions of the culture
3. Change in turbidity of a culture with the aid of a colorimeter, spectrophotometer, or nephelometer
4. Change in dry weight per unit volume of the culture
5. Change in volume of packed cells after standard conditions of centrifugation
6. Change in amount of metabolic activity, such as evolution of carbon dioxide, exhaustion of oxygen, production of acids, etc.
7. Change in any of the chemical constituents of the cell population, such as the protein, RNA, DNA, and polysaccharide content.

One of the reasons it is possible to follow growth of a culture by so many criteria is that there is an equal proportional (orderly) increase in every constituent of the cell, e.g., every measurable component of the cell increasing by 25 percent. However, this situation of balanced growth may not hold true for the macromolecules during all phases of the growth cycle. For example, bacterial cells are larger when growing rapidly than when growing slowly, so that in the growth cycle they are larger cells during the logarithmic growth phase than during the stationary phase. Such faster-growing cells have a higher total RNA content when expressed as a RNA/protein ratio or a RNA/DNA ratio. In the light of present knowledge, this higher RNA content is due to one species of RNA, the ribosomal RNA. Thus rRNA/DNA ratio may vary over a ten- to twentyfold range while the sRNA/DNA ratio may be less than twofold.

During the logarithmic growth phase, certain important attributes of cellular growth may be summarized as follows:

1. Protoplasmic substances increase as an exponential or logarithmic function of time.
2. The generation time remains constant.
3. The specific growth rate (quantity of protoplasm produced per unit of time by a unit quantity of protoplasm) is proportional to the reciprocal of the generation time.

Many aspects of microbial growth can be reduced to mathematical expressions. Starting with a single cell, the total population N at the end of a given time period would be expressed as

$$N = 1 \times 2^n \qquad [1]$$

where 2^n is the bacterial population after the nth generation (since a cell divides by binary fission). This can be clarified further by considering the increase in population by the one cell as follows:

$$1 \text{ cell} \rightarrow 2 \ \rightarrow 4 \ \rightarrow 8 \ \rightarrow \text{no. of cells}$$
$$1 \text{ or } 2^0 \text{ cell} \rightarrow 2^1 \rightarrow 2^2 \rightarrow 2^3 \rightarrow \text{no. of cells}$$
$$0 \text{ generation} \rightarrow 1 \ \rightarrow 2 \ \rightarrow 3 \ \rightarrow n \text{ no. of generations}$$

Thus expressed exponentially, the population after n generations becomes 2^n. Since, in practice, microbial physiologists do not study just one cell because of their particular laboratory techniques, 1 in Eq. [1] becomes

$$N = N_0 \times 2^n \qquad [2]$$

where N_0 represents the number of organisms at zero time, or the initial population of the culture. Solving Eq. [2] for n, we have

$$\log N = \log N_0 + n \log 2 \qquad [3]$$

and rearranging we have

$$n = \frac{\log N - \log N_0}{\log 2} \qquad [4]$$

Since $\log 2 = 0.301$,

$$n = 3.32 (\log N - \log N_0) \qquad [5]$$

or

$$n = 3.32 \log \frac{N}{N_0} \qquad [6]$$

One of the reasons why logarithms to the base 10 are used is convenience. Most workers are familiar with them, and the original inoculum N_0 contains a thousand or more bacteria. Other workers like Monod have suggested using logarithms to the base 2 because an increase of one logarithmic unit corresponds to one doubling or one generation. If this is done,

$$\log_2 N = \log_2 N_0 + n \qquad [7]$$

Solving for n gives

$$n = \log_2 N - \log_2 N_0 \qquad [8]$$

Natural logarithms, $\log_e$ or ln, may also be used, since Eq. [2] is an exponential curve. (Tables are available for all these logarithmic bases.) Regardless of the base used, they all bear a constant relation to each other, and the equations take the same form. Bear in mind also that conversion from one base to another can be made by multiplying or dividing by a constant, i.e.,

$$\log_2 x = 3.32 \log_{10} x$$

and

$$\log_e x = \frac{\log_{10} x}{0.43}$$

The average generation time G during the same interval can be determined by substituting for n so that

$$G = \frac{\text{time elapsed}}{\text{no. of generations}} = \frac{t}{n} = \frac{t}{3.32 \log_{10} N/N_0}$$

$$= \frac{0.3010t}{\log_{10} N - \log_{10} N_0} \qquad [9]$$

The multiplication rate r, or number of generations per unit of time, can be obtained simply by dividing the number of generations n by the same time interval (between inoculation and time of final population sampling):

$$r = \frac{n}{t} \qquad [10]$$

Substituting for n with Eq. [6] gives

$$r = \frac{3.32 \log_{10} N/N_0}{t} \qquad [11]$$

Since the generation time G is the time for the population to double, it is the reciprocal of the doublings per unit time,

$$G = \frac{1}{r} \qquad [12]$$

The specific growth rate k, defined previously as the amount of protoplasm produced per unit of time by a unit amount of protoplasm, is equal to $0.693/G$. Let us see how this is obtained.

During the growth of a culture, the amount of material which is growing is continuously increasing and may be described by

$$\frac{dC}{dt} = kC \tag{13}$$

where

C = cell no. or quantity of material
t = time, hr
k = specific growth rate

Integrating over an interval t_0 to t_1, we get

$$\ln C_1 = \ln C_0 + k(t_1 - t_0) \tag{14}$$

Rearranging,

$$k = \frac{\ln C_1 - \ln C_0}{t_1 - t_0} \tag{15}$$

Thus k may be defined as the increase in the natural logarithm of some property of the culture divided by the time interval required for that increase. In the particular situation where the culture has doubled in the measured constituent, $t_1 - t_0$ is the generation time and $\ln C_1 - \ln C_0$ becomes equal to $\ln 2$:

$$k = \frac{\ln 2}{\text{generation time}} = \frac{0.693}{G} \tag{16}$$

The most convenient and commonly used procedure for determining the specific growth rate of a culture is to measure one of the parameters mentioned at timed intervals and then to plot the values as a function of time on semilogarithmic paper. The best straight line through the plotted points is used to read off the time required for a doubling of the measured parameter. The generation time G in hours is then divided into 0.693 to give k, the specific growth rate of the culture [Eq. (16)].

REFERENCE: F. C. Neidhardt and R. F. Boyd, "Cell Biology," Burgess, Minneapolis, 1965.

MATERIALS
SAMPLING A GROWING CULTURE

1. Trypticase-soy-broth culture of *Arthrobacter globiformis* in the stationary phase (24-hr, shaken, at 25°C)
2. Sterile 10-ml pipettes
3. 200 ml trypticase-soy broth in 1-liter Erlenmeyer flask
4. 4 large screw-cap tubes for 25-ml samples
5. Ice bath
6. Rotary or reciprocating shaker at 25°C

OPTICAL-DENSITY MEASUREMENTS

1. Bausch and Lomb Spectronic 20 spectrophotometer (or equivalent)
2. Sterile cuvettes for each sampling

DETERMINATION OF DRY
WEIGHTS

1. 8 aluminum weighing pans
2. Analytical balance
3. Desiccator
4. Bench-top centrifuge
5. 2 centrifuge tubes
6. Sterile distilled water
7. 85°C drying oven

DIRECT CELL COUNT

1. 4 sterile test tubes
2. 100 ml buffered saline (dissolve 2.88 g NaH_2PO_4 and 12.5 g Na_2HPO_4 in 100 ml distilled water; add 20 ml of this solution to 980 ml 0.9% saline)
3. 10 ml 5.0% aqueous phenol solution
4. Binocular microscope with 10X ocular and 4-mm objective or 6X ocular and oil-immersion objective with phase-contrast accessories
5. Petroff-Hauser counting chamber
6. Sterile Pasteur pipettes

VIABLE COUNT BY
PLATING

1. 32 dilution blanks with 9 ml physiological saline in each
2. Sterile 1-ml pipettes
3. Trypticase-soy-agar plates; prepared 2 to 3 days ahead
4. 25°C incubator
5. Glass spreaders in 95% ethanol in beaker

TREATMENT OF CULTURE
FOR MACROMOLECULAR
ANALYSES

1. Refrigerated centrifuge (Servall or equivalent)
2. 1 liter phosphate buffer (dissolve 9.078 g KH_2PO_4 in 1,000 ml water; dissolve 9.465 g Na_2HPO_4 in 1,000 ml water; combine 611 ml of the Na_2HPO_4 solution with 389 ml of the KH_2PO_4 solution; the pH of this $M/15$ buffer should be 7.0)
3. 50 ml 10% trichloroacetic acid
4. 4 centrifuge tubes for refrigerated centrifuge
5. 200 ml cold 5% trichloroacetic acid
6. 4 thick-walled glass test tubes
7. Boiling water bath
8. Cold water bath
9. Clean marbles

PROTEIN DETERMINATION

1. Reagents A, B, and C as described in text
2. Folin-Ciocalteu reagent
3. 10 ml 1 N NaOH
4. 100°C water bath
5. 34 test tubes for dilution
6. 250 ml $N/10$ NaOH
7. Bovine serum albumin, fraction V, standard dilutions (10 ml each) as described
8. Spectronic 20 spectrophotometer with accessories for adapting for use at 690 nm
9. 1- and 5-ml pipettes

RNA DETERMINATION

1. Reagent with orcinol as described in text
2. 17 thick-walled test tubes
3. 1- and 5-ml pipettes
4. Boiling water bath
5. Clean marbles
6. Spectronic 20 spectrophotometer with accessories for use at 670 nm (or Beckman DU or similar instrument)
7. RNA standard dilutions as described
8. Ice-water bath

DNA DETERMINATION

1. Diphenylamine reagent
2. DNA standard dilutions as described
3. 5 ml $N/50$ NaOH
4. 10 thick-walled glass test tubes
5. Clean marbles
6. Spectrophotometer as used above
7. 1- and 5-ml pipettes
8. Ice-water bath

NEGATIVE STAINING

1. 10% aqueous nigrosin (spin down at 24,150 g's for 10 min; decant gently and use supernate)
2. Slides and cover slips
3. Permount or similar mounting fluid
4. Binocular microscope

PROCEDURE
SAMPLING OF GROWING CULTURE

Members of the genus *Arthrobacter* exhibit a characteristic morphological growth cycle in which stationary-phase and older cells persist as coccoid organisms. Upon transfer to fresh medium they become rod-shaped before completing the cycle by reversion to coccoid forms. This makes *Arthrobacter* organisms very suitable for the demonstration of morphological changes at the cell level during the growth cycle of a culture.

1. You are provided with a trypticase-soy-broth culture of *A. globiformis* in the stationary phase of growth.
2. *Immediately* inoculate 20 ml into 200 ml fresh sterile trypticase-soy broth in a 1-liter Erlenmeyer flask. Mix the inoculated medium well and remove 25 ml *aseptically* into a large screw-cap tube (0-hr sample).
3. Place the sample in the screw-cap tube in an ice bath. Place the medium with *A. globiformis* on a rotary or reciprocating shaker at 25°C.
4. At 2-hr intervals remove 25 ml from the flask and place the samples in the ice bath as soon as possible. It is suggested that this be carried out for the next 6 hours (total of four samples).
5. Perform the following determinations for each sample, the procedures for which are given below. Careful organization

and good understanding of procedures are necessary for successful execution of the experiments.

a. Optical density
b. Dry weight
c. Direct cell count with the Petroff-Hauser counting chamber
d. Viable count by plating
e. Protein content
f. RNA content
g. DNA content
h. Nigrosin stain (negative-staining)

6. After all the data have been collected, plot curves of the above values (except h) against time, using semilogarithmic paper. Calculate the specific growth rate k for the culture from the curve of viable cell count vs. time.

OPTICAL-DENSITY MEASUREMENTS

Set the wavelength of the Spectronic 20 (Bausch and Lomb) at 520 nm and take the optical-density reading with a 5-ml volume of the sample, zeroing the instrument against sterile trypticase-soy broth. Be sure the cuvette with the sample is not fogged with moisture. (This same volume can be used for direct counts, viable counts, and for negative staining.)

DETERMINATION OF DRY WEIGHTS

1. Preweigh to four decimal places two aluminum weighing pans for each sample and place them in a desiccator (total of eight required).
2. Use 10 ml of your sample; centrifuge the cells down in two centrifuge tubes using a bench-top centrifuge with 5 ml sample per tube.
3. Wash the cells once with distilled water.
4. Resuspend the cells in 5 ml distilled water per tube.
5. Transfer 4 ml of the washed bacterial suspension to each of two pans.
6. Carefully place the pans in a drying oven at 85°C for about 12 hr. (This temperature will not cause boiling or spattering.)
7. Remove them and keep in a desiccator until cool.
8. Weigh the pans and calculate the dry weight per milliliter of original culture.

DIRECT CELL COUNT

1. Place 1 ml of the sample (from the cuvette used for optical-density readings) in a test tube.
2. Put in 3.5 ml buffered saline and 0.5 ml 5% phenol solution. Mix with a pipette. The dilution of the sample is now 1:5 (further dilutions may be made with buffered saline if the suspension proves too thick for counting.)
3. Place a drop of the mixture on the ruled area of a clean Petroff-Hauser counting cell. Place the thin, precision-made cover slip over the drop so as to avoid air bubbles. Alternatively, place the cover slip in place first and permit the

suspension to run underneath by capillary action from a Pasteur pipette tip.

4. Let the counting cell stand for 10 min to permit the bacteria to settle into the same focal plane as much as possible.

5. Using phase-constrast illumination, count the bacteria with a 10X ocular and 4-mm objective or with a 6X ocular and the oil-immersion objective. In order to include all bacilli in the field, focus at different levels, up and down.

6. Locate the smallest squares. Count at least 20 squares. Beginning with the first completely ruled square at the upper left hand corner, count diagonally across the counting chamber; then count a few additional squares.

7. Determine the average number per square. Three counts of the diluted suspension should be made, and if they agree within 10 percent, take their average.

8. Calculate the number per milliliter of the original suspension (undiluted) as follows:

(Average no. per square) $\times$ 5 $\times$ 20,000,000

Explanation of factors:

Area of square $= \dfrac{1}{20}$ mm $\times \dfrac{1}{20}$ mm $= \dfrac{1}{400}$ mm^2

Volume over square $= \dfrac{1}{400}$ mm$^2 \times \dfrac{1}{50}$ mm (depth) $= \dfrac{1}{20,000}$ mm^3

$$= \dfrac{1}{20,000} \text{ mm}^3 \times \dfrac{1}{1,000} \text{ ml/mm}^3$$

$$= \dfrac{1}{20,000,000} \text{ ml}$$

Dilution factor $= 5$

VIABLE COUNT BY PLATING

1. Place 1 ml of the sample (from the cuvette used for optical-density readings) in the first tube of a series of dilution tubes containing 9 ml of diluent (physiological saline).

2. Continue making a series of eight tenfold dilutions in all.

3. Make spread plates using 1-ml portions in duplicate of each of the last four dilutions.

4. Incubate the plates in an inverted position for 48 hr at 25°C before counting.

5. Calculate the number of cells per milliliter in the original culture.

TREATMENT OF CULTURE FOR MACROMOLECULAR ANALYSES

1. Wash the remaining 10 ml of the sample three times with cold phosphate buffer and resuspend it in 5 ml of buffer.

2. Add an equal volume (5 ml) of 10% trichloroacetic acid (TCA). Store the suspension at 4°C until actual determinations are run. This step separates two major fractions upon subsequent centrifugation:

   a. An acid-soluble fraction containing low-molecular-weight constituents such as inorganic cations and anions, sugars, organic acids, amino acids, nucleotides and nucleosides, organic phosphate esters, vitamins, coenzymes, polyamines, and oligopeptides

    b.   An acid-insoluble fraction containing the macromolecules of interest in this experiment, such as proteins and nucleic acids

3.   Centrifuge the cells in the cold at about 7,700 g's. Discard the supernate.

4.   Wash the pellet once with cold 5% TCA. Centrifuge and discard the supernate.

5.   Resuspend the cells in exactly 5 ml TCA, using thick-walled glass test tubes.

6.   Heat the cells at 100°C for 30 min in the 5% TCA. (This step removes the nucleic acids from the cells. The proteins remain in the hot acid-insoluble fraction.)

7.   Cool the tubes in a cold water bath.

8.   Centrifuge the mixture as before and decant the supernate carefully. The supernate is used for RNA and DNA determinations; the pellet is used for protein assay.

PROTEIN DETERMINATION

This determination is carried out according to the phenol method of Oyama and Eagle.*

1.   Make up the following reagents:
      Reagent A:
         Na_2CO_3, 20 g
         NaK tartrate or K tartrate, 0.2 g
         Distilled water, 1,000 ml

      Reagent B:
         $CuSO_4 \cdot 5H_2O$, 5.0 g
         Distilled water, 1,000 ml

      Reagent C:
         Add 50 parts reagent A to 1 part reagent B. This is to be prepared fresh before use.
      Folin-Ciocalteu reagent
         Mix 5 ml reagent with 7 ml distilled water

2.   Pipette 1 ml 1 N NaOH into the tube containing the pellet to be used for protein analysis.

3.   Put into a 100°C water bath and swirl gently until almost all cloudiness has disappeared (about 10 min).

4.   Make 1:5, 1:10, and 1:20 dilutions of this dissolved protein solution using N/10 NaOH.

5.   Prepare protein standard with 1,000 μg/ml of bovine serum albumin, fraction V (0.1 g in 100 ml distilled water). Dilute with N/10 NaOH according to the following protocol:

*V. I. Oyama, and H. Eagle, Measurement of Cell Growth in Tissue Culture with a Phenol Reagent (Folin-Ciocalteau), *Proc. Soc. Exptl. Biol. Med.*, 91: 305–307 (1956).

ALBUMIN STANDARD, ml	N/10 NaOH, ml	CONC. ALBUMIN μg/ml
1	4	200
0.9	4.1	180
0.8	4.2	160
0.7	4.3	140

ALBUMIN STANDARD, ml	N/10 NaOH, ml	CONC. ALBUMIN $\mu g/ml$
0.6	4.4	120
0.5	4.5	100
0.4	4.6	80
0.3	4.7	60
0.2	4.8	40
0.1	4.9	20
0	5.0	0

6. To 1 ml of sample add to 5 ml with reagent C. Mix and let stand for 10 min at room temperature.

7. Add in 0.5 ml Folin-Ciocalteu Reagent. Mix and let stand 30 min at room temperature for maximum color development.

8. Read optical density in the Spectronic 20 at 690 nm. Draw the protein-standard curve and from it obtain the values for micrograms of bacterial protein of your diluted samples. From one of the values, taking into account all dilutions made, calculate the micrograms of bacterial protein per milliliter of the original culture.

RNA DETERMINATION

This determination is after the orcinol method of Dische.*

1. Prepare the following reagent just before use:
   1 g purified orcinol
   100 ml concentrated HCl
   0.5 g $FeCl_3 \cdot 6H_2O$

2. Prepare a RNA standard solution using yeast RNA at a concentration of 200 $\mu g/ml$ in distilled water. Assist solution of the RNA with several drops of N/10 NaOH.

3. Set up a series of the standard according to the following protocol in thick-walled glass test tubes:

STANDARD SOLN., ml	WATER, ml	μg RNA/1.5 ml
0.5	1.0	100
0.4	1.1	80
0.25	1.25	50
0.1	1.4	20
0	1.5	0

4. Make 1:5, 1:10, 1:20 dilutions with distilled water and place samples in thick-walled glass tubes.

5. Make up to 1.5 ml with water.

6. Add 3 ml reagent to the samples and to the standard dilutions of RNA.

7. Place in boiling water bath for 20 min, capping each tube with a marble.

8. Cool the tubes in an ice-water bath. Read at 670 nm using the Beckman DU or similar spectrophotometer.

9. Draw the standard curve and deduce the RNA values of the samples tested. Calculate the micrograms of bacterial RNA per milliliter of original culture.

*Z. Dische. Color Reactions of Nucleic Acid Components, in E. Chargaff and J. N. Davidson (eds.), "The Nucleic Acids," vol. 1, Academic, New York 1955.

DNA DETERMINATION

This determination is by the diphenylamine method (Dische*).

1. Prepare the reagent as follows. Dissolve 1 g purified diphenylamine in 100 ml glacial acetic acid. Add 2.75 ml concentrated H_2SO_4.
2. Prepare a DNA standard solution with salmon sperm DNA at 1,000 $\mu g/ml$ in $N/50$ NaOH.
3. Set up a series of the standard according to the following protocol in thick-walled test tubes.

STANDARD SOLN., ml	WATER, ml	μg DNA/1.5 ml
0.5	1.0	500
0.4	1.1	400
0.2	1.3	200
0.1	1.4	100
0.05	1.45	50
0	1.5	0

4. Place 1.5-ml sample in thick-walled glass test tube.
5. Add 3 ml reagent.
6. Boil for 10 min in a boiling water bath with a marble on each tube.
7. Within 5 min of cooling read at 600 nm with a spectrophotometer after cooling in an ice-water bath.
8. Draw the standard curve and deduce the DNA values of the samples tested. Calculate the micrograms of bacterial DNA per milliliter of original culture.

*Ibid.

NEGATIVE STAINING

1. Take a small loopful of cells (from the cuvettes used for optical-density readings) and place it on a cover slip.
2. Add 1 to 2 drops 10% aqueous nigrosin.
3. Mix with a loop thoroughly.
4. Stand it on edge and allow to dry.
5. Reverse the cover slip on a slide with a drop of Permount.
6. Examine under oil immersion. Draw the morphology of the cells for each sampling time and comment with reference to the growth of the culture.

RESULTS

OPTICAL-DENSITY MEASUREMENTS

1. Use the blank space provided to collect your data. Employ appropriate graph paper where required. Then fill in the results in the tables.

SAMPLE		OD
0-hr		
2-hr		
4-hr		
6-hr		

DETERMINATION OF DRY WEIGHTS

SAMPLE	AVERAGE DRY WEIGHT, mg/ml
0-hr	
2-hr	
4-hr	
6-hr	

DIRECT CELL COUNT

SAMPLE	NUMBER OF CELLS PER MILLILITER
0-hr	
2-hr	
4-hr	
6-hr	

**VIABLE CELL COUNT
BY PLATING**

SAMPLE	NO. OF COLONY-FORMING UNITS PER MILLILITER
0-hr	
2-hr	
4-hr	
6-hr	

PROTEIN DETERMINATION

SAMPLE	MICROGRAMS OF PROTEIN PER MILLILITER
0-hr	
2-hr	
4-hr	
6-hr	

RNA DETERMINATION

SAMPLE	MICROGRAMS OF RNA PER MILLILITER
0-hr	
2-hr	
4-hr	
6-hr	

DNA DETERMINATION

SAMPLE	MICROGRAMS DNA PER MILLILITER
0-hr	
2-hr	
4-hr	
6-hr	

NEGATIVE STAINING

Draw the morphology of cells of each sample:

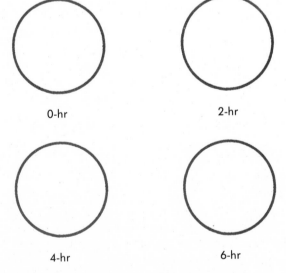

0-hr

2-hr

4-hr

6-hr

Comment on the morphology with reference to the stage of growth of the culture.

2. Plot the above values in the tables against time using semilogarithmic paper (with appropriate cycles).

3. Calculate the specific growth rate k for the culture using data from the curve of viable cell count vs. time.

QUESTIONS

1. What is meant by balanced growth?

_____

_____

_____

_____

_____

2. What is the chemical basis of the assays for DNA, RNA, and protein?

_____

_____

_____

_____

_____

_____

_____

_____

_____

3. Discuss the advantages and disadvantages of each parameter used for following cell (culture) growth.

_____

_____

_____

_____

_____

_____

_____

_____

_____

_____

_____

_____

4. Why were different wavelengths of light used in the various
spectrophotometric measurements?

_____

_____

_____

_____

_____

_____

_____

APPENDIXES

A. LIST OF CULTURES
B. STAINING SOLUTIONS AND MISCELLANEOUS REAGENTS
C. MEDIA
D. NOTES TO INSTRUCTOR BY EXERCISE
E. GENERAL BIBLIOGRAPHY

APPENDIX A
LIST OF CULTURES

Bacteria, molds, yeasts, algae, protozoa, and viruses can be obtained from the American Type Culture Collection, Rockville, Md. 20852.

Protozoa and algae (living specimens as well as prepared slides) can be obtained from Carolina Biological Supply Co., Elon College, N.C.; General Biological Supply House, Inc. (Turtox), Chicago 60620; and Wards Natural Science Establishment, Inc., P.O. Box 1712, Rochester, N.Y., and P.O. Box 1749, Monterey, California.

ALGAE

Chlamydomonas sp.
Chlorella sp.
Nostoc sp.

BACTERIA

Aerobacter aerogenes
Agrobacterium tumefaciens
Alcaligenes faecalis
Alcaligenes viscolactis
Arthrobacter globiformis
Bacillus cereus
Bacillus coagulans
Bacillus megaterium
Bacillus stearothermophilus
Bacillus subtilis
Bacillus subtilis var. *globigii*
Brevibacterium linens
Chromobacterium violaceum
Clostridium butyricum
Clostridium perfringens
Clostridium sporogenes

Clostridium tetani
Clostridium tetanomorphum
Corynebacterium diphtheriae (avirulent or atoxigenic strain)
Corynebacterium xerosis
Diplococcus pneumoniae
Escherichia coli
Escherichia coli (bacteriophage host)
Escherichia coli ATCC 15939
Escherichia coli ATCC 23590
Escherichia coli ATCC 23716
Escherichia coli ATCC 23717
Escherichia coli ATCC 23718
Escherichia coli ATCC 23719
Escherichia coli ATCC 23720
Escherichia coli ATCC 23724
Flavobacterium capsulatum
Haemophilus influenzae
Halobacterium salinarium
Klebsiella pneumoniae
Microbacterium flavum
Micrococcus agilis
Micrococcus luteus
Mycobacterium phlei
Mycobacterium smegmatis
Neisseria catarrhalis
Neisseria gonorrhoeae
Neisseria meningitidis
Neisseria perflava
Pasteurella multocida
Proteus sp. (nonswarming)
Proteus vulgaris
Pseudomonas aeruginosa
Pseudomonas fluorescens
Salmonella typhimurium
Salmonella sp.
Sarcina lutea
Serratia marcescens
Shigella sp.
Spirillum itersonii
Spirillum serpens
Staphylococcus aureus
Staphylococcus aureus ATCC 6538P
Staphylococcus epidermidis
Streptococcus durans
Streptococcus faecalis
Streptococcus lactis
Streptococcus liquefaciens
Streptococcus mitis
Streptococcus pyogenes
Streptococcus salivarius

Streptococcus viridans
Streptomyces albus

MOLDS

Aspergillus niger
Mucor mucedo
Penicillium notatum
Phycomyces blakesleanus (+ and − strains)
Rhizopus stolonifer

PROTOZOA

Amoeba sp.
Euglena sp.
Paramecium sp.
Tetrahymena pyriformis

VIRUS

Escherichia coli bacteriophage

YEASTS

Geotrichum candidum
Rhodotorula rubra
Saccharomyces cerevisiae
Saccharomyces cerevisiae var. *ellipsoideus*
Schizosaccharomyces octosporus

STAINING SOLUTIONS

1. *Acid alcohol*
   3% by volume concentrated hydrochloric acid in 95% alcohol

2. *Alcohol, ethyl (95%)*

3. *Bouin's fluid (fixative)*
   Picric acid, saturated aqueous solution, 75 ml
   Formalin, 25 ml
   Glacial acetic acid, 5 ml

4. *Carbolfuchsin (dilute)*
   Carbolfuchsin (Ziehl's), 1 ml
   Distilled water, 19 ml

5. *Carbolfuchsin (Ziehl's)*
   SOLUTION A:
      Basic fuchsin (90% dye content), 0.3 g
      Ethyl alcohol (95%), 10 ml
   SOLUTION B:
      Phenol, 5 g
      Distilled water, 95 ml
   Mix solutions A and B

6. *Cetylpyridinium chloride solution*
   Use $M/100$ or 0.34% aqueous solution (mol. wt. 357.99)

7. *Congo red solution*
   Use a saturated aqueous solution

8. *Copper sulfate solution*
   20% $CuSO_4 \cdot 5H_2O$ in distilled water

9. *Crystal violet—ammonium oxalate (Hucker's)*
   SOLUTION A:
      Crystal violet (90% dye content), 2 g
      Ethyl alcohol (95%), 20 ml
   SOLUTION B:
      Ammonium oxalate, 0.8 g
      Distilled water, 80 ml
   Mix solutions A and B

*Reference: MMM.

10. *Crystal violet (Tyler's)*
    Crystal violet (85% dye content), 0.1 g
    Glacial acetic acid, 0.25 ml
    Distilled water, 100 ml

11. *Flagella mordant (Gray's)*
    SOLUTION A:
    Saturated aqueous solution potassium alum, 5 ml 20% aqueous tannic acid, 2 ml (This must be preserved in the icebox with a few drops of chloroform if a large amount is kept on hand.)
    Saturated aqueous solution mercuric chloride, 2 ml
    SOLUTION B:
    Saturated alcoholic solution of basic fuchsin, 0.4 ml
    Mix solutions A and B on the day the mordant is to be used. Filter through paper before flooding on slide.

12. *Giemsa stain*
    Azur II eosin, 3 g
    Azur II, 0.8 g
    Glycerol, 125 g
    Methanol (acetone-free), 375.0 ml

13. *Hollande's stain*
    MORDANT:
    Tannic acid, 5 g
    Glacial acetic acid, 5 ml
    Ethyl alcohol (95%), 50 ml
    Distilled water, 50 ml
    PYRIDINE-SILVER SOLUTION:
    Silver nitrate, 5 g
    Distilled water, 100 ml
    Pyridine, 2 ml
    Allow crystallization to take place (several hours) and decant the clear solution, which keeps well in the dark.

14. *Iodine solution (Gram's)*
    Iodine, 1 g
    Potassium iodide, 2 g
    Distilled water, 300 ml

15. *Malachite green*
    Malachite green, 5 g
    Distilled water, 100 ml

16. *Methylene blue, alkaline (Loeffler's)*
    SOLUTION A:
    Methylene blue (90% dye content), 0.3 g
    Ethyl alcohol (95%), 30 ml
    SOLUTION B:
    Dilute KOH (0.01% by weight), 100 ml
    Mix solutions A and B

17. *Neisser's stain*
    SOLUTION A:
    Methylene blue, 0.1 g
    Absolute alcohol, 2.0 ml

Glacial acetic acid, 5.0 ml

Distilled water, 93.0 ml

SOLUTION B:

Crystal violet, 0.3 g

Absolute alcohol, 5.0 ml

Distilled water, 95.0 ml

SOLUTION C:

Bismark brown, 0.2 g

Distilled water, 100 ml

18. *Nigrosin solution (Dorner's)*

Nigrosin, water-soluble, 10 g

Distilled water, 100 ml

Immerse above mixture in boiling-water bath for 30 min; then add, as a preservative, formalin, 0.5 ml. Filter the solution twice through double filter paper. Store in small tubes.

19. *Safranin*

Safranin 0 (2.5% solution in 95% ethyl alcohol), 10 ml

Distilled water, 100 ml

20. *Toluidine blue (for nuclear stain)*

Toluidine blue, 0.1 g

Ethyl alcohol, 10 ml

Water, 90 ml

MISCELLANEOUS
REAGENTS

1. *Bromothymol blue indicator solution*

Bromothymol blue, 0.4 g

Ethyl alcohol (95%), 500 ml

Distilled water, 500 ml

Dissolve the bromothymol blue in alcohol and then dilute with water.

2. *Diphenylamine reagent*

Diphenylamine, 0.7 g

Sulfuric acid (concentrated), 60 ml

Water, 28.8 ml

Hydrochloric acid (concentrated), 11.3 ml

Dissolve the diphenylamine in sulfuric acid, and then add the water. Cool the mixture, and add the hydrochloric acid slowly. Allow to stand overnight.

3. *Kovacs' reagent (for detection of indole)*

p-Dimethylaminobenzaldehyde, 5 g

Amyl alcohol, 75 ml

Hydrochloric acid (concentrated), 25 ml

4. *Mercuric chloride solution*

Mercuric chloride, 15 g

Water, 100 ml

Hydrochloric acid (concentrated), 20 ml

5. *Methyl cellulose (10%)*

6. *Nessler's reagent*

Follow directions on manufacturer's label.

7. *Nitrite test reagents*
   SOLUTION A:
   Sulfanilic acid, 8 g
   Acetic acid (5 N; 1 part glacial acetic acid to 2.5 parts water), 1,000 ml
   SOLUTION B:
   Dimethyl-1α-1 naphthalamine, 5 g
   Acetic acid (5 N), 1,000 ml

8. *Paraffin-petrolatum mixture*
   Paraffin, 30 g
   Petrolatum, 70 g

9. *Physiological salt solution (saline solution)*
   Sodium chloride, 8.5 g
   Distilled water 1,000 ml

10. *Tetramethyl-p-phenylenediamine dihydrochloride solution (1%)*

11. *Trommsdorf's reagent (for nitrites)*
    a. Add 20 g zinc chloride to 100 ml water, boil, and then add this boiling solution to a mixture of 4 g starch in water.
    b. Dilute with water, and add 2 g zinc iodide.
    c. Dilute to 1,000 ml with water, filter, and store in tightly stoppered bottles.

Formulas of all the media used in exercises of this manual are listed below. Most of the media, with the exception of the in-organic-salts type of formula, are available commercially in powdered form. Specific directions for putting the powdered products into solution, the method of sterilization, and other details are provided on the labels.* If the media are prepared from the individual ingredients, the general procedures described in Exercise 8 may be followed. *Formulas are in grams per liter of distilled water unless otherwise stated.*

1. *Ascitic agar slopes (slants) and plates*
   To 500 ml molten heart-infusion agar (45 to 50°C), add 25 ml sterile ascitic fluid.†

2. *Azotobacter medium*
   Saccharose, 10
   K_2HPO_4, 0.5
   $MgSO_4 \cdot 7H_2O$, 0.2
   NaCl, 0.2
   $MnSO_4 \cdot H_2O$, trace
   $FeSO_4$, trace
   $Na_2MoO_4 \cdot 2H_2O$, trace
   $CaCO_3$, 5.0
   Agar, 15

3. *Blood agar base‡*, pH 7.3 $\pm$
   (Heart infusion agar)
   Beef heart muscle, infusion from 375
   Tryptose or thiotone peptic digest of animal tissue, 10
   Sodium chloride, 5
   Agar, 15
   Cool to 50°C after autoclaving and add 5% defibrinated sheep or rabbit blood. (Defibrinated blood may be prepared by putting fresh blood into a flask and shaking vigorously with glass beads for about 5 min.)

*Two very useful handbooks on microbiological culture media are "BBL Manual of Products and Laboratory Procedures," Baltimore Biological Laboratory, Division of BioQuest, Cockeysville, Maryland 21030 (in Canada, Becton, Dickinson & Co., Canada, Ltd., Clarkson, Ontario), and "Difco Manual," Difco Laboratories, Inc., Detroit, Mich., 48232. The "Manual of Clinical Microbiology" is also useful.
†Available commercially; use aseptic technique to add to sterile medium. Incubate media 24 hr at 37°C for sterility check.
‡These media are available commercially.

NOTE: Prepoured disposable blood agar plates are also available commercially.

4. *Brain heart infusion broth‡*, pH 7.4 ±
Calf brain, infusion from 250
Beef heart, infusion from 250
Peptone, 10
Sodium chloride, 5
Disodium phosphate, 2.5
Dextrose, 2.5

5. *Calcium nitrate–salts agar (for algae)*
Calcium nitrate, 1.0
Potassium chloride, 0.25
Magnesium sulfate, 0.25
Monopotassium phosphate, 0.25
Ferric chloride, 0.01
   Dissolve above chemicals in tap water. Dilute further (1 part of salt solution with 2 parts tap water) and add agar to a concentration of 1.5%.

6. *Casein solution*
Sodium caseinate, 2
Glucose, 1
Dipotassium phosphate, 0.2
Magnesium sulfate, 0.2
Ferrous sulfate, 0.01
   NOTE: Use tap water for preparation of this medium.

7. *Chocolate agar*
Pancreatic digest of casein, 7.5
Peptic digest of animal tissue or other peptone, 7.5
Cornstarch, 1.0
Dipotassium phosphate, 4.0
Monopotassium phosphate, 1.0
Sodium chloride, 5.0
Agar, 10.0
   Prepare sterile base (above). Add sterile 5 to 10% defibrinated blood and heat at about 80°C for 15 min or until the color is chocolate brown. (Variations of supplement exist depending upon use.)

8. *Cystine-trypticase agar (CTA) medium‡*, pH 7.3
Cystine, 0.5
Trypticase, 20.0
Agar, 2.5
Sodium chloride, 5
Sodium sulfite, 0.5
Phenol red, 0.017
   For fermentation reactions carbohydrates may be incorporated at 0.5 – 1.0% as preferred.

9. *Czapek-Dox agar‡*, pH 7.3
Sucrose, 30
Sodium nitrate, 3
Dipotassium phosphate, 1

Magnesium sulfate, 0.5
Potassium chloride, 0.5
Ferrous sulfate, 0.01
Agar, 15

10. *Deoxycholate agar‡*, pH 7.2
Polypeptone, 10
Lactose, 10
Sodium chloride, 5
Dipotassium phosphate, 2
Ferric citrate, 1
Sodium citrate, 1
Sodium deoxycholate, 1
Agar, 16
Neutral red, 0.033

Add 46 g of the dehydrated medium per liter of distilled water. Allow the material to stand for 5 min and mix thoroughly. After the suspension is homogeneous, heat gently with occasional agitation. Boil for 1 min or until solution is complete. The dissolved medium is ready for use when it has cooled to 42 to 44°C. Do not autoclave.

11. *Deoxycholate solution*
Sodium deoxycholate, 1
Distilled water, sterile, 9 ml

Use fresh solution for bile-solubility test.

12. *Eosin — methylene blue agar‡*, pH 7.1
Peptone, 10
Lactose, 10
Dipotassium phosphate, 2
Eosin Y, 0.4
Methylene blue, 0.065
Agar, 15

13. *Fildes enrichment‡*
Sodium chloride, 0.85%, 150 ml
Hydrochloric acid, 6 ml
Defibrinated sheep blood, 50 ml
Pepsin, granular, 1 g

Available commercially and added at 4 to 10 ml to 200 ml of sterile nutrient agar melted and cooled to 56°C.

14. *Fluid thioglycolate‡*
Trypticase, 15
L-Cystine, 0.5
Glucose, 5
Yeast extract, 5
Sodium chloride, 2.5
Sodium thioglycolate, 0.5
Resazurin, 0.001
Agar 0.75

For fluid thioglycolate with calcium carbonate, add approximately 0.1 g calcium carbonate to each tube prior to addition of medium.

15. *Gelatin agar*, pH 7.0

Laboratory Exercises in Microbiology

Peptone, 5
Beef extract, 3
Gelatin, 30
Agar, 15

16. *Glucose-acetate medium*, pH 4.8
Glucose, 1
Yeast extract, 2.5
$CH_3COONa \cdot 3H_2O$, 8.2
Agar, 15

17. *Glucose broth*, pH 7.3
Peptone, 10
Glucose, 5
Sodium chloride, 5

18. *Heart infusion broth‡*
(Same as Blood agar base but without agar.)

19. *Iron-agar stabs*
Tryptone agar, 500 ml
Ferric ammonium citrate, 250 mg
Sodium thiosulfate, 250 mg
Make sure all salts dissolved. Distribute into tubes and autoclave at 121°C for 15 min.

20. *Lactose broth‡*, pH 7.0
Peptone, 5
Beef extract, 3
Lactose, 5
NOTE: Double-strength lactose broth contains twice the amounts of the above ingredients in 1 liter.

21. *Litmus milk*
Fresh skim milk or rehydrated skim-milk powder, 1,000 ml
Azolitmin, 0.5
NOTE: The azolitmin should be dissolved in about 10 ml water with the aid of a few drops of 1 *N* sodium hydroxide. Add this solution to the skim milk.

22. *Loeffler's medium‡*
Mammalian serum, nonhuman, 750 ml
Infusion broth, 250 ml
Dextrose, 2.5 g
a. Mix well but carefully to avoid bubbles.
b. Dispense and slant in an autoclave with a manually operated air-escape valve. Close the door and air-escape valve, to avoid foaming, and raise the pressure immediately to 15 lb. After 10 min, open the valve *very slightly* so that steam enters and air escapes slowly, maintaining 15 lb pressure.
c. When the temperature reaches 121°C, close the valve and hold for 15 min.
d. Turn off the steam but do not open the autoclave until the pressure slowly falls to zero and the autoclave is cool.
e. Admit air *slowly* to the cooled autoclave.

23. *MacConkey's (or MacConkey) agar‡*
    Sodium taurocholate, 5
    Peptone, 20
    Sodium chloride, 5
    Lactose, 10
    1% aqueous neutral red solution, 5 to 7 ml
    Agar, 15
    a. Dissolve the sodium taurocholate, peptone and salt in a liter of distilled water by steaming.
    b. Adjust the reaction to pH 7.8 and add the agar.
    c. Autoclave at 10 lb for 20 min.
    d. Filter and adjust the reaction to pH 7.5.
    e. Add the lactose and sufficient neutral red to give a reddish brown color.
    f. Bottle and autoclave at 10 lb for 20 min.

24. *Malt-extract broth, pH 4.7*
    Malt extract, 20

25. *Milk agar, pH 7.2*
    Peptone, 5
    Beef extract, 3
    Milk powder, 100
    Agar, 15

26. *Milk-protein-hydrolysate agar, pH 7.0*
    Milk protein hydrolysate, 9
    Glucose, 1
    Agar, 15

27. a. *Minimal agar*
    Water agar, 75 ml
    Minimal salts (x4), 25 ml
    Glucose (20%), 1 ml
    Melt agar by placing into boiling water bath. Add warmed sterile salts and glucose. Medium is now ready to be dispensed into plates.

    b. *Minimal medium, liquid*
    Minimal salts (x4), 25 ml
    Glucose (20%), 1 ml
    Sterile water, distilled, to 100 ml
    Mix the three components under aseptic conditions just before use.

    c. *Water agar*
    Agar powder, 20 g
    Water, to 1,000 ml
    Suspend and steam at 100°C until dissolved. Adjust pH to 7.2 (to prevent hydrolysis). Dispense in 75-ml volumes into 100-ml bottles. Autoclave at 121°C for 20 min.

    d. *Minimal salts (x4 concentrate), pH 7.2*
    NH_4Cl, 20 g
    NH_4NO_3, 4
    Na_2SO_4, anhydrous, 8

K$_2$HPO$_4$, anhydrous, 12

KH$_2$PO$_4$, 4

MgSO$_4$·7H$_2$O, 0.4

Water, distilled, to 1,000 ml

Dissolve each salt in cold water in the order indicated, waiting until the previous salt is dissolved before adding next (a light precipitate will be formed). Filter 25-ml aliquots into storage bottles. Autoclave at 121°C for 15 min.

e. *20% glucose* (x100 concentrate)

D-Glucose, 200 g

Distilled water to 1,000 ml

Dissolve in warm water. Dispense into 100-ml bottles (for storage). Autoclave at 5 lb (109°C) for 10 min.

28. *Motility-test agar, pH 7.0*

Peptone, 10

Sodium chloride, 5

Agar, 3.5

29. *Nitrate-salts medium*

Glucose, 10

Dipotassium phosphate, 0.5

Calcium chloride, 0.5

Magnesium sulfate, 0.2

Potassium nitrate, 1.0

NOTE: Use tap water for preparation of this medium.

30. *Nitrogen-free liquid medium*

Dipotassium phosphate, 1.0

Magnesium sulfate, 0.2

Sodium chloride, 0.01

Ferrous sulfate, 0.01

Manganese sulfate, 0.01

Glucose, 20.0

Calcium carbonate, 30

31. *Nutrient agar‡, pH 7.0*

Peptone, 5

Beef extract, 3

Agar, 15

32. *Nutrient broth‡, pH 7.0*

Peptone, 5

Beef extract, 3

33. *Nutrient gelatin‡, pH 7.0*

Peptone, 5

Beef extract, 3

Gelatin, 120

34. *Peptone solution*

Peptone, 2

Dextrose, 1

Dipotassium phosphate, 0.2.

Magnesium sulfate, 0.2

Ferrous sulfate, 0.01

NOTE: Use tap water for preparation of this medium.

35. *Phenol red–dextrose broth, pH 7.4*
    Trypticase, 10
    Sodium chloride, 5
    Glucose, 0.5
    Phenol red, 0.018
    Other carbohydrate-fermentation broths can be prepared using this same formula by replacing the glucose with the carbohydrate desired, e.g., sucrose, lactose, or maltose.

36. *Phenylethyl alcohol agar‡, pH 7.3*
    Trypticase, 15
    Phytone, 5
    Sodium chloride, 5
    Phenylethyl alcohol, 2.5
    Agar, 15

37. *Sabouraud's agar‡, pH 5.6*
    Peptone, 10
    Glucose, 40
    Agar, 15

38. *SIM (sulfide, indole, motility) agar, pH 7.3*
    Trypticase, 20
    Thiotone, 6
    Ferrous ammonium sulfate, 0.2
    Sodium thiosulfate, 0.2
    Agar, 3.5
    NOTE: This medium can be used for detection of hydrogen sulfide, indole, and motility.

39. *Skim milk*
    Use fresh skim milk or rehydrated skim-milk powder according to directions given for this product.

40. *Spirillum medium, pH 7.6*
    Peptone, 1
    Yeast extract, 1
    Sodium acetate, 1
    Cystine (1%), 5 ml
    Agar, 15

41. *Starch broth, pH 7.2*
    Soluble starch, 10
    Beef-heart-infusion broth, 1 liter

42. *Starch-agar medium‡, pH 7.0*
    Peptone, 5
    Beef extract, 3
    Soluble starch, 2
    Agar, 15

43. *Todd Hewitt broth‡, pH 7.8*
    Beef-heart infusion, 500
    Peptone component, 20
    Dextrose, 2
    Sodium chloride, 2
    Disodium phosphate, 0.4
    Sodium carbonate, 2.5

44. *Tributyrin agar*
Peptone, 5
Beef extract, 3
Agar, 15
Tributyrin, 10
> NOTE: The tributyrin is added to the other ingredients after they have been dissolved and cooled to 90°C and then emulsified using a Waring blender.

45. *Trypticase agar,* pH 7.3
Trypticase, 10
Sodium chloride, 5
Dipotassium phosphate, 2.5
Agar, 15

46. *Trypticase broth,* pH 7.3
Trypticase, 10
Sodium chloride, 5
Dipotassium phosphate, 2.5

47. *Trypticase-nitrate broth,* pH 7.2
Trypticase, 20
Disodium phosphate, 2
Glucose, 1
Agar, 1
Potassium nitrate, 1

48. *Trypticase-soy agar‡,* pH 7.3
Trypticase, 15
Phytone, 5
Sodium chloride, 5
Agar, 15

49. *Trypticase-soy broth‡,* pH 7.3
Trypticase, 17
Phytone, 3
Sodium chloride, 5
Dipotassium phosphate, 2.5
Glucose, 2.5

50. *Tryptone agar,* pH 7.4
Tryptone, 20
Sodium chloride, 5
Agar, 15

51. *Tryptone water sugar,* pH 7.4
Tryptone, 10
Bromothymol blue (0.2%), 12 ml
Sugar, 5
> Autoclave at 115°C (10 lb) for 12 min. after dispensing into test tubes.

52. *Yeast-extract broth,* pH 7.0
Peptone, 5
Yeast extract, 5
Beef extract, 3
Sodium chloride, 5

APPENDIX D
NOTES TO INSTRUCTOR
BY EXERCISE

EXERCISE 1
MICROORGANISMS IN
THE ENVIRONMENT

This first exercise is intentionally short because there is so much else to do in the first laboratory period. Organization of the class usually takes up much of the time.

However, if time is still available, it is helpful to include an introductory film on microbiology. The chapter on visual aids in the Instructor's Manual to accompany "Microbiology," 3d ed., by Pelczar and Reid, will be useful to help in choosing and obtaining films. Canadian instructors may find useful the Medical and Biological Film Library Catalogue, Information Services Division, Department of National Health and Welfare, Ottawa, Ontario and Catalogue de Films Microbiologiques avec Résumés Français et Anglais, by G. Nogrady and V. Fredette, Département de Bactériologie de la Faculté de Médecine, Université de Montréal, Montréal, Québec.

In addition to the 16-mm sound films noted in the above sources, cartridged films in microbiology are also available today. They are convenient to use but require special projectors. Ealing film loops with subtitles but no sound can be obtained from Harper & Row, New York, 10016, or from Ealing Scientific Limited, Dorval 760, Quebec, Canada. Fairchild film loops with sound can be obtained from Modern Learning Aids, New York, 10036.

EXERCISE 2
THE USE OF THE
MICROSCOPE

Types of microscopy other than light may be set up as a demonstration. (In order to avoid multiple setups or crowding around a single demonstration table in a large class, a movable table on casters can be used successfully provided sufficient electric outlets are built into it. The demonstration can then be moved around to each group of students for a fixed period.) For example, phase-contrast microscopy and dark-field microscopy can easily be demonstrated if the equipment is available. *Spirillum serpens* would be a good organism for this examination. (Instruction manuals that come with the instrument show how these types of microscopy can be set up. In addition, the references on microscopy in the general bibliography will be helpful.) Electron micrographs may be provided to show the fine structures of microorganisms. A picture of an electron microscope should also be exhibited unless, of course, an electron microscope is available.

**EXERCISE 3
MICROSCOPIC
EXAMINATION OF
MICROORGANISMS**

Algae and protozoa can be obtained from a biological supply house such as Turtox, Chicago, Ill. 60620. Delivery dates for living materials should always be given the company.

**EXERCISE 4
MEASUREMENT OF
MICROORGANISMS**

If focusing oculars and ocular and stage micrometers are in short supply, this exercise may be set up as a demonstration. Microscope 1 has an ocular micrometer. Microscope 2 has a stage micrometer. Microscope 3 has an ocular micrometer superimposed on a stage micrometer under the oil-immersion objective. The student can compute from this microscope the number of ocular-micrometer divisions that are equivalent to one stage division. He can then determine how many micrometers are superimposed by each division of the ocular micrometer. Microscope 4 has an ocular micrometer superimposed on some stained bacterial cells.

Using stained (gram or another stain) cells for measurement of cell size can be criticized, but all methods have limitations. If phase-contrast is used, organisms, especially viable ones, do not present a sharp outline. If ordinary light-microscopy is used, diffraction prevents the organisms from appearing distinct. In using stained cells, distortion does occur, depending upon the nature of the fixative and the stain. Some workers feel that negative staining is the most reliable for giving the true cell size. Others prefer chemical fixation followed by a simple stain.

**EXERCISE 5
STAINING THE
WHOLE CELL**
A. THE SIMPLE STAIN

The petri-dish mixed cultures may be spread-plate cultures of the pure cultures used, namely, *Bacillus subtilis*, *Staphylococcus aureus*, and *Spirillum itersonii*. The medium may be trypticase-soy agar.

The purpose of fixation is to kill the microorganism, coagulate the protoplasm of the cell, and cause it to adhere to the slide. Gentle heating is the most commonly used method. Chemical fixatives, such as osmium tetroxide, may also be used.

Some useful terms are:

Simple staining: the organism is stained by immersion in the stain.

Mordant: the "link" between organism and stain; it fixes the stain so that it will be retained by the organism being stained.
Selective stain: selective for a specific structure or material.
Differential stain: stains differentially with two colors or stains one type of organism and not another.
Vital staining: the staining of living cells.
Metachromatic staining: the organism or part of the organism is stained a color different from that of the stain itself.

Cultures used for staining, especially for the gram reaction, should be less than 24 hr old (except for very slow growing cultures).

B. THE NEGATIVE STAIN

The negative stain works because the coloring part of the dye is in the negative ion and does not readily combine with another negative ion; thus the negatively charged bacterial cell is not stained. Instead, the dye forms a deposit around the cell.

C. THE GRAM STAIN

This method of staining was described by Gram, a Danish physician, in 1884. It divides bacteria into two groups, depending on whether they can be decolorized with acetone, alcohol, or aniline oil after staining with one of the p-rosaniline dyes such as crystal violet, methyl violet, or gentian violet and treating with iodine.

There are several modifications of the gram-stain procedure today with respect to reagent composition and timing, but all require four reagents: a basic dye (see above); a mordant, usually iodine; a decolorizing agent, acetone or alcohol or a mixture of both; and a counterstain, a basic dye which has a different color from the first one used.

Most recent evidence suggests that the basis of the gram stain lies in permeability differences between gram-positive and gram-negative bacteria. In gram-positive bacteria, the crystal violet-iodine complex appears to be trapped in the wall following ethanol or acetone treatment, which presumably causes a diminution in the diameter of the pores in the wall mucopeptide. Walls of gram-negative bacteria have less mucopeptide, and it is less extensively cross-linked than that in the walls of gram-positive bacteria. The pores in the mucopeptide in the walls of gram-negative bacteria are thought to remain sufficiently large, even after ethanol treatment, to allow the crystal violet–iodine complex to be extracted.

D. THE ACID-FAST STAIN

The property of acid-fastness appears to be due to the large amount of lipids (especially a lipid fraction called mycolic acid) and causes not only acid-fastness but a resistance to ordinary staining methods.

In gram-stained preparations acid-fast bacteria appear to be gram-positive. It is said that the fundamental basis of the gram-positive staining in these organisms is not the same as that of other gram-positive bacteria in that it is quite independent of the iodine mordant, depending instead on the high lipid content of the cells.

Tubercular sputum, which can be obtained from a nearby hospital, should be autoclaved before use by students. Autoclaving time should be 30 min at 121°C. (Autoclaving does not greatly alter the staining properties of acid-fast bacteria.) If the sputum is not contaminated with many bacilli, it may be necessary to concentrate them by adding a 5% solution of sodium hydroxide to the sputum, allowing it to stand for 1 hr, then centrifuging the solution and using the sediment as the material to be stained.

Some laboratories dislike the use of blotting paper in staining procedures because discarded strips of paper may clog up the drains. The use of paper is obviated if sufficient stain is kept over the smear during the heating procedure.

EXERCISE 6
STAINING FOR CELL STRUCTURES
A. THE SPORE STAIN

Two useful demonstrations can be set up for this exercise. A gram-stained preparation under the light microscope will show spores as clear unstained spaces in otherwise stained bacteria. The high light refractivity of the spores should be noted. The other demonstration may be a wet mount of the sporeforming organisms under the phase-contrast microscope. The appearance of the preparation with this type of illumination is quite striking.

The use of a blotting-paper strip is optional provided the stain is not allowed to dry up during the steaming.

B. THE CAPSULE STAIN

Capsules may sometimes be confused with artifacts. Clear areas around cells may not be capsules at all but merely the spaces resulting from retraction of the surrounding medium from the cells on drying (or heating). For this reason the best method of demonstrating capsules is to stain them by a procedure which differentiates them from the cells themselves.

The capsule has a low affinity for dyes and is not usually visible in stained smears unless a suitable mordant is used. The copper sulfate solution serves this purpose and probably also has some dehydrating effect to render the capsule more discrete.

C. THE FLAGELLA STAIN AND DETECTION OF MOTILITY

In bright-field microscopy, the flagella are not seen except in preparations intensely stained following the use of a mordant. This treatment increases the density of the flagella, their thickness, and the contrast with the background.

Sometimes depression slides are in short supply in large classes. In such a case, a hanging-drop preparation can be made with an ordinary slide and a well made with petroleum jelly about the size of a cover slip. This well is then inverted over the cover slip with the droplet suspension of bacteria.

The motility-test agar tube can be modified to give more clear-cut results by having an upright piece of glass tubing in the medium. The semisoft agar in the inner tube should be continuous at the bottom with that of the main outer tube. A straight needle is used to inoculate the agar in the inner tube to a depth of about 1 in. (Care must be taken not to contaminate the surface of the main body of medium.) The growth of a nonmotile organism is confined to the site of inoculation in the inner tube, while that of a motile organism extends downward and out into the main body of the medium.

D. THE CELL-WALL STAIN

The cell wall is positively charged by treating it with a cationic surface agent such as cetylpyridinium chloride, which dissociates in water to give a positively charged cetylpyridinium cation and a negatively charged chloride ion. The cations neutralize the negative surface charges of the bacterial cell surface (wall), and the surface becomes positively charged because of the absorption of the cations. It then takes on the acid dye with a negatively charged chromophore.

Electron micrographs of sectioned bacteria showing the difference between gram-positive and gram-negative bacterial cell walls are easily obtained (from many published papers or elsewhere) and can be demonstrated to the class.

EXERCISE 8
PREPARATION OF
NUTRIENT BROTH,
GLUCOSE BROTH,
YEAST-EXTRACT
BROTH, AND
NUTRIENT AGAR

The precise measurement of pH should first be demonstrated with a potentiometric method, using a pH meter equipped with glass electrodes. (The instructor should emphasize that the instrument must be adjusted first to the specific pH of a standard buffer solution before it can be used for any measurement.)

Commercial preparations of dehydrated media may also be set up for demonstration.

EXERCISE 9
PREPARATION OF A
CHEMICALLY DEFINED
MEDIUM

Commercial preparations of pure biochemicals may be put up for demonstration.

Since ingredients of chemically defined media may be called for in very small amounts, it may be useful to demonstrate to students the *proper* use of an analytical balance.

EXERCISE 10
EVALUATION OF
MEDIA FOR ABILITY
TO SUPPORT
GROWTH OF
BACTERIA

To make this exercise more meaningful, the "American Type Culture Collection, Catalogue of Strains" should be brought to the attention of students. Appendix V of the Catalogue is particularly relevant since it gives a key to the preferred medium (and incubation temperature) of all cultures in the ATCC.

EXERCISE 12
THE STREAK-PLATE
METHOD FOR
ISOLATION OF PURE
CULTURES

The mixed culture is obtained by mixing together fluid pure cultures of bacteria just before the laboratory begins. Equal numbers of each organism in the mixture are *approximated* by using equal densities (turbidities) of the pure cultures estimated by visual inspection.

EXERCISE 13
THE POUR-PLATE
METHOD FOR
ISOLATION OF PURE
CULTURES

The availability of vortex shaking or mixing instruments makes the even distribution of cells in a fluid contained in a tube much more accurate and easier. If they are not available for class use, one such instrument (available from Fisher Scientific or any supply house) should at least be demonstrated.

EXERCISE 14
ANAEROBIC-CULTURE
METHODS

For incomparable convenience, the BBL GasPak Anaerobic System is recommended for the cultivation of anaerobic micro-organisms (especially on petri dishes). In use, inoculated plates or tubes are simply placed in the jar with one GasPak Envelope (for generating gases) and an indicator containing methylene blue (an oxidation-reduction indicator). Water is added to the envelope, and the lid and clamp are placed in position. The screw need only be secured hand-tight. This apparatus is available from: Baltimore Biological Laboratory, Division of Becton, Dickinson and Co., Cockeysville, Md. 21030, or Becton, Dickinson & Co., Canada, Limited, Clarkson, Ontario.

If available, a modern anaerobic incubator (as shown in the photograph in the exercise) should also be demonstrated.

EXERCISE 15
CULTURAL
CHARACTERISTICS

An excellent manual for demonstration of cultural characteristics is S. Stanley Schneierson, "Atlas of Diagnostic Microbiology," Abbott Laboratories, North Chicago, Ill.

EXERCISE 18
FERMENTATION OF
CARBOHYDRATES

Media containing different carbohydrates can be color-coded by painting on the metal caps of the test tubes. Different colored cotton can be used by instructors who still prefer cotton plugs.

Durham tubes are simply inserted into each test tube containing liquid media. On autoclaving, the air is expelled from the Durham tubes, which become filled with broth.

Microbiologists use over 20 different carbohydrates as substrates for bacterial catabolism. The sugars commonly employed are glucose (dextrose), lactose, sucrose, maltose, salicin, and mannitol.

The word "fermentation" needs some clarification. Although anaerobiosis is often considered as synonymous with fermentation, it is better to restrict the term to those pathways in which the terminal electron acceptor is an organic compound (as is the case in this exercise). Where the terminal acceptor is oxygen or an inorganic compound, the pathway is regarded as oxidative and the process is one of respiration. Thus respiration can be aerobic where oxygen is the acceptor or can be anaerobic where inorganic compounds other than oxygen are used for the same function.

EXERCISE 20
ADDITIONAL
BIOCHEMICAL
CHARACTERISTICS
B. PRODUCTION OF
INDOLE

The chemical reaction indole undergoes in the test for its presence is an aldehyde reaction. Indole and its derivatives give strongly colored products with a number of aromatic aldehydes. In the test carried out by the student indole reacts with p-dimethylaminobenzaldehyde in hydrochloric acid to give a red color.

Extraction of the indole from the liquid culture increases the sensitivity of the test. Petroleum, xylol, and ether can be used; but they are potentially dangerous if, following aseptic technique, the mouth of the tube is flamed. Kovacs' reagent (as used in the exercise) has the advantage that the solvent (amyl alcohol) is present in the test solution.

Sometimes this particular test may be negative even with organisms that do produce indole from tryptophan, because (1) the indole could have volatilized away or (2) the organism broke it down (used it) very quickly. This can be confirmed by the more sensitive paper-strip method, in which paper strips soaked with oxalic acid or p-dimethylaminobenzaldehyde are held in the mouth of the test tube by the cotton plug or metal cap.

C. REDUCTION OF NITRATE

In the exercise carried out, nitrate served as a terminal electron acceptor. (Sometimes when an organism makes use of nitrate as a nitrogen source, the nitrate is assimilated instead.) The products of reduction may include nitrite, hyponitrite, hydroxylamine, ammonia, nitrous oxide, or gaseous nitrogen, although most bacterial species do not carry the reduction beyond the stage of nitrite. For these organisms simple testing of the medium for nitrite at a fixed time after inoculation is valid. With the other organisms that produce other reduced nitrogen compounds the detection of nitrite will depend on the degree to which it accumulates at any time during growth. The first test applied aimed at showing the presence of nitrite.

The reduction of nitrate will not occur if the organism receives an adequate oxygen supply for all respirational needs, e.g., in shallow-medium cultures and in aerated cultures. This is due to one of the following factors: the nitrate-reducing enzyme is not formed in the presence of an adequate oxygen supply, and the enzyme, once formed, is not functional in such an environment.

The principle for the measurement of nitrite is based on the formation of a red azo compound. This involves, first, the reaction in acid solution of a primary amine such as sulfanilic acid with nitrite to form a diazonium salt. The salt is then coupled to an aromatic amine to yield the red azo dye. (An azo compound has the chemical group —N≡N— in it.)

EXERCISE 22
MORPHOLOGICAL AND CULTURAL CHARACTERISTICS OF MOLDS

Cultures of the molds used by the student should be set up for demonstration by point inoculation (to form a single radial colony) on Sabouraud's agar plates.

The morphology and appearance of these cultures can be examined in greater detail by using a few binocular dissecting microscopes (stereomicroscopes). When examined in this manner, many cultures in petri dishes are very beautiful and this will stimulate enthusiasm for further study.

For instructors with an interest in teaching mycology, valuable notes on simple methods of preparing cultures, demonstrations, and slides can be found in the H. A. Dade and Jean Gunnell, "Class Work with Fungi," Commonwealth Mycological Institute, Kew, Surrey, a paperback.

EXERCISE 24
MORPHOLOGY OF YEASTS

The attention of the student should be drawn to the manner by which each of the species studied reproduces asexually. *Saccharomyces cerevisiae* and *Rhodotorula rubra* reproduce by budding, *Geotrichum candidum* by arthrospore formation (breaking up of a hypha into separate cells), and *Schizosaccharomyces octosporus* by transverse binary fission.

The "true" yeasts produce sexual spores, e.g., ascospores in *S. cerevisiae* and *S. octosporus*. Ascospores are retained in the parent cell, the ascus, which eventually breaks open to free them. Ascospore formation is stimulated by growth on glucose-acetate agar. A heavy inoculum from Sabouraud's medium is spread on glucose-acetate agar plates and incubated for 1 to 2 weeks at room temperature; abundant ascospores should be formed.

A microscopic demonstration of ascospores can easily be set up. Stain the yeast smear after heat fixation with the malachite green spore stain (no steaming is required because ascospores stain easily with simple stains). Counterstain with safranin. The ascospores are stained green with a red ascus while the vegetative cells are stained red.

EXERCISE 28
THE VIRUSES
A. BACTERIAL LYSIS BY BACTERIOPHAGE

Virulent phages are supplied lyophilized as bacteria-free lysates from the American Type Culture Collection. Be sure to have an actively growing broth culture of the proper host *E. coli* strain ready before opening the specimen.

To open the ampul, file a groove in it approximately 1 in. from the sealed tip. Wipe the ampul with alcohol-soaked gauze. Using two pieces of dry sterile gauze, grasp the ampul, one end in each hand, and with the groove outward, snap open.

Using a sterile Pasteur pipette, add to the dried material in the ampul 0.5 ml trypticase broth and mix well. Transfer a drop of the rehydrated phage suspension into a tube of exponential phase *E. coli* cells in trypticase broth. Incubate until lysis occurs or overnight. (The remaining rehydrated phage suspension can be preserved by keeping it in the cold at 2 to 10°C in a sterile screw-capped tube.)

Centrifuge the culture (to remove any unlysed cells) and filter through a Seitz filter or a Millipore filter with 0.22-μm membrane (see Exercise 34). Store the filtrate at 4°C.

A phage titration may be performed as follows.

1. Prepare tenfold dilutions in trypticase broth of the phage filtrate.
2. Add 0.1 ml of dilutions 10^{-3} to 10^{-10} to 2.5 ml of soft trypticase agar (0.7% agar) contained in small test tubes in a water bath at 43 to 45°C.
3. Add 0.1 ml of an 18-hr culture of *E. coli*.
4. Mix well and pour over dry 1.5% agar plates (trypticase agar) and incubate overnight at 35°C.
5. Count the number of plaques with background light and determine the final titer in your original suspension by multiplying their number times dilution factor.

A useful text giving detailed procedures for handling phage is M. H. Adams, "Bacteriophages," Interscience, New York, 1959.

Electron micrographs of free phage particles and particles attached to bacterial cells may be demonstrated.

B. TISSUE-CULTURE TECHNIQUES AND VIRUS PROPAGATION

Tissue-culture cell lines and tissue cultures are readily obtained from Flow Laboratories, Inc., Rockville, Md., 20852; Microbiological Associates, Bethesda, Md.; Difco Laboratories, Inc., Detroit, Mich. 48232; and Baltimore Biological Laboratories, Cockeysville, Md. 21030 (in Canada, Becton, Dickinson & Co., Canada, Ltd., Clarkson, Ont.).

It may be difficult for a laboratory not doing routine virus work to show tissue cultures with CPE, e.g., plaque formation caused by poliovirus following infection of a monolayer of monkey kidney cells with a high dilution of a virus suspension. In such a case, pictures showing such an effect may be demonstrated. Of course, if a public health or similar laboratory is nearby, such tissue cultures can easily be obtained.

EXERCISE 31
STERILIZATION WITH
AUTOCLAVE AND
HOT-AIR OVEN

Specific instructions for the use of sterilization equipment are supplied by the manufacturers.

The working principle of the autoclave is that pure saturated steam at pressures above atmospheric is used to heat the contents in a closed chamber. (Autoclaves for routine laboratory sterilization are usually set for 15 lb pressure, giving a temperature of 121°C.) When saturated steam hits a cooler object, it condenses to form water and liberates its latent heat of condensation so that the temperature of the object rises quickly. Condensation is also accompanied by a contraction in volume, which draws more steam to inner parts of the contents. Autoclaving does not dehydrate materials like rubber or paper, which may be damaged by sterilization in a hot-air oven.

For a detailed discussion of sterilization procedures in microbiology, the instructor should refer to the chapter on Sterilization in G. G. Meynell and E. Meynell, "Theory and Practice in Experimental Bacteriology," 2d ed., Cambridge University Press, London, 1970.

EXERCISE 33
EFFECT OF HIGH
CONCENTRATIONS
OF SALT AND SUGAR
ON MICROBIAL
GROWTH

The term percent is often used incorrectly. The correct uses are the following: % or %(w/w) is g/100g of solution. For percent of volume, i.e., ml/100 ml, the term %(v/v) should be used, and for weight of a substance in 100 ml of solution, the term %(w/v). For example, 5%(w/v) means weighing out 5 g, dissolving this amount, and taking it up to 100 ml (usually in a volumetric flask for precise work).

EXERCISE 36
ANTIBIOTICS

Perhaps the student should be reminded that other chemical substances can inhibit microorganisms besides disinfectants and antibiotics. The effect of dyes and heavy metals can easily be demonstrated.

EFFECT OF DYES ON THE
INHIBITION OF BACTERIAL
GROWTH

A petri dish, one half of which contains nutrient agar and the other half nutrient agar with 1:50,000 dilution of gentian violet, is streaked with Escherichia coli and Staphylococcus aureus. The inhibitory effect of the dye on the growth of S. aureus is shown after incubation.

EFFECT OF HEAVY METALS
ON BACTERIAL GROWTH

A sterile dime (silver) is placed on nutrient agar seeded with Bacillus subtilis. Note the zone of inhibition caused by the antimicrobial action of silver.

The mode of action of an antibiotic is easily shown by the use of penicillin. If low concentrations of penicillin are added to a growing bacterial culture, synthesis of the cell wall is inhibited and spherical bodies, protoplasts, are formed. Only if the medium is hypertonic, are the protoplasts stabilized and saved from bursting. A method for the preparation of such proto-plasts for demonstration is as follows.

1. Inoculate 0.2 ml 10^7/ml *Bacillus megaterium* (overnight culture) into each of two test tubes containing 1.5 ml broth and incubate with shaking at 37°C for 2 to 3 hr.
2. Add to the first test tube 0.5 ml penicillin 100 units/ml in 30% sucrose (dissolved in broth).
3. Add to second test tube 0.5 ml broth, to serve as control.
4. Take samples after 10 and 30 min incubation.
5. Observe with a phase-contrast microscope and demonstrate these protoplasts to the class.

**EXERCISE 37
IMMUNOLOGY AND
SEROLOGY**
A. PRECIPITATION: RING TEST

Although antihuman rabbit serum was mentioned in the exercise to add human interest, antibovine albumin rabbit antiserum may be used. (Lyophilized antiserum can be obtained from commercial sources, such as Nutritional Biochemicals Corp., Cleveland, Ohio 44128.)

The antigen is obtained by making a 0.2% (w/v) bovine albumin solution in normal saline. The other antigen or extract used can be egg albumin or simply saline solution.

The optimal dilution of antiserum to be given out for student use (taking into account the cost; i.e., highest dilution consistent with a good ring precipitate is best) can be titrated beforehand. Do halving dilutions of the reconstituted antiserum and dispense it into narrow tubes. Layer over it the antigen solution.

Halving dilutions can be performed as follows:

1. To a series of tubes add 1.0 ml saline.
2. To the first tube add 1.0 ml reconstituted antiserum. Mix thoroughly by sucking the solution up and down in your pipette.
3. Transfer 1.0 ml of this mixture to the second tube in the series.
4. Mix the contents of tube 2, transfer 1.0 ml to tube 3, and proceed in the same way for the required number of tubes (nine for example).

D. COMPLEMENT-FIXATION

This is a rather long exercise and the instructor may not want the class to run all the titrations. In such a case, it is recommended that the titrations for hemolysin, complement, and antigen be carried out prior to the laboratory session by the instructor. Only the modified Wasserman test then will be carried out by the class.

Complement-fixation reagents (complement, hemolysin, sheep red blood cells) may be purchased from commercial sources such as Grand Island Biological Company, Grand Island, New York 14072.

Again, to heighten student interest, Wasserman antigen and syphilitic serum were mentioned in the text or exercise. However, this test can be carried out by using chicken egg albumin as antigen and anti-chicken egg albumin antiserum (obtainable from Nutritional Biochemicals Corp.).

**EXERCISE 38
AIRBORNE
INFECTIONS
A. THE CORYNEBACTERIA
AND THE GRAM-POSITIVE
COCCI**

Blood-agar plates, antigens, antisera, and other such supplies are readily obtained from BBL or Difco.

Diplococcus pneumoniae may lose its capsule on prolonged artificial cultivation, but it may be possible to induce it to form capsules by inoculating 0.1 ml of a 24-hr broth culture of the organism into the peritoneal cavity of a mouse. Overnight the mouse is sacrificed and the washing (with saline plus some broth) used for capsule staining.

For detailed description of any procedure in clinical methods of medical microbiology, the instructor is advised to consult the American Society for Microbiology, "Manual of Clinical Microbiology."

**B. THE MYCOBACTERIA,
NEISSERIAS, AND
BRUCELLAE**

THE OXIDASE TEST

Oxidases differ from dehydrogenases in that they transfer hydrogen directly to oxygen to form water whereas the dehydrogenases transfer hydrogen to an acceptor other than oxygen. The enzymes are metalloproteins, containing iron or copper. Iron is quantitatively the most important metal in enzymatic activity. The enzymes do not act under anaerobic conditions.

The reagent 1% tetramethyl-*p*-phenylenediamine dihydrochloride should not be used if it has turned deep blue. The autooxidation of the reagent may be retarded by the addition of 0.1% ascorbic acid (a reducing agent) if it is to be kept in a refrigerator protected from the light for a while.

The oxidase reaction is based upon the ability of certain bacteria to produce indophenol by the oxidation of the reagent. Production of a purple color within 10 sec is positive; its development in 10 to 60 sec is a delayed positive; the absence of coloration or its later development is a negative reaction.

**EXERCISE 39
FOOD- AND WATER-
BORNE DISEASES**

A dramatic demonstration of phagocytosis in vivo is possible. A white mouse is injected before students with 1.0 ml 0.5% aqueous trypan blue intraperitoneally. Watch the development of generalized staining of the animal, which will be apparent on superficial examination as a striking blue discoloration of the skin. Cells in the skin are phagocytosing the dye. (No harm is done to the mouse; the blue color will disappear after about 2 months.)

Throughout these exercises on medical microbiology, the instructor is reminded of the wealth of medical films available for screening to the class. Such films are not only helpful but will also enhance student interest.

**EXERCISE 42
ENUMERATION OF
BACTERIA BY THE
PLATE-COUNT
TECHNIQUE**

The *median* of a group of measurements is the middle measurement, if there is one. Thus the median for the group 1, 3, 4, 5, 7, 8, 9 is 5. For the group 2, 6, 8, 9 the median is not defined, but may be taken as 7, which is halfway between the two middle numbers 6 and 8. Thus if all the measurements of a series are numbered in order of magnitude, the magnitude of the measurement which is halfway up the series is called the *median*. The class median may be found conveniently by pairing off the largest and smallest measurements, and repeating the process until only one or two are left. If only one is left, it is the median; if two are left, the median is usually taken as the measurement halfway between them.

The class mean in the exercise is the arithmetic average of the class results. (Of course if the class is very large, only a section of the class is considered by each student.)

The average error between a series of plates, such as present in the triplicate plates of a dilution, is calculated as follows

	PLATE NO.	PLATE COUNT.	DIFFERENCE (FROM AVERAGE)
	1	120	9
	2	130	1
	3	137	8
Total		387	18
Average		129	6

Therefore, average error is ±6; the plate count of the particular dilution is 129 ± 6.

Where colonies per plate appreciably exceed 300, advise students to count colonies in portions of plate representative of colony distribution and estimate therefrom the total number per plate.

Numerous aids to plate counting are obtainable from commercial sources. For example, automatic colony registers (a probe upon contact with a surface registers a count) and petri plate rotators for surface spreading are interesting instruments to demonstrate.

**EXERCISE 43
BACTERIOLOGICAL
EXAMINATION OF
WATER**

Copies of a "Table of Most Probable Numbers" may be made available to the class to answer question 7. This table will be found in various texts, e.g., S. C. Prescott, C. E. A. Winslow, and H. McCrady, "Water Bacteriology," 6th ed., Wiley, New York, 1946.

Attractive literature on the membrane-filter technique of bacteriological examination of water is available on request from the Millipore Corporation, Bedford, Mass. This can be exhibited to the class.

EXERCISE 46
MICROBIOLOGY OF
SOIL

It is essential that a good soil sample be obtained for this exercise. A good fertile soil (from the garden) is best. Do not use soil from a store (packaged variety) because it has been sterilized prior to packaging. In northern climes the ground is covered with snow and is frozen solid when this experiment is usually conducted. Unless a greenhouse soil supply is available, it is advisable to collect soil late in the fall in a plastic bag and store it in the refrigerator until use. Such stored soil has been found satisfactory for class use.

As a demonstration preserved specimens of legumes exhibiting nodules are interesting. Commercial preparations of soil inoculum may also be put out for observation.

MICROSCOPY

Gray, P.: "The Use of the Microscope," McGraw-Hill, New York, 1967.

White, G. W.: "Introduction to Microscopy," Butterworths, London, 1966.

STAINS AND STAINING TECHNIQUES

Lillie, R. D.: "Conn's Biological Stains," 8th ed., Williams & Wilkins, Baltimore, 1969.

CULTURES

American Type Culture Collection, "Catalogue of Strains," 9th ed., Rockville, Md., 1970.

Martin, S. M. (ed.): "Culture Collections: Perspectives and Problems," University of Toronto Press, Toronto, 1963.

CHARACTERIZATION AND CLASSIFICATION OF MICROORGANISMS

Ainsworth, G. C., and P. H. A. Sneath (eds.): "Microbial Classification," Cambridge University Press, New York, 1962.

Breed, R. S., E. G. D. Murray, and N. R. Smith: "Bergey's Manual of Determinative Bacteriology," 7th ed., The Williams & Wilkins Company, Baltimore, 1957.

Emmons, C. W., C. H. Binford, and J. P. Utz: "Medical Mycology," Lea & Febiger, Philadelphia, 1963.

Gilman, J. C.: "A Manual of Soil Fungi," 2d ed., Iowa State College Press, Ames, Iowa, 1957.

Skerman, V. B. D.: "A Guide to the Identification of the Genera of Bacteria," Williams & Wilkins, Baltimore, 1959.

Skerman, V. B. D. (ed.): "Abstracts of Microbiological Methods," Wiley-Interscience, N.Y., 1969.

Whittaker, R. H.: New Concepts of Kingdoms of Organisms, *Science*, **163**: 150–160 (1969).

MICROBIAL
PHYSIOLOGY AND
METABOLISM

Seaman, G. R.: "Experiments in Microbial Physiology and Biochemistry," Burgess, Minneapolis, 1963.

Van Norman, R. W.: "Experimental Biology," Prentice-Hall, Inc.,
Englewood Cliffs, N.J., 1963.

Wilkinson, J. R.: "An Introduction to Diagnostic Enzymology," E.
Arnold, London, 1962.

VIRUSES, RICKETTSIAE
AND TISSUE
CULTURES

Cunningham, C. H.: "Laboratory Guide in Virology," 5th ed.
Burgess, Minneapolis, 1963.

Kalter, S. S.: "Procedures for Routine Laboratory Diagnosis of
Virus and Rickettsial Diseases," Burgess, Minneapolis, 1963.

White, P. R.: "The Cultivation of Animal and Plant Cells," Ronald,
New York, 1963.

APPLIED MEDICAL
MICROBIOLOGY AND
SEROLOGICAL
METHODS

Bailey, W. B., and E. G. Scott: "Diagnostic Microbiology," 3rd ed.,
Mosby, St. Louis, 1970.

Beneke, E. S., and A. L. Rogers: "Medical Microbiology Manual,"
3rd ed., Burgess, Minneapolis, 1971.

Blair, J. E., E. H. Lennette, and J. P. Truant (eds.): "Manual of
Clinical Microbiology," American Society for Microbiology,
Bethesda, Md., 1970.

Graber, C. D. (ed.): "Rapid Diagnosis Methods in Medical Microbiology," Williams & Wilkins, Baltimore, 1970.